Leadership, Popular Culture and Social Change

NEW HORIZONS IN LEADERSHIP STUDIES

Series Editor: Joanne B. Ciulla, *Academic Director, Institute for Ethical Leadership and Professor of Leadership Ethics, Department of Management and Global Business, Rutgers Business School, USA*

This important series is designed to make a significant contribution to the development of leadership studies. This field has expanded dramatically in recent years and the series provides an invaluable forum for the publication of high quality works of scholarship and shows the diversity of leadership issues and practices around the world.

The main emphasis of the series is on the development and application of new and original ideas in leadership studies. It pays particular attention to leadership in business, economics and public policy and incorporates the wide range of disciplines which are now part of the field. Global in its approach, it includes some of the best theoretical and empirical work with contributions to fundamental principles, rigorous evaluations of existing concepts and competing theories, historical surveys and future visions.

Titles in the series include:

Poor Leadership and Bad Governance
Reassessing Presidents and Prime Ministers in North America, Europe and Japan
Edited by Ludger Helms

Leadership by Resentment
From *Ressentiment* to Redemption
Ruth Capriles

Critical Perspectives on Leadership
Emotion, Toxicity, and Dysfunction
Edited by Jeanette Lemmergaard and Sara Louise Muhr

Authentic Leadership
Clashes, Convergences and Coalescences
Edited by Donna Ladkin and Chellie Spiller

Leadership and Transformative Ambition in International Relations
Mark Menaldo

Extreme Leadership
Leaders, Teams and Situations Outside the Norm
Edited by Cristina M. Giannantonio and Amy Hurley-Hanson

Community as Leadership
Gareth Edwards

Madness and Leadership
From Antiquity to the New Common Era
Savvas Papacostas

The Leadership Imagination
An Introduction to Taxonomic Leadership Analysis
Donald R. LaMagdeleine

Thinking Differently about Leadership
A Critical History of Leadership Studies
Suze Wilson

Politics, Ethics and Change
The Legacy of James MacGregor Burns
Edited by George R. Goethals and Douglas Bradburn

Global Women Leaders
Breaking Boundaries
Regina Wentzel Wolfe and Patricia H. Werhane

Leadership, Popular Culture and Social Change
Edited by Kristin M.S. Bezio and Kimberly Yost

Leadership, Popular Culture and Social Change

Edited by

Kristin M.S. Bezio

Associate Professor of Leadership Studies, University of Richmond, USA

Kimberly Yost

Visiting Assistant Professor of Business and Leadership, Lourdes University, USA

NEW HORIZONS IN LEADERSHIP STUDIES

Edward Elgar
PUBLISHING

Cheltenham, UK • Northampton, MA, USA

Chapter 1 reprinted from *Cultural Icons and Cultural Leadership*, Peter Iver Kaufman and Kristin M.S. Bezio (eds).

Published by
Edward Elgar Publishing Limited
The Lypiatts
15 Lansdown Road
Cheltenham
Glos GL50 2JA
UK

Edward Elgar Publishing, Inc.
William Pratt House
9 Dewey Court
Northampton
Massachusetts 01060
USA

A catalogue record for this book
is available from the British Library

Library of Congress Control Number: 2017950458

This book is available electronically in the **Elgar**online
Social and Political Science subject collection
DOI 10.4337/9781785368974

ISBN 978 1 78536 896 7 (cased)
ISBN 978 1 78536 897 4 (eBook)

Typeset by Servis Filmsetting Ltd, Stockport, Cheshire
Printed and bound in Great Britain by TJ International Ltd, Padstow

Contents

Contributors

Kristin M.S. Bezio is Associate Professor of Leadership Studies at the Jepson School of Leadership Studies at the University of Richmond in Virginia. Recent publications include the monograph *Staging Power in Tudor and Stuart English History Plays*, "Playing (with) the Villain: Critical Play and the Joker-as-Guide in *Batman: Arkham Asylum*" (VG 2009) and "From Rome to Tyre to London: Shakespeare's *Pericles*, Leadership, Anti-Absolutism, & English Exceptionalism" in *Leadership*.

Virginia K. Bratton is Associate Professor of Management in the Jake Jabs College of Business and Entrepreneurship at Montana State University in Bozeman, Montana. Dr Bratton teaches undergraduate courses in organizational behavior, human resource management and leadership. Her research focus is on business ethics, pay equity and performance apprais-als; and her recent publications include articles in *Ethics and Behavior* and *Leadership and Organization Development Journal*, as well as a coauthored book titled *Teaching Plagiarism Prevention to College Students*.

Patricia D. Catoira is Associate Professor of Latin American Studies at Montana State University in Bozeman, Montana. She teaches courses on literature and culture from Latin America. She is the Director of Latin American and Latino Studies at Montana State University and has been the Director of the Women's and Gender Studies Program at the same institution. She has published numerous scholarly articles and book chapters about literature, culture, gender and exile from Latin America and especially from Cuba. Her current research focuses on Latin American crime fiction that explores the legacy and violence of recent civil wars and dictatorships in the region.

Laura DelPrato works at the University of Virginia's Career Center and is pursuing her Master of Applied Positive Psychology at the University of Pennsylvania. She earned her BA in leadership studies from the University of Richmond, where she completed her thesis on light painting art. She is an avid light painting artist and creative problem-solving facilitator who has led many creativity workshops for the Creative Education Foundation and the University of Virginia.

Susan (Susie) J. Erenrich is a social movement history documentarian. She uses the arts for social change to tell stories about transformational leadership, resilience and societal shifts as a result of mobilization efforts by ordinary citizens. Susie holds a PhD in leadership and change from Antioch University and is the founder/Executive Director of the Cultural Center for Social Change. She has more than three decades of experience in non-profit/arts administration, civic engagement, community service and community organizing and has taught at universities, public schools and community-based programs for at-risk, low-income populations. Currently a professor at American University, she is also the editor of *Freedom is a Constant Struggle: An Anthology of the Mississippi Civil Rights Movement* and co-editor of *Grassroots Leadership and the Arts for Social Change* (International Leadership Association, Building Leadership Bridges series), and is the producer of *Wasn't That a Time: Stories & Songs That Moved the Nation*, a live community radio broadcast.

Kavitha Ganesan is a senior lecturer at Universiti Malaysia Sabah and works on Malaysian Literatures in English with a particular interest in life-writings and their contributions in the making of the country's history. She completed her PhD at the University of Nottingham, United Kingdom with a thesis titled, "Construction of national identity in contemporary Malaysian state narratives and life-writings in English by women writers of Malay, Chinese, and Indian ethnic origins."

Shawna Guenther is a PhD candidate in English at Dalhousie University in Halifax, Nova Scotia. Her dissertation examines early modern English medical representations of women's breasts. She is co-editor of *Mothering Canada: Interdisciplinary Voices* (Demeter Press) and recently presented a paper at "Bowie's Books" at the University of Northampton.

Eileen Mary Holowka is a writer, editor and graduate student living in Montreal. She also makes games and music. Her most recent project is an interactive narrative video game about the act of narrating sexual trauma within institutional spaces.

Kimberly Klimek, Associate Professor of History at Metropolitan State University, Denver, is currently working on a textbook, *The Global Middle Ages*, a comparative work surrounding medieval concepts on a world stage. Her other projects include the use of graphic novels in history classrooms, and PTSD and medieval Crusade veterans.

Mark A. Menaldo is Associate Professor and Director of the College of Liberal Arts at Texas A&M University-Commerce. He is author of *Leadership and Transformative Ambition in International Relations* (2013).

Holly Connell Schaaf teaches in Boston University's College of Arts and Sciences Writing Program. In her interdisciplinary seminars, she incorporates Wikipedia and other collaborative platforms. She enjoys combining technology with outside-the-classroom learning, ranging from student observation of animal behavior at local sites to student attendance at plays, concerts, readings and lectures.

Nicholas O. Warner received a BA from Stanford and a PhD from the University of California at Berkeley. After teaching at Oberlin, he came to Claremont McKenna College, where he is Professor of Literature. His current research focuses mainly on the depiction of leadership in literature and film.

Kimberly Yost received her PhD in Leadership and Change from Antioch University. She writes about leaders in science fiction narratives to discover the influence this genre has on our thinking surrounding crisis leadership and ethical behaviors. She is the author of *From Starship Captains to Galactic Rebels: Leaders in Science Fiction Television* and a contributor to *The Routledge Companion to Leadership*.

Acknowledgements

We would like to thank the remarkable scholars who participated in this volume for their imaginative and innovative ways of interpreting and making sense of leadership and leaders through popular culture. In addition, we wish to thank the editors and editorial team at Edward Elgar (including Alan Sturmer, Karissa Venne, Melanie Marshall and Michaela Doyle) for their patience and willingness to take a risk on popular culture, and the New Horizons in Leadership Studies Series Editor, Joanne Ciulla, for accepting the volume and allowing us to proceed with such a non-traditional topic. We are grateful to Elizabeth DeBusk-Maslanka for her careful eye for detail and excellent advice, and to Dean Sandra Peart and the Jepson School of Leadership Studies for their support. Kim would also like to thank Kristin for her mentorship, unflagging efforts and friendship, and Kristin is similarly appreciative of all Kim's hard work and tracking down of possible contributors, editing, commenting and writing two superb chapters (one on very short notice), in addition to coming up with the genesis for the volume in the first place. Finally, we would like to thank our friends and family, of both the human and furry varieties, for their patience and understanding as we put together this volume.

Introduction to *Leadership, Popular Culture and Social Change*

Kristin M.S. Bezio

Civilization is made up of many components, including religion, politics, social structure and historical narrative. Michael Harvey, in an essay on "Leadership and the Human Condition," explains that "One way by which humans construct their reality is through storytelling . . . Stories connect reason, emotion, intuition, and the subconscious . . . A story offers an account of reality that seeks either to affirm or contest an existing terrain of meaning" (Harvey, 2006, p.43). Leadership studies recognizes the significance of such stories, but outside of the fields of literary analysis (which, in many institutions, includes analysis of cinema, television and other similar media), communication studies and art history, we very often overlook an important component of any civilization's storytelling *zeitgeist*—its popular culture.

In our modern lexicon, "culture" is given an intellectual valence, associated with "the arts" as elite or spiritual pursuits. "Culture," explains Lionel Trilling, "is not a flow, nor even a confluence; the form of its existence is struggle, or at least debate—it is nothing if not a dialectic" (Trilling, 2008, p.9). In essence, Trilling argues that we can come to understand the debates of any historical time and place through an examination of its culture. Culture is therefore, by this definition, a selective representation of the higher echelons or those who form and dictate social and political mores— in other words, our leaders.

By contrast, "popular" is vulgar, widespread, something enjoyed or participated in by the proverbial unwashed masses. "Popular" as a modifier is applied to a variety of terms, and typically contains a derogatory or dismissive valence. The addition of "popular" to "culture" thus diminishes it, reduces it from the pinnacle of artistic creation to something shallow, "pure entertainment" such as that offered by pop stars, pop music or pop art. "Popular culture" is therefore commonly associated with the young, the uneducated, the mob. Popular culture includes music, television, movies, social media, Internet culture and video games. In any given year, we are able to list titles, celebrities and genres, the vast majority of which we likely dismiss as valueless or shallow.

However, to do so, to view popular culture as vulgar entertainment without deeper meaning or purpose, is to profoundly misapprehend the value and role of popular culture to civilization and to leadership. Put simply, through the practice of leadership, popular culture helps to both reinforce and question our understanding of who "we"—both as individuals and as members of a civilization—are and what we should strive to become or accomplish as citizens, leaders and followers. Furthermore, as Trilling suggests of culture more generally, popular culture engages on multiple levels with contextual social and political concerns, capturing and driving debates on core issues of religion, economics, security and domestic and international politics, as well as questions of personal and relational identity. In short, popular culture provides a distillation of the concerns facing a civilization at a particular sociohistorical moment. As such, a civilization's popular culture provides an image of its conflicts concealed within a package of "popularity" designed to neutralize its criticisms behind the mask of "entertainment."

For the sake of this project, it is vitally important to remember that the distinction between "culture" and "popular culture" is entirely fabricated. "Culture," as it appears in art and literature, is "popular culture" with an elitist veneer; for example, William Shakespeare, widely considered to be the epitome of Western high literary culture, was in his own day lambasted for his vulgarity and popularity. Furthermore, Shakespeare has reappeared in the popular cultures of every historical era from his own to the present day. This is not to say that every work of popular culture has equal depth or complexity to Shakespeare—but it is a caution against dismissing all popular culture as irrelevant or vapid. All cultural artifacts are or have been popular; they would not have power or meaning without some level of popularity.

This notion of popularity, of requiring an audience, brings us back to the relationship of popular culture to leadership studies. If a leader requires followers to be effective, a work of popular culture similarly requires an audience to disseminate meaning. Thus, fans of a particular work of popular culture are the most devoted of followers, but any consumer of pop culture becomes a follower in the act of reading, watching, viewing or playing.

This linkage between followership and consumption presents an interesting, and problematic, opportunity to consider leadership (and leaders) as a product, although that is not our project here. Rather, we use this link as a means of determining a work's influence; the higher the level of consumption, the more followers a work of popular culture reaches and the larger its potential sphere of influence. What this means is that the more popular a work is, the more potential influence—the more power—it has.

One of the most notorious examples of popular culture enacting leadership for social change concerns the publication of Harriet Beecher Stowe's *Uncle Tom's Cabin* (1852), a novel which galvanized the abolition movement in the United States. In 1852, Stowe's novel sold more than 300,000 copies in the United States (Hagood, 2012, p. 71), meaning that it was purchased by 1.5 percent of the non-slave population (approximately 3 percent of the literate population) (U.S. Department of Commerce, 1975). For comparison, a book published today would need to sell 4,738,761 copies in its first year in order to match the popularity of *Uncle Tom's Cabin*. For Southern plantation readers, Stowe's novel was lambasted as slander, and, Hagood notes, "Alabama burned shipments of it" and "Maryland jailed a free Negro preacher for having a copy" (2012, p. 72). However, in other parts of the country—and even some parts of the South—it was widely popular, "and a bookseller in Columbia, South Carolina 'complained that he could not keep up with demand for it'" (Hagood, 2012, p. 72).

In addition, Stowe's novel initiated a wave of 'response novels' and critical publications, including Mary Eastman's *Aunt Phillis's Cabin* (1852), Caroline Lee Hentz's *The Planter's Northern Bride* (1854) and Stowe's counterpoint, *A Key to Uncle Tom's Cabin* (1854), in addition to any number of more typical reviews in journals and newspapers (Hagood, 2012, p. 73). The widespread publication of the novel—and its reception, as it was both beloved and hated by its readership, depending on their demographic origins—offers a quantitative measure of its influence, while readers' responses suggest the equal significance of a qualitative analysis.

As Hagood observes, *Uncle Tom's Cabin* "opened the floodgates for open conversations about the pros and cons of slavery—floodgates that decades of American male politicians had struggled to keep shut" (2012, p. 71). According to the diary of one Susan Bradford, a woman writing in 1861 Florida, Stowe's novel was responsible in no small part for the antislavery politics that produced the American Civil War: "If Mrs. Harriet Beecher Stowe had died before she wrote 'Uncle Tom's Cabin,'" wrote Miss Bradford, the daughter of a plantation owner who also owned more than 300 slaves, "this would never have happened . . . she has kindled a fire which all the waters of the earth cannot extinguish" (Hagood, 2012, p. 71). We cannot, of course, directly attribute, as does Miss Bradford, the Civil War to the publication of *Uncle Tom's Cabin*, but we can certainly recognize the cultural influence of the novel in galvanizing widespread discussions of abolition around the country.

The example of Stowe's *Uncle Tom's Cabin* demonstrates that our impulse to dismiss popular culture as "just" entertainment, particularly the more popular it is, reveals a profound disconnect between what influences us the most and what we identify as influential. Interestingly, this disconnect is part of what enables popular culture as leadership to be so powerful, particularly as a vehicle for ideological subversion. Although much popular culture reinforces the status quo of its time, even to the degree of becoming propagandistic, popular culture has also been responsible—as with Stowe's *Uncle Tom's Cabin*—for profound cultural and ideological rebellion throughout history.

At its core, the study of popular culture is the study of social history through a society's stories—an examination of the ideological dialectic between those with and those without power concealed within fictional and fictionalized representations and narratives of identity. When we analyze and interrogate popular culture with a critical eye, then, we focus on both the positive and problematic aspects of our socio-political milieu. Such an examination is particularly important in leadership studies in dual terms. First, and most obviously, it tells us what we expect of—and fear from—our leaders. Second and, we argue, more importantly, the study of popular culture opens up a critical space in which to question the oppressive and exclusive structures in place in our society in the interest of inclusivity and social justice. It is the second of these which we find most valuable to—and, unfortunately, most neglected in—leadership studies.

THIS VOLUME

It is our intention to demonstrate that popular culture, rather than being peripheral to civilization, in fact occupies a focal point at its center, both reflecting and shaping the ideological traces which run through, support and potentially even undermine dominant paradigms. The chapters in this volume examine a collection of examples of popular culture—both in the United States and around the globe—as such galvanizers of social change, both within their specific contexts and in a larger, more universal sense. With this mingled parochial and global sense of culture in mind, we have divided the volume into generic sections, each of which addresses a broad category of popular culture.

The first section—"Written Leadership"—is the most traditional, examining works of literature which directly engage with social concerns across a global context. As a genre, literature is among the most commonly studied forms of popular culture, typically placed in an historical context which distinguishes between "literature" and "pulp," "popular" or "genre" fiction. Our examination of the power of popular written works transects these "sub-genres," presenting examples from around the globe which engage with traditional and modern works of literature openly advocating for social transformation.

We begin with an example of "old school" popular culture—a play from the sixteenth century by playwright Christopher Marlowe, a contemporary of William Shakespeare. According to early modern scholar Kristin M.S. Bezio, in Marlowe's play *The Massacre at Paris*, the playwright uses contemporaneous events in Paris to comment on the need for change in English governmental policies surrounding religious intolerance. From the sixteenth century, we jump forward and across oceans to the writings of Malay-Muslim author Abdullah Munsyi, whose work in the nineteenth century, according to Kavitha Ganesan, created a framework for modern Malay writers to explore their cross- and inter-cultural identities and advocate for increased tolerance and diversity in post-colonial Malaysia.

The remaining two chapters in the "Written" section are more modern, looking at novels from the twentieth and twenty-first centuries. Mark A. Menaldo's examination of Mario Vargas Llosa's *The Feast of the Goat* situates Llosa's historical fiction about Dominican dictator Rafael Trujillo as an expression of the national trauma that still resonates in the Dominican Republic following his assassination. Kimberly Yost's chapter on the *Harry Potter* series by J.K. Rowling identifies Rowling's young adult series as a modern epic narrative drawn from Classical and fairy tale traditions that encourages its readers to engage in the leadership practice of resistance.

In the second section, we move from the written word to the sung, with chapters that contextualize and analyze song lyrics and music which reflect and challenge dominant ideological paradigms. The "Aural Leadership" section draws upon a tradition of music of resistance and protest, featuring chapters which examine song-as-protest in both North and South America.

Susan J. Erenrich's chapter on women troubadours in the U.S. Civil Rights Movement narrates the trajectory of women singers-songwriters on the path toward Civil Rights during the Southern Freedom struggle in 1964 in the Deep South. She analyzes the work being done by these women in and through music, situating their voices at the crux of the Southern Freedom movement. Similarly, Patricia D. Catoira and Virginia K. Bratton examine the countercultural music of Mexican *narcoculture* folk ballads which valorize and celebrate the controversial figure of El Chapo. The section concludes with a chapter from Shawna Guenther, who examines the charismatic and fluid identity leadership of David Bowie, which encourages his audience to not only tolerate but also embrace Otherness.

In our third section, we add a visual component to the aural/oral, interrogating cinematic, graphic and video game works from the twentieth and twenty-first centuries. This section, "Visual Leadership," focuses on works which demonstrate the power of visual images over our collective social imaginations, foregrounding the social and cultural impacts of visual media.

Nicholas O. Warner's critical examination of leader-follower relationships in military films—specifically, *Glory* and *Twelve O'Clock High*—foregrounds the importance of "followers to the leadership process and to the social or cultural transformations that result from that process," as he writes in Chapter 8. Kimberly Yost focuses in her chapter on the science fiction films of Neill Blomkamp, a South African director whose work uses literal physical transformation to depict the process of personal change, which produces (occasionally unwilling) leadership among those impacted by the transformative process.

Kristin M.S. Bezio's chapter on video games explores the potential impact of interactive play combined with the visual and aural cues of games, suggesting that interactivity can be used to promote considerate leadership, diversity, creativity and cooperation as tools of social change. Similarly, Kimberly Klimek examines the ways in which video games, graphic novels and comics, and the popular culture practice of cosplay ("costume-roleplay") can be used in the classroom to help students of history—and leadership in history—form a more affective connection to the lessons of history and historical leadership.

Our final section, "Digital Leadership," presents analyses of digital cultures, an area of yet-undeveloped research and inquiry, examining social media and digital art and art communities. In this section, the chapters foreground digital practices, platforms and communities, all oriented at providing space in which social change can be created and fostered.

Eileen Mary Holowka's chapter on the "Sad Girls" of Instagram—a social media image-sharing platform—examines the formation of identity and community through the use of particular images and ideologies in social media spaces. Similarly, Laura DelPrato's chapter on a form of long-exposure photography known as light painting mixes analysis of images and communities to discuss the ways in which online community groups create digital space in which to share art expressly for the purpose of encouraging global cooperation and social transformation. Finally, the section concludes with Holly Connell Schaaf's examination of the world of Wikipedia and its use as a transformative tool in the classroom to teach both students and professors how to use digital communities to engage in collaborative leadership as a means of creating a more inclusive and egalitarian society.

Taken all together, this volume can offer only the briefest of snapshots of each of these generic categories and their potential to reflect, shape and even revolutionize social and political ideologies. Each category is, of course, so much broader and more diverse than we can possibly hope to contain in a single volume, and it is our hope that future scholars of leadership and popular culture will seek to fill the gaps. We believe, as this volume should make evident, that works and creators of popular culture are engaging directly with the most pressing questions and problems of their context and that their creators use these works to effect change for both themselves and the wider world around them.

As popular culture is ubiquitous, so, too, is its capacity for critical engagement with the ideas and practices that shape how we think about ourselves, our societies and—of course—our leaders and leadership practices. Put simply, popular culture helps to both reinforce and question our understanding of who "we"—both as individuals and as members of a civilization—are and what we should strive to become or accomplish.

REFERENCES

Hagood, T.C., 2012, "'Oh, what a slanderous book': Reading *Uncle Tom's Cabin* in the Antebellum South", *Southern Quarterly*, **49**, 71–93.

Harvey, M., 2006, "Leadership and the human condition", in G.R. Goethals and G.L.J. Sorenson (eds), *The Quest for a General Theory of Leadership*, New Horizons in Leadership Studies series, Cheltenham, UK and Northampton, MA, USA: Edward Elgar, pp. 39–45.

Trilling, L., 2008, *The Liberal Imagination: Essays on Literature and Society*, New York, NY: The New York Review of Books.

U.S. Department of Commerce, 1975, *Historical Statistics of the United States: Colonial Times to 1970*, Bureau of the Census, https://www.census.gov/history/pdf/histstats-colonial-1970.pdf, accessed 15 September 2017.

PART I

Written leadership

1. Marlowe's violent reformation: religion, government and rebellion on the Elizabethan stage*

Kristin M.S. Bezio

On 23 August 1572, the French Duke of Guise ordered the systematic slaughter of French Huguenots in Paris. Begun with a failed (later successful) assassination attempt on Admiral Coligny on 22 August, the St. Bartholomew's Day Massacre rapidly devolved into mob violence and spread throughout the region, leaving thousands dead. One of its witnesses was an Englishman living in Paris, Sir Francis Walsingham, then Elizabeth's Ambassador to France. During the events of August 1572, Walsingham opened his house to shelter potential victims of the Massacre.[1] The following year, Walsingham, having returned to England, was to be promoted to the position of Secretary of State and assume control of the Elizabethan spy network.

One of the spies in his service was a Canterbury man by the name of Christopher Marlowe. The Cambridge graduate and future playwright joined the government network some time between 1584, when he took his Bachelor's degree, and 1587, when the Privy Council intervened on his behalf with the university, which was refusing to grant his Master's on the grounds that he was a secret Catholic.

Beginning in 1585, Marlowe was frequently absent from classes, and it was suspected that he had traveled abroad to Rheims in France, where the Jesuit William Allen had established an English Catholic seminary.[2] During this time, biographers note, Marlowe began spending more money on food and his friends, a distinct change from his frugality in previous years.[3] This suggests, argue A.L. Rowse, David Riggs and Park Honan, that the peripatetic scholar had acquired a secret source of income commensurate with the pay expected of an Elizabethan secret agent.[4]

When coupled with the apparent coincidence of many of Marlowe's acquaintances being themselves in the employ of the government—among them Richard Baines, Robert Poley, Gifford Gilbert, Nicholas Skeres and Ingram Frizer (the last of whom was personally responsible for Marlowe's untimely death)—or in positions of considerable political power—Francis and Thomas Walsingham, Sir Walter Raleigh and Henry Percy, Earl of Northumberland—it seems likely that Marlowe, too, was a government agent.

As such, Marlowe would have been in a position not only to have heard Walsingham's account of the St. Bartholomew's Day Massacre (either personally or second-hand), but to have been a first-hand witness to the violence and cruelty occasioned by the question of religion in Reformation England. Although only an eight-year-old boy at the time of the Massacre, Marlowe was clearly impacted by the event, both imaginatively and professionally. As David Riggs notes, the word "massacre" itself—French in origin, meaning "slaughterhouse"—was imported into the English language by the French Huguenots fleeing persecution, some of whom ended up in Marlowe's native Canterbury.[5] The association of the Massacre with a slaughterhouse came from the fact that when French soldiers refused to participate in the killing, the task was given to the butchers.[6] Furthermore, Riggs remarks, "The eight-year-old Christopher Marlowe, living on the edge of the town shambles, could readily grasp the sense of this metaphor. Armed men butchered their prey in a killing field; the carnage reduced human beings to the status of livestock; blood and body parts littered the streets."[7] These images recurred frequently in Marlowe's dramatic works, including *Edward II*, *Jew of Malta*, *Doctor Faustus* and, of course, *Massacre at Paris*.

MARLOWE AS CULTURAL LEADER

So how, then, ought we to consider Marlowe as a figure for cultural leadership? Certainly, his dramatic innovations paved the way for the future of Elizabethan and Jacobean drama, and, by extension of his influence on one William Shakespeare, all of English literature. But of greater interest to me is the way in which Marlowe sought to lead—to use the term somewhat loosely—through the influence of his work.

Marlowe's leadership, in the sense in which I use it here, took place on the public stages and through the printed pages of early modern London, both during and after his life. As an agent of Elizabeth's all-but-totalitarian government, Marlowe was most likely a party to political and courtly details which would have been beyond the rank of the majority of his peers, whether at Cambridge or in Southwark. As such, Marlowe's plays are uniquely political and particularly critical, with an edge of cynicism and a lack of regard for his own reputation that only an agent secure in his position could attempt.

Repeatedly—as we have seen—throughout his career Marlowe was accused of and even formally charged with offenses which would have meant fines, imprisonment and even death for others. *Doctor Faustus* transgressed the boundaries of both propriety and religious tolerance by actively staging a demonic summoning complete with ritual words; *Jew of Malta* contains contentious depictions of Christians and non-Christians alike, including Barabas's diatribe against religion; *Edward II* stages the graphic and sodomitical death of an anointed king; and *Massacre at Paris* depicts a political event which happened during the lifetimes of most living adults and includes reference to the living English Queen. In so doing, Marlowe changed the face of the English stage, not simply in terms of defining the genre, but in actively promoting his own political, social and (anti-)religious agenda.

The theatrical stages of early modern London played to a public audience of approximately one thousand patrons a day, affording dramatists like Marlowe a distinctive opportunity to engage the public en masse.[8] And this engagement—although ostensibly regulated by the Office of the Revels under the control of the Privy Council—came to define both the value and the danger of the theaters; they could serve both to circulate propaganda and to subvert the dominant paradigm, often (and, especially in Marlowe's case) simultaneously:

> In short, while offering a site of governmental ideological dissemination, play-houses nevertheless implicitly threatened the very regime that sanctioned their authority, in large part because of the scope and impressionability of the audience contained within their walls, but also because of the potential for the plays themselves to influence that audience.[9]

As a playwright, then, Marlowe had the ability to speak—through the actors performing his plays—to an audience of thousands; as a government agent of some value, he was given the license (literally, from the Office of the Revels) to be even more subversive than his contemporaries, an opportunity of which he took full advantage, writing plays which staged material that bordered on the seditious and heretical. His followers—his audience—were more than receptive, making Marlowe's drama among the most popular in early modern England.

AGENT AND "ATHEIST"

By January of 1593, when *Massacre at Paris* appeared on the stage of Philip Henslowe's Rose Theatre to great popular acclaim, Marlowe was an experienced spy and playwright, a rising star on the Elizabethan dramatic stage. It was Marlowe who was responsible for the introduction of blank verse to the public theaters and who, Roy Kendall explains, "began the move that eventually led to the play form being taken up by some of the keenest minds of their respective generations" as not simply a pastime, but a career.[10] As one of early modern drama's first published and named playwrights, Marlowe helped to shape not only the form, but the frequently subversive content of the early modern public theaters.

As a government agent, Marlowe's intellect was both an asset and, if his behavior stateside is any indication, a liability. While in the Netherlands, Marlowe and Baines were both found guilty of currency forgery and functionally deported. Years later, Baines accused Marlowe of atheism, a charge that led to a warrant for his arrest in 1593, although both "the minutes of the Council, as well as the warrant for Marlowe's apprehension, are silent about the nature of the charges."[11] Arrested on 20 May, Marlowe was immediately released, suggesting that "the Council did not take the matter too seriously, very probably," Samuel Tannenbaum argues, "because it knew that Marlowe was one of the Queen's secret agents."[12] Nine days later, the Privy Council received the Baines Note, a document which details Marlowe's (supposed) heretical opinions, including the infamous statements "that Moyses was but a Jugler & that one Heriots being Sir W Raleighs man can do more then he" and "That Christ was a bastard and his mother dishonest."[13]

The Baines Note tells us more than just Marlowe's (probably drink-induced) views on religion; it reveals his intimacy with Sir Walter Raleigh, prominent courtier, sometime favorite of the Queen, part-time spymaster and member of the "atheistic" School of Night. The School was a group of men surrounding Raleigh and which included the poet George Chapman, mathematician Thomas Heriot, and the "Wizard Earl" of Northumberland, Henry Percy. The charge of atheism leveled at these men came specifically from a Jesuit, Robert Parsons, a man who undoubtedly had reason to harbor distaste for men like Raleigh and Marlowe, whose job it was to root out and expose Catholic agents like Parsons. As such, the Baines Note shows a picture of a man who not only sought to impress his companions with his daring opinions, but who was intimate with some of the leading—and politically powerful—"atheists" of his time.

It is worth noting that "atheism" in early modern parlance is not the same as modern atheism (a lack of belief in a God or gods). To early moderns, "atheism" included "the denial of the validity of the Scriptures, deism, agnosticism, Arianism, and sometimes, it would seem, any extreme or radical religious belief," explains George T. Buckley.[14] As such, Marlowe's claim that "Moyses was but a Jugler" and, especially, that "Christ was a bastard" would easily have fallen within such a definition.

But what did Marlowe really believe? Although it is difficult to ascertain for certain just how seriously Marlowe believed the assertions in the Baines Note (assuming Marlowe did indeed say any of the things recorded therein), there is evidence to suggest that Marlowe's beliefs were unconventional, even "radical." In addition to the Note, the Privy Council's search of the chambers Marlowe shared with another playwright, Thomas Kyd, revealed a heretical treatise which Kyd—undoubtedly wanting to save his own skin—claimed belonged to Marlowe. The contents of this tract appear to have been Socinian, a branch of Protestantism which formed in Poland in the sixteenth century and ultimately gave rise to Unitarianism.

The tenets of Socinianism "rejected not only the central doctrines of the Trinity and the deity of Christ, but a raft of subordinate doctrines, including original sin, total depravity, predestination, vicarious atonement, and eternal punishment," explains Leonard Smith, any of which would have earned it the label of "atheism" in Elizabethan England.[15] Although we cannot be certain of Marlowe's personal beliefs, there are hints throughout his plays which suggest his familiarity with Socinian doctrine. *Massacre at Paris* contains several references to Poland, the birthplace of Socinianism and Faustus Socinus, its founder, whose name seems too coincidental not to have had some connection to Marlowe's *Doctor Faustus*. Furthermore, *Doctor Faustus* mentions one "princely Sigismund" (*DF*b 3.1.146), which Edgar C. Knowlton suggests—contrary to popular readings—refers to a sixteenth-century Polish king (rather than the presumed fourteenth-century German Emperor):

> If we recall that Marlowe's was the century of Popes Julius II and Julius III, and that Sigismund I was King of Poland from 1506 to 1548, and that Sigismund II was King of Poland from 1548 to 1572, the possibility that a Polish Sigismund might be relevant is hard to overlook.[16]

Since Socinus completed his *De Sacrae Scripturae Auctoritate* around 1575, the suggestion that "princely Sigismund" refers to a contemporary Polish king rather than the German emperor (whose reign did not overlap with a Julian papacy) seems reasonable.[17] When examined as one of several allusions to Socinianism—which was also popular among the School of Night—it seems an intentional reference. Whether Marlowe believed in its doctrine we cannot know, but its radicalism and rejection of Christ's divinity would certainly have appealed to his contrarian nature.

When we consider Marlowe's work, then, it is important to remember his incredulity in matters of religion. In particular, when we examine characters of faith, we must consider them from Marlowe's perspective, not just the perspective of the accepted orthodoxy of his day. For Marlowe,

Protestant zealotry would have been as worthy of derision as Catholic devotion: indeed, if Baines is to be believed, Marlowe was of the opinion "That if there be any god or any good Religion, then it is in the papistes."[18] Given this, it becomes difficult to read *Massacre at Paris*—the most directly anti-religious of Marlowe's plays—as anything but a criticism of both Catholics and Protestants which seeks to expose the hypocrisy found in adherents of both.

MASSACRE AT PARIS

Henslowe's Diary gives the weekly income for a play referred to as the "*tragedy of the gvyse*," played by Lord Strange's Men on 30 January 1593 as £3 14s, an income that, Kristen Poole notes, "was the highest of the season," exceeding by £2 the average weekly income for a play, concluding that this "initial and sustained popularity indicates that *The Massacre at Paris* profoundly resonated with Elizabethan interests and concerns."[19] Gruesome and bloody, *Massacre at Paris* has been widely maligned by critics for its macabre content, as well as the poor state of the only extant text, generally believed to be an actor's copy.[20] Yet the seeming propagandism and anti-Catholic sentiment of the play ought to be questioned, as Julia Briggs astutely observes, since "in Marlowe's dramaturgy things are so seldom exactly what they seem."[21] Like Briggs, I find Marlowe's "obviousness" to be highly suspect, and instead argue that what appears to be trite propaganda catered to the tastes of the lowest common denominator is in fact a scathing denouncement of Elizabethan religious policy.[22]

The play, with Marlovian irony, opens with the marriage of Henry of Navarre to Margaret, sister of King Charles IX of France. Charles blesses the wedding as a union of both family and religion, saying: "I wish this union and religious league, / Knit in these hands, thus join'd in nuptial rites, / May not dissolve till death dissolve our lives" (1.3–5). The wedding concludes with a mass, and the Queen Mother, Catherine de Medici, gives an aside in which she says she will "dissolve" the union "with blood and cruelty" (1.25). This early reference to the mass links the Catholic sacrament with the impending slaughter of the massacre, as, John Guillory argues, "for Marlowe the St. Bartholomew's Day Massacre and the Catholic mass can be understood as joined at the root, socially if not linguistically," as "mass" quite literally begins the word "massacre."[23] The mass also serves here as a kind of Black Mass, a ritual consumption of flesh and blood partaken prior to an act of treason or witchcraft. For Elizabethans, the one was barely separable from the other in popular culture, and the reference to Catholic ritual would immediately vilify the participants.

The ritual provides the frame for the rest of the play, the general plot of which would have been familiar to Marlowe's audience, since, according to Paul Voss, "the wars in France received more extensive coverage in the press than any other news event during the reign of Elizabeth I," including the defeat of the Spanish Armada in 1588.[24] In 1593, the year in which *Massacre at Paris* first appeared on stage, the French religious wars were not yet over, and Elizabeth had recently sent the Earl of Essex—with whom Marlowe, as a government agent, was likely also acquainted—to assist Henry IV in liberating Rouen from Catholic forces.[25] This also meant, of course, that Marlowe's audience likely understood far too well the consequences of religious wars across the Continent, as it was from their numbers that the soldiers were sent to assist the Protestant cause abroad. So while *Massacre at Paris* is certainly propagandistic in places, it also provides a reminder to the English audience that they, too, were being asked to risk their lives in foreign wars.

In order to mitigate this criticism, however, Marlowe provides an appropriate villain for his play: the Machiavellian Duke of Guise, who, Navarre explains once the Catholic royals have left the stage, "seeks to murder all the Protestants" (1.30). Yet Marlowe does not vilify the Guise alone, attributing violence to Catholicism more generally when Condy explains that "what he doth the Pope will ratify – / In murder, mischief, or in tyranny" (1.39–40). Navarre is quick to remind him—and the Elizabethan audience—that:

> NAVARRE He that sits and rules above the clouds
> Doth hear and see the prayers of the just,
> And will revenge the blood of innocents
> That Guise hath slain by treason of his heart
> And brought by murder to their timeless ends. (1.41–45)

Navarre's prediction thus serves two purposes: first, to remind the audience that they are among God's chosen; and, second, to introduce the play's central villain-hero.

The Guise himself appears almost immediately following Navarre's naming of him, a demon summoned to the stage upon being invoked. He also immediately confirms the audience's expectations of his villainy by proclaiming his aspirations to "the diadem of France" (2.41) in full Machiavellian style:

> GUISE For this, hath heaven engender'd me of earth;
> For this, this earth sustains my body's weight,

> And with this weight I'll counterpoise a crown
> Or with seditions weary all the world;
> For this, from Spain the stately Catholics
> Sends Indian gold to coin me French ecues;
> For this, have I a largess from the Pope,
> A pension and a dispensation too;
> And by that privilege to work upon,
> My policy hath fram'd religion.
> Religion: *O Diabole!* (2.53–63)

Here, Marlowe's play smacks strongly of propaganda, situating Navarre (Elizabeth's ally) in direct opposition to the Guise and Spain (Elizabeth's avowed enemy). For the early portions of the play, Marlowe maintains the appearance of Protestant nationalism, although it is a nationalism he complicates in *Massacre at Paris*'s final scenes.

In the following scene, the Guise and Catherine propose the Massacre to Charles as a means "to seek your country's good" (3.19). Charles protests, explaining that:

> KING CHARLES my heart relents that noble men,
> Only corrupted in religion,
> Ladies of honour, knights, and gentlemen,
> Should for their conscience taste such ruthless ends. (4.9–12)

These lines, divorced from a specific religious (or theatrical) context, could apply equally to either Elizabeth or Charles, and serve as an indication that it is violence in the name of religion, rather than a specific religion in and of itself, that is Marlowe's target in *Massacre at Paris*. In his argument for the Massacre, the Guise equates France with Catholicism, combining church and state in a manner much more reflective of the English theocratic monarchy than of France. Furthermore, it was an argument that would have resonated with the Elizabethan government, which, in the years leading up to the play's appearance, had executed Mary Queen of Scots (1587), convicted nobles involved in the Babington Conspiracy against Elizabeth (1586/7), and purged Catholic sympathizers in anticipation of the arrival of the Armada (1588).[26] Like the Guise, Elizabeth's government chose their "country's good" rather "Than pity or relieve these upstart heretics" (4.20).

But Marlowe does not allow the audience much time to dwell on such ideological similarities, and immediately plunges into the carnage of the Massacre. Although Joan of Navarre is arguably the first victim—poisoned (ahistorically, it is worth noting) by a pair of gloves in Scene III—the Admiral's death in Scene V is the first "official" death in the Massacre. He is stabbed by Gonzago with the injunction to "kiss this cross" (5.28), and his body thrown into the street at the Guise's command.[27] Anjoy orders the soldiers to "cut off his head and hands – / And send them for a present to the Pope" (5.42–43).[28] The deed being done, the Guise commands that the signal be given to initiate the Massacre city-wide:

> GUISE Mountsorrell, go shoot the ordinance off,
> That they which have already set the street
> May know their watchword; then toll the bell
> And so let's forward to the massacre. (5.53–56)

The Massacre proper begins with a preacher—Loreine—perhaps a reflection of the Elizabethan government's active pursuit of Catholic priests. The next is Seroune, whose occupation is unknown, followed by the scholar Ramus.[29] Following Ramus's death, the Guise calls out:

> GUISE My Lord of Anjoy, there are a hundred Protestants
> Which we have chas'd into the river Seine
> That swim about and so preserve their lives:
> How may we do? I fear me they will live.
> DUMAINE Go place some men upon the bridge
> With bows and darts to shoot at them they see,
> And sink them in the river as they swim. (9.56–62)

Next, the Guise and his men kill two schoolmasters, tutors to Prince Condy, then *"five or six* Protestants *with books"* (12.0.1). Thus far, it is worth noting the demographics of Marlowe's Massacre victims—those in the Seine aside. As Paul Kocher remarks,

> Marlowe is particularly profuse with the blood of scholars and preachers, all five of the persons he chooses for extinction being one or the other. Scholars, perhaps, Marlowe was personally interested in; preachers helped to emphasize the religious quarrels involved, and their deaths would evoke the strongest indignation of the English audience.[30]

This is to say nothing of the fact that Marlowe, as a government agent, would have been particularly cognizant of the role of both scholars—as those likely to defect to Rheims—and preachers—like the Jesuits he was paid to hunt—in the religious cold war between English Protestants and Catholics.

It is perhaps unsurprising, therefore, that Marlowe returns to the idea of the "country's good" following these scenes of murder; Cardinal Lorraine, at the coronation of Henry III (formerly Anjoy), urges Catherine to "insinuate with the King / And tell him that 'tis for his country's good, / And common profit of religion" (14.57–59). The Cardinal's language mimics the sentiments contained in the Elizabethan Bond of Association (1584)—requiring Elizabeth's subjects to defend her with their lives, targeted specifically at Recusants and, particularly, at Mary Queen of Scots, whose death it assured.[31] The Bond, like the Cardinal's exhortation, prioritized the sovereign not only as the head of the nation, but—as Elizabeth herself reminded Parliament at its closing in 1585—of "the Church, whose overruler God hath made me, whose negligence cannot be excused if any schism or errors heretical were suffered."[32] As in the earlier scene in which the Guise invokes the "country's good," however, Marlowe moves on swiftly, not dwelling too long on a statement at once treasonous and—given the close ties between the Elizabethan church and state—heretical.

At this point, the play abruptly jumps forward historically, juxtaposing the Massacre of 1572 with the deaths of the Guise in 1588 and Henry III in 1589, two events much more contemporary to the play's composition. Mere pages later, at the opening of Scene XVI, Navarre's discourse echoes the language of providential justification with which he began the play, and he, interestingly, repeats the refrain of "country's good" (16.11) employed earlier by the Guise and Lorraine:

> NAVARRE My Lords, sith in a quarrel just and right
> We undertake to manage these our wars
> Against the proud disturbers of the faith –
> I mean the Guise, the Pope, and King of Spain,
> Who set themselves to tread us under foot
> And rent our true religion from this land
> (But for you know our quarrel is no more
> But to defend their strange inventions
> Which they will put us to with sword and fire) –
> We must with resolute minds resolve to fight
> In honour of our God and country's good. (16.1–11)

The fact that Navarre, too, draws upon the language of the common weal further problematizes an already fraught expression in the play. If both sides can claim the "country's good," then the only thing that becomes clear is that neither has its "country's good" at heart; war in the name of religion, although justified in the name of country and common good, can, by extrapolation, only do the country (and her people) harm, a point *Massacre at Paris* goes on to illustrate with further bloodshed.

Protestant retribution for the earlier Massacre begins with the death of Henry III's General Joyeux offstage, the announcement of which spurs the play's first direct reference to England:

NAVARRE But God, we know, will always put them down
That lift themselves against the perfect truth,
Which I'll maintain so long as life doth last,
And with the Queen of England join my force
To beat the papal monarch from our lands. (18.12–16)

In the notes to the *Revels* edition of the play, Oliver observes that Elizabeth "and Navarre, of course, did share a concern to defeat Catholicism in Europe," a concern in which Marlowe, as an English agent, served.[33] On the surface, this, too, seems overtly propagandist, but if we remember that Navarre has already been tied to both Lorraine and the Guise through their mutual use of the phrase "country's good," this passage gains a darker valence. If Navarre is as untrustworthy as the Cardinal and the Guise, then how should the audience perceive his connection to Elizabeth? On the one hand, the alliance between Navarre (Henry IV) and Elizabeth was a political fact of 1592/3. On another, as Penny Roberts astutely observes,

> Henry of Navarre was to embrace Catholicism the year after Marlowe is thought to have written the play, lending his remarks about upholding the true faith as hollow a ring as Henry III's declarations of affection for the Guises. It may be argued that Marlowe, anticipating the conversion which was widely rumoured, was demonstrating yet again the cynical use of religion as a cloak for personal political gain—a cynicism which runs as a theme throughout the play.[34]

If, as Roberts suggests, Marlowe was aware of these rumors, then his mitigation of Navarre's heroism makes sense; however, there is still the matter of his relationship to Elizabeth, made more complicated by Henry III's (formerly Anjoy, and historically a former suitor of the Queen) sudden reversal of loyalty from the Guise to Navarre (and, by extension, Elizabeth).

When Henry discovers the Guise's intent to supplant him, he turns against his erstwhile ally, recognizing that the Guise's loyalty to Spain and the Pope opposes his role as a subject of France. This dichotomization of loyalty to religion versus loyalty to the state was commonplace in Elizabeth's England as an argument against permitting the practice of Catholicism, and Epernoun's claim that the Guise has acted "for the Pope's sake" (14.23) makes him a "traitor to the crown of France" (14.21), just as Recusancy marked English Catholics as (potential) traitors.

Henry's response to the Guise's protestations of loyalty once again summons the ghost of Mary Queen of Scots and the Bond of Association to the play: like Elizabeth's government, Henry convinces the Guise to pledge his loyalty upon pain of death, thereby justifying—as did the Privy Council with Mary—his execution for treason. Although Henry proclaims that "Guise, the King and thou are friends" (14.66), only a few lines later he tells Epernoun and the audience that "as I live, so sure the Guise shall die!" (14.94). Two scenes later, Henry literally invites the Guise to his death, reassuring him that "I am resolute – / . . . / Not to suspect disloyalty in thee" (16.44–46) moments before he is murdered at Henry's command.

Standing over the Guise's corpse, Henry proclaims the end of religious broils in France, making explicit reference to a Protestant alliance between France and England:

> KING HENRY This is the traitor that hath spent my gold
> In making foreign wars and civil broils.
> Did he not draw a sort of English priests
> From Douai to the seminary at Rheims
> To hatch forth treason 'gainst their natural Queen?
> Did he not cause the King of Spain's huge fleet
> To threaten England and to menace me?
> Did he not injure Monsieur that's deceas'd?[35]
> Hath he not made me the Pope's defence
> To spend the treasure that should strengthen my land,
> In civil broils between Navarre and me? (21.99–109)

It is worth remarking that the description of the Guise offering patronage to English Catholic sympathizers to migrate from England to Rheims was, Oliver observes, "historically correct – if hardly appropriate to Henry III, whose hatred of Guise had nothing to do with England."[36] Furthermore, as Clayton MacKenzie explains, "Henry's effusive praise for England and its queen is repeatedly undermined by his poverty of judgment, his ludicrous self-mythologization, and by the general moral treachery that pervades the play."[37]

The injection of an Anglo-Gallic alliance thus serves as yet another indication of Marlowe's distrust of the Elizabethan government's religious policy. Like Henry, Marlowe's text seems to suggest Elizabeth was more than willing to play politics with religious belief, making use of anti-Papal discourse when—and only when—it suited her interests. Similarly, neither regime shied away from ostensibly religiously-motivated violence when it helped to maintain their power; as Mathew Martin suggests,

> It is precisely the amnesia of *realpolitik* that the play invites its audience to interrogate. The play does not give its Elizabethan audience the moral luxury of complete identification with the massacre's victims but, rather, presses the audience to recognize its own complicity in the historical trauma it dramatizes.[38]

Interestingly, Marlowe implicates himself in this accusation of complicity, quite literally, through the figure of the silent English Agent who appears in the play's final scene. Some critics even suggest that the Agent is meant to be Marlowe, although I would argue that the Agent is symbolic of the Elizabethan government's reach rather than a specific figure for the playwright himself.[39] Yet as an agent of the English government, Marlowe participated in the perpetuation of religious violence in the service not of God or of the common good, but of politics. *Massacre at Paris* demonstrates that in the political game, no one is safe, and no one's hands are clean.

Once Henry begins to kill the Guisians, the clergy turn murderous, as well, as a Friar declares his intent to murder the King in order to revenge the deaths of Guise and Lorraine: "I am a friar of the order of the Jacobins, that for my conscience' sake will kill the King" (23.23–25). The Friar stabs Henry—"*He stabs the King with a knife as he readeth the letter, and then the King getteth the knife and kills him*" (24.33.1–33.3)—but the King survives long enough to send a warning to England: "I'll send my sister England news of this, / And give her warning of her treacherous foes" (24.50–51). As he is dying, Henry sends for an English Agent, who acts as a witness of Henry's death to England. As such, it is possible to imagine that Henry's dying speech is being recited to the Queen by the Agent, rather than the king himself—a scenario made all the more plausible by the fact that Marlowe was not the only English Agent to participate in the public theaters:[40]

> KING HENRY Tell her, for all this, that I hope to live,
> Which if I do, the papal monarch goes
> To wrack, and antichristian kingdom falls.
> These bloody hands shall tear his triple crown
> And fire accursed Rome about his ears.
> I'll fire his crazed buildings, and incense
> The papal towers to kiss the holy earth.
> Navarre, give me thy hand: I here do swear
> To ruinate that wicked Church of Rome
> That hatcheth up such bloody practices,
> And here protest eternal love to thee,
> And to the Queen of England specially,
> Whom God hath bless'd for hating papistry. (24.57–69)

Henry's dying proclamation—prophesying the (historical) continuation of France's religious wars—acts as much as a warning to the Elizabethan government as it is an historical observation of France; this point is made especially evident through the presence of the English Agent throughout this final scene, as he—and, through him, Elizabeth—presides over the death of Henry III and the transition of power to Henry IV (Navarre). That Henry's last words are to Elizabeth—"Salute the Queen of England in my name, / And tell her, Henry dies her faithful friend" (24.104–105)—further suggests the parallelism between French and English religious policies, and, furthermore, questions the intentions of both. Like many of Marlowe's plays, *Massacre at Paris* ends with a false resolution that promises not peace and security, but a future fraught with violence. As his audience was well aware, the religious wars in France would continue to rage (and would not end until after Marlowe's death) and the alliance between England and France would be tentative at best.

So, in light of the political nihilism of *Massacre at Paris*, how do we return to the idea of Marlowe as a cultural leader? Put simply, Marlowe was an advocate for peace and tolerance in an age where both were considered tantamount to treason. Interested in the unconventional—as a scholar, an author, a secret agent and a believer—Marlowe was a seeker of knowledge whose role as playwright and spy led him to see the things which divided his world and those things which united it. Through plays like *Massacre at Paris*, Marlowe sought to show his audience the price of their supposed safety: bloodshed, death and the division of friends and family against one another. In the process, he was willing to accept his own culpability—as the English Agent—in the machine of Elizabethan government, a responsibility that, some argue, led to his death on 30 May 1593 in the back room of a tavern at the hands of other agents. Whether we choose to believe that Marlowe was murdered in a brawl over a tavern bill or assassinated for finally having crossed one too many of the Privy Council's lines, Marlowe's legacy was one of testing boundaries—of propriety, of censorship, of belief and of loyalty. And in the process, he helped to reshape the world in which he lived.

NOTES

*   This chapter has been reprinted from *Cultural Icons and Cultural Leadership*, edited by Peter Iver Kaufman and Kristin M.S. Bezio (Cheltenham, UK and Northampton, MA, USA: Edward Elgar, 2017). Original formatting has been retained.

1. Mark Abbott, *The Massacre at Paris: With the Death of the Duke of Guise*, An Overview of Marlowe's Works (The Marlowe Society, 2011), 34.

2. Charles Nicholl, *The Reckoning: The Murder of Christopher Marlowe* (New York: Harcourt Brace & Company, 1992), 100.

3. Marlowe attended Cambridge on a scholarship, as he would otherwise have been unable to afford to attend. The buttery kept careful records of student spending, particularly for scholarship students, in order to keep them within their allotted budget. Starting in 1585, Marlowe appears to have been in possession of additional cash that enabled him to spend money more freely.

4. Park Honan, *Christopher Marlowe: Poet & Spy* (Oxford: Oxford University Press, 2005); David Riggs, *The World of Christopher Marlowe*, A John Macrae Book (New York: Henry Holt and Company, 2004); A.L. Rowse, *Christopher Marlowe: His Life and Work* (New York: Harper & Row, 1964).

5. Riggs, 32.

6. Riggs, 32.

7. Riggs, 33.

8. Andrew Gurr, *Shakespeare's Opposites: The Admiral's Company 1594–1625* (Cambridge: Cambridge University Press, 2009), 95.

9. Kristin M.S. Bezio, *Staging Power in Tudor and Stuart English History Plays: History, Political Thought, and the Redefinition of Sovereignty* (Aldershot: Ashgate Publishing, 2015).

10. Roy Kendall, *Christopher Marlowe and Richard Baines: Journeys through the Elizabethan Underground* (Madison, NJ: Fairleigh Dickinson University Press, 2003), 154.

11. Samuel A. Tannenbaum, *The Assassination of Christopher Marlowe*, Reprint (1928) (Hamden, CT: The Shoe String Press, 1962), 27.

12. Tannenbaum, 28.

13. Quoted in Kendall, 332.

14. George T. Buckley, *Atheism in the English Renaissance* (New York: Russell & Russell, 1965), 50.

15. Leonard Smith, "Truth in a Heresy? 5. Socinianism," *The Expository Times* 112, no. 7 (1 April, 2001), 223.

16. Edgar C. Knowlton, "Marlowe and Poland," *The Polish Review* 28, no. 1 (1 January, 1983), 14; edition of *Doctor Faustus* used: Christopher Marlowe, *Doctor Faustus: A- and B-Texts (1604, 1616)*, eds David Bevington and Eric Rasmussen, The Revels Plays (Manchester: Manchester University Press, 1995).

17. During the reign of Emperor Sigismund (1368–1437), the papacy was held by Urban V, Gregory XI, Urban VI, Boniface IX, Innocent VII, Gregory XII, Martin V and Eugene IV. Julius I was pope from 337–52, Julius II from 1503–1513, Julius III from 1550–1555 (overlapping with Sigismund of Poland for the entirety of his papacy).

18. Quoted in Kendall, 332.

19. Philip Henslowe, *Henslowe's Diary*, ed. Walter W. Greg (London: A.H. Bullen, 1904), 15; Kristen Elizabeth Poole, "Garbled Martyrdom in Christopher Marlowe's *The Massacre at Paris*," *Comparative Drama* 32, no. 1 (Spring 1998), 4. David Potter notes that the play would be bought by Edward Alleyn and taken to the Lord Admiral's Men and replayed from 1594 until 1601 ("Marlowe's *Massacre at Paris* and the Reputation of Henri III of France," in *Christopher Marlowe and English Renaissance Culture*, eds Darryll Grantley and Peter Roberts (Aldershot: Scholar Press, 1996), 71).

20. Potter, 70.

21. Julia Briggs, "Marlowe's *Massacre at Paris*: A Reconsideration," *The Review of English Studies*, New Series, 34, no. 135 (1 August 1983), 259.

22. Briggs, 258.

23. John Guillory, "Marlowe, Ramus, and the Reformation of Philosophy," *ELH* 81, no. 3 (2014), 708.

24. Paul J. Voss, *Elizabethan News Pamphlets: Shakespeare, Spenser, Marlowe, and the Birth of Journalism* (Pittsburgh, PA: Duquesne University Press, 2001), 42.

25. Abbott, 52–3.

26. It is also well worth noting that Mary Stuart (Queen of Scots) was related by marriage to the Guises, a familial tie that further cements the link in the play between Mary and the Guise.

27. Presumably, the murder would have been staged on the gallery above the stage, then a dummy corpse thrown down to the main performing area below.

28. H.J. Oliver includes a note which reads: "Varamund says the head *was* sent to the Pope, and adds, 'Other cut off his hands, and other his secrete partes' (x, f.14v). One wonders whether it was Marlowe or the reporter who omitted the last gruesome detail" (note contained in Christopher Marlowe, *Dido Queen of Carthage and The Massacre at Paris*, ed. H.J. Oliver, The Revels Plays (London: Methuen & Co., 1968), 112).

29. Ramus's death is itself extended and quite interesting. For further details, see John

Ronald Glenn, "The Martyrdom of Ramus in Marlowe's *The Massacre at Paris*," *Papers on Language and Literature* 9 (1973), 365–79.

30. Paul H. Kocher, "François Hotman and Marlowe's *The Massacre at Paris*," *Publications of the Modern Language Associations of America* 56, no. 2 (1 June, 1941), 365.

31. Elizabeth I, *Elizabeth I Collected Works*, eds Leah S. Marcus, Janel Mueller and Mary Beth Rose (Chicago, IL: The University of Chicago Press, 2000), 183–5.

32. Elizabeth I, 182.

33. Oliver, 139 (note).

34. Penny Roberts, "Marlowe's *The Massacre at Paris*: A Historical Perspective," *Renaissance Studies* 9, no. 4 (December 1995), 439.

35. The "Monsieur" mentioned in line 106 is the Duke of Alençon (d. 1584), brother to Henry III and Elizabeth's sometime suitor to whom she affectionately referred as her "Frog."

36. Oliver, 151 (note).

37. Clayton G. MacKenzie, *Deathly Experiments: A Study of Icons and Emblems of Mortality in Christopher Marlowe's Plays*, AMS Studies in the Renaissance 49 (New York: AMS Press, 2010), 77.

38. Mathew R. Martin, "The Traumatic Realism of Christopher Marlowe's *The Massacre at Paris*," *English Studies in Canada* 37, no. 3/4 (September 2011), 38.

39. Andrew M. Kirk, "Marlowe and the Disordered Face of French History," *Studies in English Literature, 1500–1900* 35, no. 2 (1 April 1995), 193.

40. Anthony Munday, another playwright and actor, and the author of a pamphlet which included an account of the St. Bartholomew's Day Massacre, *The Mirrour of Mutabilitie* (1579), also served as an agent for the Elizabethan government (Anthony Munday, *The Mirrour of Mutabilitie, or Principall Part of the Mirrour for Magistrates Describing the Fall of Diuers Famous Princes, and Other Memorable Personages*, Early English Books Online (London: Iohn Allde, 1579), ₵2r–₵3v); Stephen Alford, *The Watchers: A Secret History of the Reign of Elizabeth I* (New York: Bloomsbury, 2012), 67.

2. Abdullah Munsyi's nineteenth-century travelogue and its continued influence on Malaysian Literature in English

Kavitha Ganesan

By examining the writing tradition that nineteenth-century Malay-Muslim teacher, copyist and translator Adbullah Munsyi introduced to Malaysia, this chapter addresses how Malaysian Literature in English (MLE), a small but growing body of writing, can create a sense of belonging within this ethnically and linguistically divided, multicultural country.[1] MLE, an obvious reminder of the colonial legacy in Malaysia, has been freely produced for more than 60 years, a relatively short period compared to other postcolonial nations, such as India, New Zealand and Singapore, where literatures in English have thrived since the departure of the British Raj. MLE has suffered from slow growth because of the perception that English cannot serve as a unifying nationalist discourse for nation-formation.

Opponents of MLE argue that a collective national identity can only be promoted through use of *Bahasa Malaysia*. For example, writings in *Bahasa* are given the generic "National Literature" label, while works in other languages are labelled as "Sectional Literature." Nationalism is prominent in Malaysia's nation-building process because it reiterates colonial departure and constantly reminds the descendants of Chinese and Indian migrants of the citizenship rights the Malays accorded to their ancestors during the 1950s decolonizing period. This chapter argues that Abdullah's writing tradition provides a platform for both Malay and non-Malay writers to narrativize their sense of belonging by appropriating English-language writing through expansion, and, to a large extent, reconstruction. In so doing, this chapter jettisons the idea of a rooted, nationalist identity and, in its place, examines how this nineteenth-century written tradition continues to provide an identity that is de-territorial, hybrid and global, and in which Fanon's idea of a "national consciousness for international dimension" connects people, regardless of their ethnicity, age, religion and language (1961, p. 199).

THE INFLUENCE OF COLONIALISM ON MALAYSIAN LANGUAGE AND LITERATURE

Modern Malaysia and its emergent identity as a nation resulted from a long colonial history. Peninsular Malaysia's 11 states and two federal territories used to be individual Malay kingdoms. The Portuguese and Dutch took advantage of early contests for power and territory among local chieftains and sultans to establish rule in Melaka, an important trade port within the Malay Archipelago, in 1511 and 1641, respectively. As Dutch imperialism spread in the region, it was considered a threat to other Western colonial powers seeking to gain control of the trade route in the Archipelago. Additionally, disputes among chieftains in the local Malayan kingdoms gave plausible cause for the British to arrive in Penang in 1786 and in Singapore in 1819.

British rule was officially marked by the Anglo-Dutch Treaty, signed in 1824, which divided the territorial interests of the Dutch and English, leaving the Malay states in the peninsula—Melaka, Singapore and Penang—to the British. British influence soon extended to the other states of the peninsula. By the turn of the twentieth century, the formation of the Federated and Unfederated Malay States brought together individual Malay kingdoms under a British administrative system (Andaya and Andaya, 2001). In the mid-nineteenth and early twentieth centuries, indentured laborers from mainland China and India were brought to British Malaya to fill labor shortages in the tin mines and plantation estates. This period of immigration has caused a major point of contention in present-day Malaysia, as a person's origin is reiterated through terms like "*pendatang*" (new arrival/immigrant) and "*bumiputera*" (son/ daughter of the soil). People of Chinese and Indian descent—collectively known as non-Malays due to their migrant ancestry—are considered outsiders, even after many generations. Malays, who are Muslims, are accepted as insiders due to their status as *bumiputeras*.[2] The justification that the period when the Chinese and Indians settled in Malaya should accord them the status of immigrants or new arrivals is disputable (Hooker, 2003; Cheah, 2002). Even if the period of arrival is taken into consideration, it reflects the massive wave of migration, thus the question of belonging as it pertains to those Chinese and Indians who stayed back and whose descendants eventually made Malaya (later Malaysia) their only home remains unanswered.

The way each ethnic group was represented during the height of the Malayan decolonizing period, 1945–57, is constantly revisited to explain the skewed recognition between the Malays and non-Malays in present-day Malaysia. After World War II, the cost of defending the land against communist insurgencies increased for the British, so the colonial government set inter-ethnic unity as a prerequisite condition for Malayan freedom. Since each ethnic group was already politically represented, the UMNO (United Malays National Organisation), the MCA (Malayan Chinese Association) and MIC (Malayan Indian Congress) came together to form the UMNO-MCA-MIC Alliance. The Alliance won the general elections in 1955, two years before Malayan independence, with a sweeping majority, displaying the Malayan people's faith in self-rule. Nonetheless, this political support was neither a representation of inter-ethnic unity nor an adequate foundation for the construction of Malaya's future nationhood. This reality was evident in the Malays' explanation of the Alliance as the coming together of MCA and MIC with UMNO; they explained that non-Malays would gain citizenship rights *in return* for the guarantee of the Malays' special position. This explanation is used time and again to legitimize the Malays' hegemonic position in the country.

This agreement has led to conflict in modern Malaysia between the desire for a united national identity and the desire for equal recognition, particularly since ethnic identity is used as the key signifier among Malaysians, leaving a yawning gap between Malays and non-Malays. Classification based on ethnicity was introduced during British rule for census data collection purposes, but it has remained in practice in Malaysia since that time. In fact, ethnic classification has escalated in the past 20–30 years as part of the affirmative action plan of the policies introduced in the 1970s; as a result, ethnocentric division between Malays and non-Malays has spilled into the everyday lives of Malaysians; it impacts the purchase of properties, employment, the awarding of scholarships, student enrollment in universities, high-ranks in civil service and dividend/interest rates.

In the context of language and literature, Malaysia's disregard for English and English-language literature is not dissimilar to that of other postcolonial nations trying to come to terms with independence through linguistic decolonization. One overlooked point about the inception of MLE is that it, too, sought to create a spirit of unity among Malayans to resist colonial rule. MLE was envisioned as "a Malayan language" that could play a common political role in the creation of the nation through the printed publication of *The New Cauldron*, a literary journal at the University of Malaya in Singapore ("The way to nationhood," 1950, p. 5). Although the motive of the undergraduates at the university was akin to that of the nationalists, they chose English as their creative medium and, therefore, differed vastly from the pro-Malay nationalists. However English-language education was attributed to a colonialist attitude and was perceived as a privileged form of education accessible to a select few, so despite its pro-nationalist visions, MLE failed to gain the socio-political support necessary for its growth. To date, the prevailing notion in the local literary scene is that a neocolonial mindset is pervasive in MLE. This chapter shows that, in spite of its medium, MLE can rise above its supposed colonial and neocolonial ideologies because of its ability to both abrogate colonial values and appropriate a Malay writing tradition; in doing so, it disengages a preoccupation with a rigid, territory-based nationalist identity and may be placed among other world literatures that are increasingly borderless and transnationalist in nature.

Moreover, at present, Malaysia, like other nations of the world, is actively involved in a wave of economic globalization in which English is the main tool of communication. This may explain the State's recent policy shifts to reinstate English in the country's education system in order to make English more accessible to the wider population. Malaysia has also made peace with its hostility towards the English language, as English no longer poses a threat to *Bahasa*'s status as the national language. Quayum (2007) calls the 1960s and 1970s the most trying period for English and MLE; however, the bitter war, which resulted in *Bahasa* reaching a revered status, is now over. Malaysia's status as a plural, polyglot society creates potential for English writing and reading to cross ethnic boundaries and provides a space that enables the construction of more challenging issues consistent with global change. Even more significantly, such writings, due to the medium in which they are written, may offer a textual dialogue with the wider audience of the modern world in which multiple forms of belonging and transnationalism are expected ways of life.

ABDULLAH MUNSYI AND MLE

Abdullah Munsyi lived and wrote at a time when the land was under the influence of the colonial power. Because of his occupation as a translator and copyist, he was in close contact with the Christian missionaries, a position that has until now earned him scorn among scholars of Malay Literature. (Munsyi was not recognized on Malaysia's National Museum's listing of past Malay-language writers to whom it attributes the foundation of nationalist principles.)[3] Nonetheless, Abdullah is accepted by most as the Father of Modern Malay Literature, and scholarly researchers continuously attempt to trace his contributions to Malay Literature (Mohd. Tahir, 2012; Haji Salleh, 2010). Abdullah's writings offer glimpses of the Malay world through realism. He documented personal experiences, specifics about the places he visited and the way of life in the Malay states, as well as detailed descriptions of the customs and belief systems of the Malays (Milner, 1995). These accounts are used by historians to chronicle the Malacca Sultanate and the Malay world and are often read together with the Malay Annals (Andaya and Andaya, 2001).

Abdullah's autobiographies, *Kisah Pelayaran Abdullah* (The Voyage of Abdullah, 1838) and *Hikayat Abdullah* (Abdullah's Story, 1840), were a departure from the Malay literary preoccupation with myths, legends and superstitions. In place of this preoccupation, the autobiographies introduced a new genre based on Abdullah's travels. The genre of travel narratives, either literal or figurative, continues to influence MLE writers. For instance, Muthammal Palanisamy's *From Shore to Shore* (2002) is a narrative about migrant Indian indentured labor identity; in *From Shore to Shore*, national belonging is narrativized from the perspectives of crossing, geographic relocation and diaspora. Palanisamy's work concentrates on how the author, a postcolonial, diasporic Indian female, problematizes and legitimizes the hybridity caused by migrant travels; life-writing and textual devices disrupt normative constructs of national identity as fixed within one's homeland and place of origin. Similarly, Christine Wu Ramsay's *Days Gone By* (2007) is a narrative told from the perspective of transnationalism. The narrative's multi-location setting (China, Malaya, Singapore and Australia) may be used to examine a sense of belonging from the perspective of multiple identities in a way that resonates with the contemporary global citizen whose identity is driven by movement. Unlike Palanisamy and Ramsay, Amin's *This End of the Rainbow* (2006) depicts the protagonist's figurative travel as she gains agency as a Malay female nationalist at the moment of textualization, which may be viewed as a point of arrival in the text.

Although the hard to define narrative style makes Abdullah's writing problematic, it has—to a great extent—prompted contemporary MLE to use generic forms such as autobiographical travelogues, feature articles, journals, travel records, musings, anecdotes, occasional writings, rantings, observations and jottings. The realistic depictions in Abdullah's writings offer a common pool of consciousness among the heterogeneous communities of MLE. This point is particularly important considering MLE's growth between the 1950s and 1970s, which was mainly a result of non-Malay writers' contributions to the genre; nonetheless, there was a huge shift among Malay writers in the 1980s as they began experimenting with writing in English.[4]

Malay writers' crossing of linguistic boundary is a consequence of a national education policy that provided educational opportunities in

English-speaking countries for many young Malay writers—to name a few, Farish Noor, Karim Raslan and Dina Zaman. These writers have composed narratives akin to Abdullah's tradition and are often used to examine the resurgence of Malay writers in English (Ganesan, 2014).

The volatile publication culture in Malaysia may also explain why English continues to provide an avenue for literary expression for both Malay and non-Malay writers. Numerous English-language written materials have been circulated widely in the local markets but are banned when they appear translated into the Malay language. The Home Ministry's official website lists a total of 1,532 "prohibited publications," which range from a translated Malay version of Charles Darwin's *On the Origin of Species* to a Malay edition of Karen Armstrong's *Islam: A Short History*. The English editions of both books are available in bookstores. The ministry's justification is that the Malay editions of these books go against the principles of Islam. Such restrictions imply that the dissemination of knowledge is somewhat thwarted when the medium is Malay. It is a case where Malay readership is perceived as vulnerable to intellectual expansion.

Even though the state continues to suppress the use of English because of its colonial legacy, the recent restrictions imposed on the use of Malay may justify why writers have become involved in more straightforward travelogue/autobiographical/journalistic writings. Abdullah's tradition enables writers to find a voice and potential readership within these imposed limitations, thus allowing the emergent English-language writer to fit within the country's current socio-political establishment. More importantly, in the continued negotiation for belonging within Malaysia, Abdullah's writing tradition provides a common consciousness among multi-ethnic writers that extends beyond nationalism to a belonging based on the multiplicity of difference found in textual space. This is a crucial point of interest because the twenty-first-century common person is primarily an international wanderer whose geographic and cultural affiliations have become more divided, displaced and uncertain. Boehmer (2005) sums up the causes for such an unprecedented scale of demographic shifting as "anti-imperialistic conflict, the claims of rival nationalisms, economic hardships, famine, state oppressions, [and] the search for new opportunities" (p. 226). In Malaysia, not only past journeys of migrants but also the criss-cross between languages (Malay to English and/or English to Malay) within the present generation of writers have provided literary transplantation and cross-fertilization, changing, to an extent, the very nature of what is known as Malaysian Literature in English. Since Abdullah's writing tradition has been instrumental in making this process possible, a cosmopolitan rootlessness may be understood to be at the heart of the evolving MLE.

The written tradition inherited from Abdullah is not without problems. Critics like Quayum (2007) categorize it as "occasional writings" and asserts that this tradition-bound writing has prevented other writers from getting involved in "serious literary activities" (p. 21). Likewise, Che Dan and Omar (2009) claim that the "polemic of [Malay] national language and identity" has limited both Malay and non-Malay writers to "one-hit wonders" (p. 153). In other words, the openness created by the genre is seen as delimiting literary output in the country. However, if this argument is considered from a postcolonial perspective, Abdullah's narrative style's construction of an autonomous self and sovereign subject may be ascertained as a strength. Van der Putten (2006) explains that Abdullah's use of the first-person pronoun emphasizes the authorial self, giving his work a sense of individualism otherwise absent from Malay writings of that era. For example, the following excerpt appears in *Hikayat Abdullah*:

> *Syahdan adalah nama kampung yang tempat aku diperanakkan itu Kampung Masjid. Maka adapun saudaraku seibu itu empat orang laki-laki, semuanya itu abangku, maka aku inilah yang bungsu.* (1840, p. 8)

> The name of the village where I was born was called Kampung Masjid. My mother had four boys, all older than me, so I was the youngest. (my translation)

The use of "I" gives Abdullah's work a sense of modernity. It introduced the Western form of autobiography into the local literary circle, where it was deployed as a tool for seeking self-definition. Because his works existed at a time when colonial accounts were recorded, Abdullah's writings provided literary agency and a point of view that stressed the colonized individual rising above the exotic yet uncivilized representation imposed upon him or her by colonial administrators.[5] In this regard, Abdullah's writings differed not only from those of his contemporaries who engaged with superstition and myth but also from the Western writings after which they were modeled.

Abdullah's adoption and appropriation of the autobiography in the Malay language continues to provide solidarity to MLE writers by reaching out to those seeking self-representation through literature. As a matter of fact, the genre has been expanded and reproduced as a volume of poetry in Nor Faridah Abdul Manaf's *The Art of Naming* (2006). On the other hand, in *Footprints in the paddy fields* (2010), Tina Kisil incorporates pictures and punctuates her narrative with riddles and folk songs that closely resemble her Dusunic indigenous culture. This shows that Abdullah's autobiographical form has not only been appropriated, but also, to a large extent, reconstructed to befit Malaysia's changing climate of literary writing. Therefore, narratives about life in Malaysia may not necessarily be in a rigid prose form, but may exist in a mosaic structure through a combination of literary devices, such as photographs, letters, poetry and folklore. As such, the continued intermingling of forms—derived from nationalist, indigenous and European literary traditions—can be attributed to the writing tradition Abdullah introduced and left behind. The genre of autobiography—regardless of its composite quality as exemplified through MLE—allows everyday circumstance to become universal experience, bringing global citizens closer through the common call for recognition, identity, rights, endurance and survival.

Although Abdullah's close association with the colonizers has been subject to much scrutiny, the abrogation of colonial values can be said to have existed in Abdullah's writing as early as the 1840s. He writes:

> *makanan yang diaturkan [. . .]empat ekor ayam kembiri dibakar, dan empat ekor itik digoreng, dan kambing dimasak cara Keling. Anak-anak ayam dimasak sup, dan perkara sayur-sayur seperti kubis, telur, dan terung dimasak bulat-bulat.*
> (p. 154–5)

> the wide array of food [. . .] four neutered chickens roasted, and four fried ducks, and mutton cooked in Indian style. Baby chicks cooked in soup, and things like vegetables such as cabbage, egg, and eggplants cooked whole. (my translation)

Abdullah's excerpt describes the spread of food prepared at his home in anticipation of some British guests. On one hand, the spread displays his wealth, but, on the other, it shows how he emphasizes the fusion of local ethnic cuisines. For example, Abdullah's descriptions of ingredients and cooking methods—"neutered chicken" and "cooked in Indian style"—bring to the fore his position—albeit literary—as a custodian of local tradition; while Abdullah could have offered his guests—mostly his friends—Western food, he instead favored his multicultural surroundings. Thus, he highlighted keeping cultural integrity intact when receiving foreign guests.

In Lydia Teh's *Still Honking: More Scenes from Malaysian Life* (2014), a similar style of linguistic and cultural abrogation is obvious:

> Afterwards the hanger spoil I cannot afford to pay you back. What, you can buy new one and claim from company ah? Like that oso can ah? Wah, you flers very lucky lor. Everything oso can claim. I tell you what. Afterwards we don't go *mamak*. I take you to five-star Chinese restaurant. (p. 27)

Teh's writing, like that of other MLE writers, embraces dramatic shifts—between high and low registers, colloquial expressions and compounded language—that work against the unifying Western linearity, creating a point of abrogation in the text. Describing a typical day in a Chinese Malaysian's life, the excerpt uses colonial language to weave together creatively what is native ("ah," "oso," "wah," "flers," "lor") with a mix of humor and local Malaysian culture through Indian-Muslim street food ("mamak"). Teh boldly confronts Malaysians' language (Manglish) and practices, at once embracing and demonstrating the impurity caused by the coming together of migrant postcolonial conditions in a country immersed in old Malay traditions. With its stress on the mixing of multiple expressions and cultures, Teh's work also depicts a fissured, hybrid form consistent with the invariably polyglot nature typical to other world languages and cultures.

The modernity in Abdullah's writing is also apparent in his use of ideas and criticism to convince Malay readers of his time against blindly following the Malay rulers and their firm beliefs in old feudal traditions. He writes the following in *Kisah Pelayaran Abdullah* (1838):

> *tiada juga lepas hati sahaya daripada memikirkan segala perkara yang sahaya lihat di-Terengganu, saperti [. . .] 'adat bodoh dan jahat saperti memakai senjata pada tiap-tiap hari dan sabagainya . . . hanya satu perkara yang menyesakkan dalam fikiran saya, yaitu jalan yang termat jahat sebab kekurangan pelajaran anak raja-raja itu tatkala ia lagi kechil. Bahwa inilah akar segala kelemahan kerajaan Melayu dan sengsara atas segala ra'yat-nya.* (p. 57)

> I did not have the heart to forgo what I had seen in Terengganu, such as the silly and evil practices of carrying weapons at all times and so on . . . only one thing keeps bothering me, that is, the very evil road undertaken by the princes due to a lack in education, even though they are so young. This is the root of all weaknesses in the kingdom that causes suffering to all its people. (my translation)

The satirical form Abdullah used in his approach to the living conditions of the Malay people of his time, subsequent to Malay rule, is reflected in the style used by contemporary MLE writers. For example, Karim Raslan's *Journeys Through Southeast Asia: Ceritalah 2* and Farish Noor's *The Other Malaysia: Writings on Malaysia's Subaltern History*, both published in late 2002, are narratives that engage with the increasingly ethno-religious conditions of present-day Malaysia. Charlene Rajendran's *Taxi Tales* (2009) and Lee Su Kim's *A Nyonya in Texas* (2007) go even further in their use of satirical forms. Although Rajendran's writing is based in Singapore and Lee's in the United States, both writers translocated—a tradition brought to light through Abdullah's writing—to incorporate their personal experiences in foreign countries. In this way, the tradition has evolved into a self-actualizing form of writing, highlighting that the cosmopolitan is— or can be—apolitical.

While Abdullah's nineteenth-century writing tradition may have been new and alien to his contemporaries, it has helped the nation's Malay and non-Malay writers find their voices and reach out to the wider population. English does not belong to any particular ethnic group in Malaysia, so using it in a writing tradition rooted in Malay culture and social practice is perhaps the best form of acculturation for Malaysia, a progress-driven postcolonial nation. By internalizing the tradition Adbullah introduced, modern writers have managed to straddle sensitive issues and survive in the country's increasingly restrictive socio-political and cultural environment. Presumably, Abdullah's written tradition is a primary platform for the cross-fertilization of languages and cultures as multi-ethnic and multi-religious communities come into contact with one another. For now, Abdullah's tradition is the only writing style in Malaysia that allows literary continuity, which may in turn reach a larger pool of foreign readership and result in the creation of a global, hybridized and cosmopolitan consciousness. Most importantly, Malay and non-Malay English-language writings may be understood through a continuum of transformation—especially in relation to MLE—because Abdullah's writing enables the dismantling of rigid nationalist representations and replaces them with observational autobiographical travelogues. The emergence of such postcolonial literatures in English is crucial because the divisive East/West forms of reading may be overtaken by a new post-imperial expression in which a country's internal socio-political challenges are considered. A new dimension of the internationalization of such literatures may evolve spontaneously and even overcome, to an extent, cultural untranslatability and elements of inaccessibility to a global English readership.

NOTES

1. The term "ethnicity" is used rather than "race" because in Malaysia the classification is not used to distinguish one through his/her biological features but rather as a political construct of collective identity that involves socio-religious practices and rituals as accorded by Article 160 of the Malaysian Constitution.
2. The term "Melayu" (Malay) has undergone various conceptual changes. The word seems to have first appeared in the artifacts of the early Hindu-Buddhist Empire of Srivijaya. At one point to be "Malay" meant to be a "Melakan," a name derived from the rise of Melaka as a port city. "Melakan" eventually included Islam. During the period of British rule, the term "Malay" was formalized to distinguish the Malays from the Chinese and Indian immigrants, as well as from the inhabitants of the Borneon region. During discussions of independence, there was a suggestion to call those wishing to become Malayan citizens collectively "Malay," but this idea was dropped, leaving the description introduced by the British intact. See Andaya and Andaya (2001), pp. 340–41. In Malaysia, the Federal Constitution defines a "Malay" as a person who habitually speaks the Malay language, conforms to the Malay customs, and professes Islam as his/her religion; thus in Malaysia, all Malays are Muslims (Article 160).
3. The information was gathered by the researcher during fieldwork in August 2011.
4. In the following two decades, still prior to the country's independence, MLE was more popular among the non-Malays as the Malays, driven by nationalistic pursuits, sought to create a homogeneous identity through the use of *Bahasa*. A small number of Malay writers who until that point had written in English chose to continue writing only in

Malay, following the likes of Kenyan writer Ngugi wa Thiong'o, who has opted to write in his native language, Gikuyu. The situation was reversed among the non-Malay writers who wrote in English, particularly during the 1960s and 1970s. These writers either went into long periods of silence or left the country for good. K.S. Maniam, the Raja Rao Award winner for outstanding contribution to the literature of the South Asian Diaspora (2000), had at least a ten-year gap between his first published novel, *The Return* (1981), and the second one, *In A Far Country* (1993). Poet Ee Tiang Hong immigrated to Australia, from where he continued writing until his death. Poet, novelist and academic Shirley Lim left for the USA in the 1970s. So did poet Hilary Tham, who is well-known for her collection of poetry and memoir, *Lane with No Name: Memoirs and Poems of a Malaysian-Chinese Girlhood* (1997).
5. Some of the colonial writers were Hugh Clifford, Richard Winstedt and Frank Swettenham. For a good account of writings in colonial Malaya, see Yap, *A Brief Critical Survey of Prose Writings* (1971).

REFERENCES

Abdul Kadir Munsyi, A. (1840 [1974]), *Hikayat Abdullah Jilid 1*, 6th edition, Kuala Lumpur: Penerbitan Pustaka Antara.

Abdul Kadir Munsyi, A. (1838 [1964]), *Kisah Pelayaran Abdullah*, 3rd edition, Kuala Lumpur: Oxford University Press.

Abdul Kadir Munsyi, N.F. (2006), *The Art of Naming: A Muslim Woman's Journey*, Subang Jaya: Awards Publishing.

Amin, K.A. (2006), *This End of the Rainbow*, Penang: Phoenix Press.

Andaya, B.W. and L.Y. Andaya (2001), *A History of Malaysia*, 2nd edition, Basingstoke and London: Macmillan.

Boehmer, E. (2005), *Colonial and Postcolonial Literature: Migrant Metaphors*, 2nd edition, Oxford: Oxford University Press.

Che Dan, W. and N. Omar (2009), "Writing Malaysia in English: A critical perspective," in G.L. Sui and E. Thumboo (eds), *Sharing Borders: Studies in Contemporary Singaporean-Malaysian Literature II*, Writing Asia: The Literatures in Englishes series, vol. 2, Singapore: National Library Board in partnership with National Arts Council, pp. 151–67.

Cheah, B.K. (2002), *Malaysia: The Making of a Nation*, Singapore: ISEAS.

Fanon, F. (1961 [1967]), *The Wretched of the Earth*, preface by Jean-Paul Sartre, translated by C. Farrington, England: Penguin Classics.

Ganesan, K. (2014), *Constructions of national identity in contemporary Malaysian state narratives and life-writings in English by writers of Malay, Chinese, and Indian ethnic origins*, unpublished dissertation.

Haji Salleh, S.H. (2010), *Malay Literature of the 19th Century*, Kuala Lumpur: Institut Terjemahan Negara.

Hooker, V.M. (2003), *A Short History of Malaysia: Linking East and West*, New South Wales: Allen and Unwin.

Kisil, T. (2010), *Footprints in the Paddy Fields*, Petaling Jaya: MPH Publishing Sdn Bhd.

Lee, S.K. (2007), *A Nyonya in Texas: Insights of a Straits Chinese Woman in the Lone Star State*, Malaysia: Marshall Cavendish.

Malaysian Home Ministry (n.d.), "Prohibited publications," accessed May 6, 2016 at http://www.kdn.gov.my/index.php/en/2012-08-08-00-54-58/penerbitan-larangan.

Milner, A. (1995), *The Invention of Politics in Colonial Malaya: Contesting Nationalism and the Expansion of the Public Sphere*, Cambridge: Cambridge University Press.

Mohd. Tahir, U.M. (2012), "The construction and institutionalisation of Abdullah bin Abdul Kadir Munsyi as the father of modern Malay Literature: the role of westerners" in D. Smyth (ed.), *The Canon in Southeast Asian Literature: Literatures of Burma, Cambodia, Indonesia, Laos, Malaysia, Philippines, Thailand and Vietnam*, London and New York: Routledge, pp. 99–113.

Noor, F.A. (2002), *The Other Malaysia: Writings on Malaysia's Subaltern History*, Kuala Lumpur: Silverfish Books.

Palanisamy, M. (2002), *From Shore to Shore*, Kajang: VGV Management.

Quayum, M.A. (2007), *One Sky Many Horizons: Studies in Malaysian Literature in English*, Shah Alam: Marshall Cavendish.

Rajendran, C. (2009), *Taxi Tales: On A Crooked Bridge*, Petaling Jaya: Matahari Books.

Ramsay, C.W. (2007), *Days Gone By: Growing Up in Penang*, Victoria: Macmillan.

Raslan, K. (2002), *Journeys Through Southeast Asia: Ceritalah 2*, Singapore: Times Books International.

Teh, L. (2014), *Still Honking: More Scenes from Malaysian Life*, Petaling Jaya: MPH Publishing Sdn Bhd.

"The way to nationhood," *The New Cauldron* (Hilary Term, 1949–50), pp. 3–6.

Van der Putten, J. (2006), "Abdullah Munsyi and the missionaries," *Bijdragen tot de Taal*, Land- en Volkenkunde **162** (4), 407–40.

Yap, A. (1971), *A Brief Critical Survey of Prose Writings in Singapore and Malaysia*, Singapore: Educational Publications Bureau.

3. Totalizing tyranny: Mario Vargas Llosa's *The Feast of the Goat*

Mark A. Menaldo

Leadership scholars tend to focus on models that seek to improve the psychological and ethical lives of both leaders and followers. Such perspectives take for granted pre-existing environments that observe Western ethical and democratic norms. Rarely do scholars focus on the moral and psychological consequences of destructive leadership and toxic conditions, and when they do, they focus on microenvironments, such as business and managerial contexts (Einarsen et al., 2007; Schyns and Hansbrough, 2010). There are totalizing contexts that manifest bad leadership: where bad leaders are characteristically bad, while followers who deliberately allow bad leaders to operate are, in a way, also bad (Kellerman, 2004). These toxic leaders create toxic environments that have a poisonous effect on individuals, groups, communities and entire societies (Lipman-Blumen, 2005). In Latin America, dictatorship has historically been an all too common example of bad leadership.[1] For scholars interested in the conditions and effects of bad, destructive and toxic leadership, Latin American authors supply a treasure trove of insights, especially those of the 1960s Latin American Boom, a revolution in cultural production. In Latin America, the author plays a key role in defining issues within the swirling debate that is Latin America's identity and political ideology. Usually found on the left, they have aligned with Cuba's past revolutionary and anti-imperialist stance. Latin American authors tend to embrace ideological perspectives because their countries have been beset by similar problems: endemic poverty, lack of political accountability and participation, persistent encroachments of the military in political life and dictatorial rule.

Since the time of independence, dictatorship has predominated as Latin America's main form political organization (Castellanos and Martinez, 1981). As a result, it contributes significantly to authorial production. As a genre, the dictator novel has its roots in Domingo Faustino Sarmiento's classic *Facundo* (1845), a critique of the Argentine dictator Juan Manuel de Rosas. In 1967, Boom authors Carlos Fuentes (Mexico) and Mario Vargas Llosa (Peru) designed a collective literary undertaking that they called the "Fathers of the Nations," in which the foremost Latin American authors would write a novel about dictators from their respective countries (Fradinger, 2010). The project did not materialize, but the period did spark some literary accomplishments and continued into the twenty-first century.[2]

A gem of this genre is Mario Varga's Llosa's political and literary masterpiece *The Feast of the Goat* (2000), which fictionally recreates the 1961 assassination of Rafael Trujillo, who ruled the Dominican Republic for three decades. Vargas Llosa's experience is integral to his realistic depiction of dictatorship in *The Feast of the Goat*. Living under a dictatorship in Peru, he was an early proponent of socialism and was even part of Fidel Castro's famous "kitchen cabinet." He became disillusioned with socialist politics and officially disavowed Castro in 1971 after Cuba's persecution of the poet Heberto Padilla.

Unlike most Latin American intellectuals, writers and social critics, Vargas Llosa is a stalwart defender of liberal politics and economic policies. He advanced this agenda in Peru by heading the *Frente Democrático*, which lost in the 1990 presidential election to Alberto Fujimori, who then assumed dictatorial control over Peru in 1992 after dissolving parliament through a military coup. After his electoral loss, Vargas Llosa retreated from political life and dedicated himself fully to writing fiction, journalism and essays. In 2010, the Swedish Academy awarded him the Nobel Prize in Literature, praising him "for his cartography of the structures of power and his trenchant images of the individual's resistance, revolt and defeat" (Bosman and Romero, 2010).

In *The Feast of the Goat*, Vargas Llosa artfully generates an archetype of dictatorship and its deleterious effects on civic society. Unlike social science theories that seek value neutrality, the novel does not suffer from semantic sanitization. Vargas Llosa uniquely provides insight to how dictatorship operates, coerces, cajoles and seduces. However, as a writer of fiction, Vargas Llosa provides an in-depth portrait of both the interior and exterior the dictator. That is, he shows the nature of tyranny in both primordial and modern manifestations.

As Waller Newell (2013) observes, human beings have a tendency toward primordial politics, which is "not only the idea that politics serves the passions, but also the ontology that establishes the primacy of the passions" (p. 32). For ancient Greek thinkers, potential tyrants have two competing passions: spiritedness (*thumos*) and eros. Spiritedness is an aggressive, masculine and potentially violent energy that seeks mastery. For Homer's heroes in the *Iliad*, it is the source of martial aggression and valor. In Plato's *Republic*, spiritedness is the central passion of the Guardian class, which needs taming by philosophy. On the other hand, eros manifests as sexual appetite or as a sublime quest such as ennobling of the city or the study of philosophy. However, in the case of what Plato called a deformed soul, "the zeal and aggressiveness of spiritedness allies with eros for tyrannical possession of the city" (Newell, 2013, p. 34).

For Newell, primordial politics contrasts sharply with transcendental politics, which lifts people from their finite and embodied passions towards a goal that is eternal and permanent, such as the austere aristocratic and republican regimes conceived by Plato and Aristotle. For modernists like Thomas Hobbes, transcendental politics take shape through a sovereign power that uses the state apparatus to construct a vast rational order. Transcendental politics can lead to excesses, as the will to dominate over society is made easier by the control of society's political and cultural life. In modernity, bad leaders who tend toward transcendental politics have made use of technology, propaganda and culture to seize total control over politics and society.

Primordial and transcendental politics, I argue, are appropriate for describing the case of Vargas Llosa's depiction of Trujillo and the power he exerted over Dominican society. Moreover, the classic conception of the tyrannical soul and the modern apparatus necessary for total control over society are helpful aids to contemporary leadership theories that try to account for bad, destructive and toxic leadership. The novel illustrates how Trujillo enveloped himself with power to serve his passions, especially his insatiable appetite for women. This side of Trujillo is spirited, aggressive, maniacal and capricious. The novel presents examples of Trujillo's sexual perfidy, the humiliation of collaborators, violent oppression against those who he thinks might threaten his rule. At the same time, the novel presents the dictatorship's transcendental and totalizing force that penetrates all dimensions of life. The Trujillo regime uses the State's power to police its citizens and generate propaganda through language, symbols and popular culture.

Before exploring the essence of Trujillo's destructive primordiality, I first turn to a discussion of the characters uniquely affected and disaffected by the dictatorship. They provide a frame to understand the deleterious effects of toxic environments. Moreover, these characters are essential to the novel, which follows three interrelated plot lines that involve shifting temporal and narrative perspectives.

SUFFERING THE TYRANT: URANIA AND THE CONSPIRATORS

Urania Cabral, who is the daughter of Agustín Cabral, Trujillo's close advisor, is the novel's main fictional protagonist who has ended her 35-year self-imposed exile after her attempted rape by Trujillo. Her narrative opens and closes the book. She has come back to the Dominican Republic to face her father, who offers the 14-year-old virgin to Trujillo after being marginalized by the dictator. Forty-nine-year-old Urania is the voice of the present; her character is the traumatic witness of the legacy of destruction left by Trujillo's practices, especially women. Urania has spent her life making sense of Trujillo's will to power, violence and grotesque degradation of women and men. Vargas Llosa explores the full spectrum of Trujillo's tyranny. For example, Trujillo revels in what he considers his act of high statesmanship, which included killing 20,000 unarmed Haitians; strategizing about how to use his secret police force on perceived threats; feeding murdered victims to sharks; assassinating exiles and forcing himself on his collaborators' wives and young girls.

After this incident, Urania is spirited away to the United States by Catholic nuns. Study becomes her coping strategy. While a student at Harvard Law School, she audits a Caribbean history course and acquires what she calls a "'perverse hobby': reading and collecting books on the Trujillo Era" (Vargas Llosa, 2000 [2001], p. 154). Speaking to her elderly father who is left immobile and mute after suffering a stroke, Urania tells him:

> But in my bedroom, only Dominican books. Testimonies, essays, memoirs, lots of histories. Can you guess the period? The Trujillo Era, what else? The most important thing that happened to us in five hundred years. You used to say with so much conviction. It's true, Papa. During those thirty-one years, all the evil we had carried with us since the Conquest became crystallized. I've become an expert on Trujillo ... my hobby has been finding out what happened during those years. It's a shame we can't have a conversation. You could clarify so many things for me, you lived them arm in arm with your beloved Chief, who repaid your loyalty so shabbily. For instance, I would have liked for you to tell me if His Excellency also took my mother to bed. (Vargas Llosa, 2000 [2001], p. 272)

The third plot line follows the arc of Trujillo's assassins. The conspirators are mostly midlevel bureaucrats, functionaries and military personnel who have benefited from the regime, although at great personal cost. For example, Amadito, a second lieutenant, undergoes one of Trujillo's infamous tests of loyalty. He denies Amadito permission to marry his beloved and orders him to execute a political subversive in a cloaked hood. Later, he discovers that the subversive was his former fiancée's brother. Antonio de la Maza, a businessman who has profited from complicity with the regime, joins the conspiracy as revenge for the death of his brother. Antonio's character describes the sapping of his will and spirit at the hands of Trujillo's dictatorship:

with a method that was slower and more perverse than when he had his prey shot, beaten to death or fed to the sharks. He had killed him in stages, taking away his decency, his honor, his self-respect, his joy in living, his hopes, and desires, turning him into a sack of bones tormented by the guilty conscience that had been destroying him gradually for so many years. (Vargas Llosa, 2000 [2001], p. 90)

At the end of the novel, months after Trujillo's death, one of the few conspirators who survived, Antonio Imbert Barrera, speaks of "the spell that had kept so many Dominicans devoted, body and soul, to Trujillo" (Vargas Llosa, 2000 [2001], p. 382). José René Román, nicknamed Pupo, embodies the individual under Trujillo's "spell." A high-ranking general who suffers Trujillo's incessant abuse, he joins the conspirators with the crucial job of initiating a military and civic junta once he receives confirmation that Trujillo is dead. However, Pupo becomes paralyzed by indecision despite his awareness of the actions he must take. After a series of mistakes, he takes stock of his situation and concludes that he is in a "somnambulistic state . . . sunk in a kind of hypnosis, he thought his inaction could be due to the fact that although the body of the Chief might be dead, his soul, spirit, whatever you called it, still enslaved him" (Vargas Llosa, 2000 [2001], p. 318–19). Trujillo's destructive power is so penetrating that it robs Pupo of the capacity to exercise his will at the decisive moment.

The most poignant example of how the dictatorship corrodes individual will is that of Agustín Cabral, a devoted follower, who falls apart when he is publicly disgraced and loses Trujillo's favor. Cabral is unaware that Trujillo is submitting him to an arbitrary test of loyalty. Utterly despondent, Cabral suffers an existential crisis; his sense of self-worth recedes without Trujillo's attention. Cabral represents the utter precariousness of living under a tyrant, especially for strong followers; the capriciousness of Trujillo's rule eliminates freedom and completely subjects followers' fortunes to chance.

In his state, Cabral desperately calls upon one collaborator after another who might help regain Trujillo's favor and finally looks to Trujillo's pimp, Manuel Alfonso. Alfonso, over the course of a few conversations, persuades Cabral to exchange his 14-year-old daughter's virginity to regain the dictator's favor. Cabral does not outright reject or even protest against such an idea. When he resolves to offer up his daughter to Trujillo, he tells Urania that Trujillo has invited her to a party. He tries to unburden himself from the weight of this fateful decision by seeming to give her a choice: "If you don't want to go, you won't go, Uranita . . . I'll call Manuel Alfonso right now and tell him you're not well, and give your regrets to the Chief" (Vargas Llosa, 2000 [2001], p. 271). Confused, young and hoping to help her despondent father, Urania agrees to go to the supposed party.

Urania, never truly having a choice, is a victim of living in the conditions of primordial politics: "things that had to do with desire, instincts, power and the infinite excesses and brutalities that a combination of those things could mean in a country shaped by Trujillo" (Vargas Llosa, 2000 [2001], p. 321).

Trujillo's act of enervating the wills of those around him renders them powerless, leaving only one avenue for social change. Vargas Llosa proffers tyrannicide as the only viable solution. He places the rationalization for this in the character of the one conspirator outside of Trujillo's fold, Salvador Estrella Sadhalá (the Turk). A devout Catholic, we see him seek legitimate reasons for killing the tyrant. Salvador claims to be neither a fanatic nor a saint, but feels compelled to respond to the oppression of Catholic priests following the issuances of the Pastoral Letter of 1961, in which the Bishops declared their opposition to Trujillo. Thinking that he must rid society of Trujillo, whom he calls "the Beast," Salvador consults his spiritual advisor, who puts him in touch with the Papal Nuntius. He refers Salvador to a passage in St Thomas Aquinas's *Summa Theologica:* "God looks with favor upon the physical elimination of the Beast if a people is freed thereby" (Vargas Llosa, 2000 [2001], p. 185).

Vargas Llosa places Salvador's moral justification for tyrannicide at a critical juncture, as his character's internal dialogue immediately precedes Trujillo's assassination (Köllmann, 2014, p. 232). Salvador articulates how Trujillo has created a toxic environment, emasculating to men and filled with desperation. Salvador thinks to himself:

> [i]t was the fault of the Beast that so many Dominicans turned to whores, drinking binges, and other dissipations to ease their anguish at leading a life without a shred of liberty or dignity, in a country where human life was worth nothing. Trujillo had been one of Satan's most effective allies. (Vargas Llosa, 2000 [2001], p. 187)

Though Salvador's notions of where personal responsibility begin and end beg the question, he gives voice to what life is in an undemocratic regime that denies basic rights.

THE GOAT: TRUJILLO'S PRIMORDIALISM

The novel follows Trujillo through the entire day culminating in his assassination. In the first scene, Trujillo has just awoken before dawn on 30 May 1961. Trained by the US Marines, he wakes every morning before 4 a.m., and keeps to a routine of exacting discipline, of which he is supremely proud. He bemoans his poor sleep, disturbed by restlessness and nightmares: "he woke, paralyzed by a sense of catastrophe" (Vargas Llosa, 2000 [2001], p. 14).Vargas Llosa, who has written about Shakespeare, is likely referring to a scene in *Richard III* when, on the eve of the Battle of Bosworth Field, Richard (also a tyrant) awakens after a night plagued by nightmares of the ghosts of his victims—Richard, too, ends his day by being killed in the overthrow of his government.[3]

Trujillo has a dark charisma, and it emanates from his belief that his military training by US Marines was his key formative experience. As he wakes he says to himself, "'I owe everything I am to discipline,' he thought. And discipline, the polestar of his life, he owed to the Marines" (Vargas Llosa, 2000 [2001], p. 13). From this obsession with discipline Trujillo cultivates a myth about his immaculate appearance, legendary virility and physical endurance, which helps to keep his followers under a spell throughout the novel. He never sleeps past 4 a.m., supposedly does not sweat and subjects his inner circle to grueling midsummer walks. Trujillo cloaks himself in these superficialities, yet attributes superhuman qualities to them. His sense of discipline is another way he exercises control over others, as he is mercilessly judgmental on those who do not keep his standards of appearance, especially those in the military.

However, Trujillo, now 70, suffers from incontinence and impotence, a painful ailment for a man who prides himself on his physical appearance, health and sexual prowess. The criminal charisma of Trujillo, sustained by martial and physical attributes, is now beleaguered by physical decline. The moral decrepitude of the regime becomes more evident as Trujillo desperately clings to his image of charismatic strongman. These physical maladies are deeply troubling for Trujillo's mental stability because he projects his health and manliness onto the nation's health. As such, he has become increasingly erratic. Trujillo tends to a ceaseless meandering of angry thoughts, which rise to the surface in his inner monologue:

> He was involved in the complicated task of securing his socks with garters so there would be no wrinkles. Now, how pleasant it was to give free rein to his rage when there was no risk to the State, when he could give rats, toads, hyenas, snakes what they deserve. The bellies of sharks bore witness to the fact that he had not denied himself the pleasure. (Vargas Llosa, 2000 [2001], p. 23)

Trujillo's ability to act on his thoughts and whims inspires terror in those who work closely with the regime; he especially relishes the fear he inspires in them when he adds to their uncertainty. Without explanation he summons one of his generals and then thinks to himself, "it cheered him to imagine the sizzling questions, suppositions, fears, suspicions he had put into the head of that asshole who the Minister of the Armed Forces . . . he would be in hell until the evening" (Vargas Llosa, 2000 [2001], p. 127).

Most of Trujillo's concern with governance revolves around his paranoia about constant conspiracies against his regime. His violent and defiant personality led to him having problems in foreign affairs. The narrator enumerates the manifold difficulties facing Trujillo's regime, which are of his own making:

> The massive dragnets of January 1960, into which so many boys and girls of the June 14 Movement fell, among them the Mirabal sisters and their husbands. Trujillo's break with his old accomplice, the Catholic Church, after the Pastoral Letter of January 1960, in which the bishops denounced the dictatorship. The attempt against President Bentacourt of Venezuela, in June 1960, that mobilized so many countries against Trujillo, including his great ally the United States, which voted in favor of sanctions on August 6, 1960, at the conference in Costa Rica. (Vargas Llosa, 2000 [2001], p. 136)

Trujillo is defiant in the face of such a perilous moment because his governing characteristic is the belief in his superiority over all other human beings. He is a narcissist who dons a superman role, as he believes, aided by intellectual collaborators, that he is a providential force in Dominican history. Trujillo recites a speech written about him from memory:

> a bold energetic will that supports, in the march of the Republic toward the fulfillment of its destiny, the protective benevolence of supernatural forces. God and Trujillo: here in synthesis, is the explanation, first, of the survival of the nation, and second, of the present-day flourishing of Dominican life. (Vargas Llosa, 2000 [2001], p. 224)

Although Trujillo did bring modern industry to the Dominican Republic, the economy was built through cronyism that primarily enriched Trujillo, his family and his supporters. His sham grandiosity is on display when asked about his greatest moment as a statesman, which he recounts vividly at a dinner party:

> He was solemn, absorbed in his memories. The silence thickened. Hieratic and theatrical, the Generalissimo raised his hands and showed them to his guests: "For the sake of this country, I have stained these with blood," he stated, emphasizing each syllable. "To keep the blacks from colonizing us again. There were tens of thousands of them, and they were everywhere. If I hadn't the Dominican Republic would not exist today. The entire island would be Haiti, as it was in 1840. The handful of white survivors would be serving the black. That was my most difficult decision in thirty years of government, Simon." (Vargas Llosa, 2000 [2001], p. 163)

Trujillo does not observe faith, lacks empathy and cannot conceive of any real political principles. Although he is the head of state, he is an apolitical creature who lacks a sense of justice and legality. For Trujillo, politics and society are things he uses to project his image of power, success and martial discipline. He magnifies his superficial attributes, and they become the emblems of public life. Urania retells the story of the 25th anniversary of Trujillo's rule. At great public cost, about half of the nation's budget, he hosted the "Fair for Peace and Brotherhood in the Free World." At the main ceremony, a bronze statue of Trujillo is unveiled, "in a morning coat and academic robes, professorial diplomas in hand" (Vargas Llosa, 2000 [2001], p. 98).

Vargas Llosa shows how far the dictator goes to maintain power over several decades. Although *The Feast of the Goat* is fiction, Vargas Llosa did meticulous research in the 1990s, and in an interview explained that "I did not invent anything that could not have happened" (Williams, 2014, p. 88). Vargas Llosa's visceral fiction shows how the interior of a dictatorship functions, free of the junk bin of abstractions and academic jargon. On the other hand, Urania represents the trauma lived by those who suffer at the hands of destructive leadership. In an interview, Vargas Llosa explains his choice: "I invented Urania's character because I did not want the novel to be told only from the point of view (the interior) of dictatorship" (Canfield, 2013, p. 258, [my translation]).

TOTALIZING TYRANNY: THE STATE APPARATUS AND POULAR CULTURE

In the novel, Trujillo's hold over Dominican society depends on a high degree of forceful coercion and fear, which manifests through his sadistic head of intelligence, Johnny Abbes García, the real historical person who headed Trujillo's infamous SIM agency. Abbes García and the SIM vigilantly guarded against any sign that could be interpreted as anti-Trujillo, systematically eliminating anything they perceived as threats to his regime through intimidation, torture and murder.

Trujillo reminisces with pleasure about all the domestic enemies that he was able to kill, even in exile. José Almoina, Jesús de Galíndez, Ramón Marrero Aristy, the famed Mirabal sisters and even a mentally insane couple who Trujillo had killed for impersonating him and his wife in public (Vargas Llosa, 2000 [2001], p. 23). Vargas Llosa shows us Trujillo's motive in murdering each one of these Dominican citizens. The Mirabal sisters spearheaded a youthful communist opposition; Aristy wrote critical articles of Trujillo in *The New York Times*; Galindez's dissertation on the Dominican Republic was deemed disrespectful; Almoina wrote a book entitled *Una satrapía en el Caribe*.

The use of violence and power is coeval with Trujillo's dictatorship, but that power extends beyond physical and legal control. Vargas Llosa shows how the dictator shapes and controls popular opinion and culture, incubating its propaganda into people's attitudes and opinions through the appropriation of cultural symbols. For example, Trujillo's name is everywhere. He insists on being called: "the Chief, the Generalissimo, the Benefactor, the Father of the New Nation, His Excellency Dr. Rafael Leónidas Trujillo Molina" (Vargas Llosa, 2000 [2001], p. 6). "The Goat," however, which people use negatively, is the nickname that has the greatest significance for the novel since it connotes Trujillo's indomitable sexual appetite. As many dictators have the tendency to do, Trujillo renames major Dominican landmarks. For example, the country's capital, Santo Domingo, became Ciudad Trujillo. Streets, parks and buildings also carry his name. Public events are dedicated to Benefactor of the Fatherland and Father of the New Fatherland. In every home, alongside every altar to the Virgin Altagracia there is a bronze sign that reads, "In this house Trujillo is Chief" (Vargas Llosa, 2000 [2001], p. 9). In honor of fecundity, Trujillo awards a prize named after his mother to the Dominican woman who has the greatest number of children: the Julia Molina Widow of Trujillo Prize to the Most Prolific Mother. In the novel, the winner of the prize, Dona Alejandrina Fransico, exclaims, "My twenty-one children will give their lives for Trujillo if they are asked to" (Vargas Llosa, 2000 [2001], p. 18).

Trujillo also demands intellectuals, historians, poets and literary figures to submit their talents to create a totalizing narrative of the regime, which also turns the upper-caste Dominican citizenry into docile and laudatory instruments. For example, his advisors create a ubiquitous slogan for the Dominican Party using the initials of Trujillo's name: Rectitude, Liberty, Work, Morality. The author of that slogan, Henry Chirinos, a lawyer who helped frame the constitution, boasted that "twenty years later it's on all the streets and squares of the country. And in the overwhelming majority of homes" (Vargas Llosa, 2000 [2001], p. 124). Another key collaborator, Joaquín Balaguer, wrote the speech about Trujillo linking his rule to God's providential will. It contains the famous phrase, "God and Trujillo," of which the dictator was so fond that it was showcased in bright luminous signs in people's homes both in the capital city and the interior (Vargas Llosa, 2000 [2001], p. 225). In the novel, Balaguer further explains his rationale behind this phrase when asked by Trujillo if he still believes in his thesis in the present day, in light of the mounting international pressures against the regime. He responds, "More than I did then, Excellency . . . Trujillo could not have carried out his superhuman mission without transcendental help. You have been, for this nation, an instrument of the Supreme Being" (Vargas Llosa, 2000 [2001], p. 225). His followers feed this egomaniacal sense of self that is one the one hand ridiculous, but is also necessary for exerting complete control over the social and cultural lives of Dominicans on the other.

At the level of popular culture, Trujillo uses popular mediums like radio and cultural forms, such as *merengue*, to support his regime and extend his influence into the Dominican countryside. Trujillo boasts about making the *merengue* fashionable in the capital and among all social classes. Before his rule, *merengue* was looked down upon since it connoted a rural lifestyle, regionalism and cultural backwardness. Urania speaks to the invidious racism that exists between its European, African and indigenous populations:

> She sees two barefoot, half-naked Haitian men sitting on boxes under dozens of vividly colored paintings displayed on the wall of a building. It's true, the city, perhaps the country, has filled with Haitians. Back then, it didn't happen. Isn't that what Senator Agustín Cabral said? "You can say what you like about the Chief. History, at least, will recognize that he has created a modern country and put the Haitians in their place. Great ills demand great remedies!" (Vargas Llosa, 2000 [2001], p. 7)

Trujillo, an inveterate racist himself, came from a rural, lower class origin and his mother was of a mixed-race background. To compensate, Trujillo banned voodoo rituals and promoted Dominican *merengue* to create a nationalistic culture in an attempt to differentiate the Dominican Republic as much as possible from Haiti, which Trujillo views as the poorest and most violent nation in the Western Hemisphere (Vargas Llosa, 2000 [2001], p. 356).

The novel supplies a litany of examples of the Trujillo regime's ever-presence in Dominican life through popular mediums. Trujillo's brother Petán owns the two radio stations and the sole television station. These media outlets serve to broadcast pro-Trujillo propaganda. In various scenes, the main radio station, "The Dominican Voice," is playing in the background. It plays pro-Trujillo *merengue* groups while interspersing publicity announcements from the Trujillo government. The novel demonstrates the regime's control of information by using the two newspapers, *La Nacion* and *El Caribe,* to decry enemies, traitors and even hapless loyalists, as we see happen to Agustín Cabral. The infamous "Public Forum," is a daily column that "kept people in a state of anxiety because their fate depended on whatever was said about them there" (Vargas Llosa, 2000 [2001], p. 36).

In another example of how the media acted as Trujillo's mouthpiece, the papers turned much of their attention to the bishops of the Catholic Church. In 1960, the Church's bishops issued a Pastoral Letter openly criticizing the regime for its human rights abuses, which led to an onslaught of societal oppression and persecution of the bishops. The reader sees Trujillo listening to two anti-Church speeches playing simultaneously on both radio stations:

> On the Dominican Voice, Pain Pichardo . . . recalled that the state had spent sixty million pesos on the Church, whose "bishops and priests are now doing much harm to the Catholic faithful of the Dominican Republic." He turned the dial. On Caribbean Radio they were reading a letter of protest . . . "against the disturbing machination of Bishop Thomas Reilly, a traitor to God, Trujillo, and his own manhood, who, instead of remaining in his diocese of San Juan de la Maguana, ran like a scared rat to hide in Ciudad Trujillo behind the skirts of American nuns at Santo Domingo Academy, a vipers' nest of terrorism and conspiracy." (Vargas Llosa, 2000 [2001], p. 20)

Trujillo appropriates these popular mediums for his propaganda, but also uses them to impart punishment and produce fear. In the example of the Bishops, he wants them to suffer for what he considers a betrayal. In the novel, he consistently goes back and forth on the topic of whether he should have them killed but stops short because he fears that the United States, once one of his staunchest allies, will punish him severely for persecuting the Church with John F. Kennedy at the helm. Nevertheless, he dispatches Johnny Abbes García, the chief of secret police, to torment Bishop Reilly and the nuns of the Catholic school for girls: "every night Colonel Abbes García's men played popular Trujillista merengues over loudspeakers directed at the school, depriving the sisters of sleep"(Vargas Llosa, 2000 [2001], p. 230). Stopping short of physical harm, he harasses them with the Trujillista *merengues,* which must serve to remind them that in the Dominican Republic, Trujillo supersedes the Church.

CONCLUSION

The Feast of the Goat helps provide an alarm to tyranny through its visceral portrait of dictatorship. It raises fundamental questions about what gives rise to tyranny and the effects of primordial and totalizing politics on an entire society. Vargas Llosa has attested to the view that this novel has a grander aim than simply telling the story of Trujillo: "with *The Feast of the Goat* I have written about all Latin American dictators, some who are dead and others, unfortunately, who are alive and kicking" (Martinez, 2000 [my translation]).[4] Citing Vargas Llosa's views about his novel, Julie Kruger has observed that Llosa's intention is explicitly political. According to Vargas Llosa, his reason for writing *The Feast of Goat* has a clear purpose:

Let's hope that my Trujillo endures. That is, always, the dream of every author . . . I hope . . . that my Trujillo provokes disgust in my readers and disdain for all dictatorships. To use it for this . . . I have a perverse gratitude for this dictator, who, one day, finally, dictated a novel to me. (Kruger, 2002 [my translation])[5]

The Feast of the Goat is not a postmodern work that depicts power simply as symbolic and anonymous discourse. Vargas Llosa blurs the lines between fiction and reality in such a way as to put his readers on guard against a general submissiveness, resignation to the loss of freedom, the malignity of fate and the banality of evil. The novel serves as a reminder that historically stable Western democracies are not the norm, and even in stable democracies, citizens might turn a blind eye to creeping authoritarianism through suppression of the press and individual rights. Although Vargas Llosa's depiction of Trujillo's bad leadership presents an extreme pole of dictatorship, it shows in an alarming dramatization that ease in which one individual can capture power and engage in abuse, while an entire society can forfeit its liberty and become an abettor in tyranny.

NOTES

1. For a primer on destructive leadership see, Padilla et al. (2007) "The toxic triangle: Destructive leaders, susceptible followers, and conducive environments," *The Leadership Quarterly*, **18** (3), 176–94.
2. The notable examples include: Augusto Roa Bastos's (1974) *I, the Supreme*, Alejo Carpentier's (1974) *Reasons of State* (1974), and Gabriel García Márquez's (1975) *The Autumn of the Patriarch*.
3. I would like to thank Kristin Bezio for pointing out this observation to me and allowing me to include it in this chapter.
4. *Con La fiesta del Chivo he escrito sobre todos los dictadores latinoamericanos, algunos muertos y otros todavía vivitos y coleando, por desgracia.*
5. *Ojalá que mi Trujillo permanezca. Eso es, desde ya, el sueno de todo escritor . . . Espero . . . que mi Trujillo provoque asco en los lectores y desprecio por todas las dictaduras. Usarlo para eso . . . Hay un agradecimiento perverso hacia ese dictador que, finalmente, un día me dictó una novela.*

REFERENCES

Bosman, J. and S. Romero (2010), "Vargas Llosa takes Nobel in Literature," *The New York Times*, accessed 1 October 2010 at http://www.nytimes.com/2010/10/08/books/08nobel.html.

Canfield, M.L. (2013), *Perù frontiera del mondo. Eielson e Vargas Llosa: dalle radici all'impegno cosmopolita/Perú frontera del mundo. Eielson y Vargas Llosa: de las raíces al compromiso cosmopolita*, Firenze, Italy: Firenze University Press.

Castellanos, J. and M.A. Martinez (1981), "El dictador hispanoamericano como personaje literario," *Latin American Research Review*, **16** (2), 79–105.

Einarsen, S., M.S. Aasland and A. Skogstad (2007), "Destructive leadership behaviour: A definition and conceptual model," *The Leadership Quarterly*, **18** (3), 207–16.

Fradinger, M. (2010), *Binding Violence: Literary Visions of Political Origins*, Palo Alto, CA: Stanford University Press.

Kellerman, B. (2004), *Bad Leadership: What it is, How it Happens, Why it Matters*, Boston, MA: Harvard Business Press.

Köllmann, S. (2014), *A Companion to Mario Vargas Llosa*, vol. 331, Woodbridge, Suffolk, UK: Boydell & Brewer Ltd.

Kruger, J. (2002), "Everyone's invited: Power and the body in 'La fiesta del chivo'," *Confluencia*, **18** (1), 52–8.

Lipman-Blumen, J. (2005), "Toxic leadership: When grand illusions masquerade as noble visions," *Leader to Leader*, **2005** (36), 29–36.

Martinez, S. (2000), "Mario Vargas Llosa indaga en la mente de los dictadores latinoamericanos: 'Escribiendo sobre Trujillo he escrito sobre todos los dictadores'," *BABAB*, accessed 1 May 2000 at http://www.babab.com/no02/vargas_llosa.htm.

Newell, W. (2013), *Tyranny: A New Interpretation*, Cambridge, UK: Cambridge University Press.

Padilla, A., R. Hogan and R. Kaiser (2007), "The toxic triangle: Destructive leaders, susceptible followers, and conducive environments", *The Leadership Quarterly*, **18** (3), 176–94.

Schyns, B. and T. Hansbrough (2010), *When Leadership Goes Wrong: Destructive Leadership, Mistakes, and Ethical Failures*, Charlotte, NC: IAP.

Vargas Llosa, M. (2000), *The Feast of the Goat*, trans. Edith Grossman (2001), New York, NY: Farrar, Straus, and Giroux.

Williams, R.L. (2014), *Mario Vargas Llosa: A Life of Writing*, Austin, TX: University of Texas Press.

4. Harry Potter and the leadership of resistance

Kimberly Yost

Contemporary leadership theories are shifting paradigms about exemplary leadership from individual leaders who create change through heroic individual actions to a model that incorporates shared or distributed leadership through the transformational efforts of the post-heroic leader. The post-heroic leader releases the intrinsic motivation of followers to achieve goals and, thus, changes the power dynamic of the group and enables the group to achieve more than expected (Northouse, 2007). Historically, leadership has been modeled through mythic heroes both real (for example, Abraham Lincoln, Jack Welch) and imaginary (for example, Odysseus, Clark Kent/Superman). For contemporary audiences, particularly those born in the 1980s and later, the explosion of young adult literature—heralded by the hugely successful *Harry Potter* series and continued with the trilogies of *Hunger Games* (Suzanne Collins) and *Divergent* (Veronica Roth)—provides additional opportunities to explore not only post-heroic leadership, but also the leadership of resistance, which opposes authority and the status quo. As 2017 marks the 20th anniversary of the publication of the first Harry Potter book, it seems appropriate to explore these narratives and their enduring qualities for leadership and social change.

Essentially, J.K. Rowling's *Harry Potter* series is a modern retelling of the classic hero myth. Like mythic heroes, Harry undertakes a journey wherein he acquires skills, experiences and knowledge that enable him to defeat the threats to his community. However, through gaining self-knowledge and overcoming obstacles, Harry develops his leadership capabilities and emerges as an example of a character that transcends the model of mythic hero to become a post-heroic transformational leader, empowering others to resist and overcome the threats to their community and bring about social change. Outside of the numerous authors who expeditiously label Harry Potter as a hero, scholarly consideration has almost exclusively identified Harry as an individual hero, neglecting the formation of relationships and the series of events that precede Harry's ability to become a transformational leader and enact social change. Behr (2005) correctly identifies "transformation [as] the key and the core" (p. 128) of the stories, but her analysis primarily relates to narrative function, relegating Harry's personal transformations to maturation. In contrast, this analysis examines the evolution of the character to transformational leader and reflects upon how popular culture can be useful in understanding the dynamics of resistance and social change. Throughout the series of novels, primary consideration can be given to the fact that Harry and his peers are demonstrating resistance and enacting change in creative ways that will bring order from chaos and a renewed stability to their community.

CHILDREN'S LITERATURE

Literature has traditionally played a role in the development of collective behaviors that socialize individuals. Stories are used as a rhetorical means to convince or instruct the audience (Feldman and Skoldberg, 2002). Children's literature, in particular, is a method of socializing young people to the common culture of norms, rituals, social boundaries, innovations and creating social cohesion through shared literary experiences (Kidd, 2007). As Chappell (2008) notes, children's literature can also help the child reader to deconstruct the ambiguities of the adult world and allow for reconstruction of institutions in meaningful ways to the child while leaving these institutions intact and upholding the status quo. More to the point, children's fantasy and folk literature is deemed a positive metaphor for human experiences (Gooderham, 1995; Thomas, 2003; Taub and Servaty-Seib, 2009), which allows readers to actively participate in the message without the constraints of space (Djupedal, 1993) while reinforcing cultural norms. Conversely, Foucault sees the socializing process of children's literature as suspect and a means of coercive power through the effects of discipline (Wolosky, 2014). Yet Wolosky (2014) points to the ways in which the *Harry Potter* stories address resistance to disciplinary structures, as well as ways in which discipline furthers agentic behaviors through strengthening selfhood via the experiences of that resistance.

The *Harry Potter* books are commonly associated with fantasy literature, but are a fusion of genres incorporating fantasy, the English boarding school story, detective fiction, sports story, adventure, hero myth, melodrama and series fiction (Alton, 2009). As Nikolajeva (2009) observes, the *Harry Potter* series both complies and deviates from the conventions of children's literature and genre fiction. For example, Rowling presents literary subgenres in new ways by offering a co-educational English boarding school and creating a series that cannot be adequately experienced out of order, unlike *Nancy Drew* or *Scooby-Doo* where the characters do not age—or even change clothes.

Literary scholars are more apt to assign the *Harry Potter* books to the literature of *Bildungsroman* or 'coming of age' novel where the protagonist is helped to reach his or her (but usually *his*) potential and destiny by unseen higher forces (Heilman, 2009; Appelbaum, 2009; Bousquet, 2009). This is not to suggest that the protagonist must develop and mature through a linear process. As Bousquet (2009) points out, an element of melodrama exists in many of these stories allowing the protagonist to come into his or her destiny through revelation instead of personal development or physical effort. However, ascribing the *Harry Potter* books to coming of age stories may be too simplistic. By characterizing the maturation of the protagonist as chronological and intrinsically natural, as opposed to a process of development that requires the efforts of the individual as well as others known and unknown, the traditional purpose of children's literature characters to be instructive role models seems diminished.

HERO MYTH

Rowling reaches beyond *Bildungsroman* motifs by incorporating the classical, as opposed to romantic, hero myth into her books. Similar to children's literature but tracing back to the earliest human storytelling, these myths provide the symbols and structures that constitute common culture (Nylund, 2007). Gehmann (2003) considers traditional myths to gain their meaning and authority from being rooted in the origins of culture, whereas modern myths are considered self-referential and linked to concepts of human progress. As noted by mythologist Joseph Campbell in his seminal work *The Hero with a Thousand Faces* (1949), the hero myth is an elemental story of humankind that crosses cultural boundaries in space and time.

These stories are identified through archetypes of characters and events within the structure of a journey. The hero journey is a process of development for the individual. Self-knowledge and overcoming internal and external obstacles are key elements. Rarely is there a *deus ex machina* resolution to the story, although a revelation of knowledge may occur. The hero cannot be passive and allow others to manipulate and order outcomes but is, instead, an active participant in obtaining the goal. Indeed, the hero must prevail based on his or her acquired knowledge and tools and almost invariably confronts the final obstacle alone. Through the journey, the hero develops a greater sense of personal power. In addition, feelings of responsibility grow as the hero fights to protect and serve his or her community.

As Napierkowski (2005) observes, "some of the most fundamental lessons of literature address the concepts of leadership and responsibility in society" (p. 504). Indeed, Natov (2001) views the *Harry Potter* series as chronicling "the process of the child's movement from the initial consciousness of himself as the central character in his story . . . to a sense of his own power and responsibility to a larger community" (p. 311). Unlike traditional romantic heroes in children's literature, mythic heroes are not obedient to strictures and passively wait for deliverance from a higher power. Chappell (2008) argues that the qualities of a postmodern childhood such as ambiguity, complexity, agency and resistance cause the conventional story binary of good/evil and passive heroism to be inadequate and poses Harry Potter as a postmodern hero capable of instructing and role modeling to contemporary readers.

The model of the hero journey is quite specific, but hero myths do incorporate variations such as isolating or enlarging an element, stringing a series of cycles into a single story, fusing elements together or ignoring certain elements that may no longer provide meaning to the audience (Campbell, 1949). Campbell's model is effectively distilled into a twelve-step pattern: The Ordinary World; Call to Adventure; Refusal of the Call; Meeting with the Mentor; Crossing the First Threshold; Tests, Allies and Enemies; Approach to the Inmost Cave; Ordeal; Reward; The Road Back; Resurrection and Return with the Elixir (Vogler, 1998). Although the pattern can have infinite refinements, at the core of the journey are the hero's values, which are exemplified through heroic symbols, such as healing potions, magic swords that can defeat dragons and treasures (Vogler, 1998). These symbols represent the hero's understanding and commitment to the universal longings for healing, peace and prosperity.

In addition to specific events in the hero journey, Campbell explores the common characters, symbols and relationships within myth in terms of archetypes formulated by psychologist Carl Jung. Jung considered these personality archetypes as part of the collective unconscious, and Campbell observed that the function of these archetypes enables the shared experience of storytelling (Vogler, 1998). The most common archetypes include the Hero, the Mentor, the Shadow, the Trickster and the Threshold Guardian, although there are many others, each typifying an aspect of human personality and either help or hinder the hero's efforts. These characters should not be understood as static or singular. The archetypes are *functions* of the story, and these functions can be performed by different characters at different moments in the story.

Upon their return, heroes are perceived as leaders within their communities and cultures as a result of the hero journey they have undertaken. Thus, hero myths are an effective means of granting authority to leadership attempts and are needed to justify existing institutions and cultural norms, while supporting particular kinds of change (Douglas et al., 2001). As Natov (2001) notes, the hero is caught in a paradoxical struggle of maintaining tradition while challenging norms to create change. By creating change, the hero overcomes obstacles and achieves goals within traditional structures. Heroes are not agents of revolution bent on overthrowing societal constructs in totality, but discover new ways of bringing order to the current dysfunctional structure and create new paradigms for stabilization and renewal.

TRANSFORMATIONAL LEADERSHIP

As change agents, transformational leaders share qualities with mythic heroes. This type of leadership mirrors the hero journey, as it is a process of personal and organizational development related to meeting challenges and enabling change. Fletcher (2004) views transformational leadership as dynamic, multidimensional, collective and an "emergent process more than an achieved state" (p. 649). Transformational leaders are concerned with the collective good, have a strong moral compass, inspire and motivate others to accomplish more than is expected, and typically emerge during times of great stress (Northouse, 2007). Ligon et al. (2008) note that "outstanding leaders generally emerge when a social system is experiencing a crisis or a set of events creating turbulence and placing institutions at risk" (p. 313). The challenge for leaders during times of crisis is similar to that of the hero, in that the achievement of goals may require transformative changes that provide innovative means for renewed stabilization.

A key characteristic of transformational leadership is the bond of trust, credibility and shared values between the leader and followers that develops over time and eventually blurs the line between traditional notions of leader-follower power structures. This obscuring of conventional roles and responsibilities leads to the understanding of transformational leadership as "post-heroic." The bond is developed through the post-heroic traits of empathy, community, vulnerability and skills of inquiry and collaboration (Fletcher, 2004). These traits are in opposition to heroic traits such as individualism, need for control, assertiveness, and the skills of advocacy and domination (Fletcher, 2004). As the traits imply, the post-heroic leader requires an emotional skill set that is based on relational skills and emotional intelligence qualities such as self-awareness, empathy, vulnerability and an openness to learn from others (Fletcher, 2004). Significantly, postheroic leaders must be able to practice their influence in a power dynamic that is more fluid than structured, reaching a relational configuration that shifts from "power over" to "power with" (Fletcher, 2004).

In positing the hero myth in relationship to transformational leadership, similar themes are discovered, such as mentors, the development of ethical and moral values, self-awareness and the challenge to power structures. A significant dissimilarity is the empowerment of others in achieving goals. In general, classical hero myths do not have a variant that involves the hero developing skills and confidence in others in order to overcome challenges or allowing others to make decisions, offer help or formulate strategies. What we find in the *Harry Potter* books is an example of empowering others to resist detrimental social change and create a renewal of the social contract.

EMPOWERMENT OF OTHERS

Kouzes and Posner (1995) describe empowerment as the ability of a leader to "enable others to take ownership of and responsibility for their group's success" (p. 181). Empowerment is a critical ingredient in transformational leadership, as the emphasis for this style of leadership is on intrinsic motivation and the development of followers (Northouse, 2007). Crucial to remember is the fact that the empowerment of others is not an element typically found in classic hero myths. More often, individual effort in the service of others exemplifies the hero's journey.

Though Harry Potter is the central focus of the story, early evidence demonstrates that Harry does not accomplish goals solely through individual heroic efforts. Even so, Harry is continually reluctant to involve others in his schemes because of the risks and must be repeatedly reminded by Ron and Hermione that others are willing and able to be involved and share their talents and knowledge in reaching objectives.

Success is clearly a team effort, even though students and adults in the wizarding world seem to give Harry the full credit and fame for the tests he has endured. Harry, Hermione and Ron are all involved in meeting the challenges of each test. Their friendship is cemented by trouncing the mountain troll, and they evolve into a team through overcoming the obstacles to retrieve the sorcerer's stone (*Harry Potter and the Sorcerer's Stone* [*Stone*], 1997[1]). The talents of each team member are used, as Ron plays wizard chess, Hermione must solve logic riddles and Harry flies a broomstick and resists the temptation of the stone. They continue this dynamic throughout the series: Ron offers knowledge and skills from growing up in wizard culture; Hermione offers knowledge and skills from academic abilities and magical talents; and Harry demonstrates the willingness to physically confront wickedness and not succumb to the darker facets of his character. Vital to their ability to function as a team is their open communication. They persistently share their worries, theories, knowledge and emotions with each other. In fact, when communication is stifled, as in *Harry Potter and the Goblet of Fire* ([*Goblet*] 2000), *Harry Potter and the Order of the Phoenix* ([*Phoenix*] 2003) and *Harry Potter and the Deathly Hallows* ([*Hallows*] 2007), conflicts surface and the trio can no longer effectively function until they verbalize and resolve their differences.

Communication is a key element for empowering others, but must work in tandem with actions. Harry displays specific empowering behaviors by telling Neville he is "worth twelve of Malfoy" (*Stone*, 1997, p. 218) and praising Ron's Quidditch skills (*Phoenix*, 2003). Because of his guilt over Cedric Diggory's death, Harry secretly gives Fred and George Weasley his tournament winnings to open a joke shop, because he believes in their entrepreneurial abilities and wants them to become successful (*Goblet*, 2000). However, Harry's ability to empower others is primarily illustrated through the formation of Dumbledore's Army, which was Hermione's concept. In *Phoenix* (2003), Umbridge revises the school curriculum to remove practical application of Defense Against the Dark Arts training. In response to a need to defend themselves against Voldemort and his Death Eaters, a small group of students want to learn defensive skills on their own. Ron and Hermione want Harry to teach everyone what he learned from his previous experiences, but he is reluctant and shouts at them:

> [B]ut all that stuff was luck – I didn't know what I was doing half the time, I didn't plan any of it, I just did whatever I could think of, and I nearly always had help–[. . .] I didn't get through any of that because I was brilliant at Defense Against the Dark Arts, I got through it all because – because help came at the right time, or because I guessed right – but I just blundered through it all, I didn't have a clue what I was doing [. . .] You don't know what it's like![. . .] The whole time you know there's nothing between you and dying except your own – your own brain or guts or whatever – you can't think straight when you know you're about a second from being murdered, or tortured, or watching your friends die. (*Phoenix*, 2003, p. 327–8)

This speech is not a humble denial of his ability; Harry is truly frightened and concerned about the consequences of having his peers confront the forces of Voldemort. Hermione must then empower Harry. She tells him: "This . . . this is exactly why we need you . . . We need to know what it's r-really like . . . facing him . . . facing V-Voldemort" (*Phoenix*, 2003, p. 328).

Harry acquiesces and begins clandestine lessons with them for learning counter-curses, patronus charms and other methods of defending themselves against attack. Harry designs the lessons so that the students are paired and learn from each other, as opposed to Harry simply demonstrating. Other students bring knowledge to the group that Harry does not possess, such as certain jinxes. Harry displays remarkable behavior in lightly correcting his peers and encouraging them even when they are obviously unskilled or struggling to master a spell.

Empowerment is also reciprocal. Dumbledore's Army has made Harry feel "as though he were carrying some kind talisman inside his chest [. . .] a glowing secret that supported him through Umbridge's classes" (*Phoenix*, 2003, p. 397). Interestingly, Rowling describes Dumbledore's Army as a *talisman* for Harry, which is neither knowledge nor an object, but a group of people, and as talismans are used by the hero to overcome obstacles, Dumbledore's Army simultaneously adheres to and alters hero myth.

Despite everything, Dumbledore's Army learns Harry has grave doubts about the capacity of his peers for fighting. Yet the students have found their personal strength and integrity, created an environment of trust and teamwork, believe in the vision of Dumbledore and Harry to resist the administration of Umbridge and to defeat Voldemort and understand that they are not powerless to achieve that vision. Empowerment has taken hold, and Harry is subsequently unable to deny his peers the opportunity to be involved.

Notably, transformational leaders are not obliged to act alone. Empowering leadership relies on delegation. The resolution of Rowling's story requires the destruction of Voldemort's horcruxes, each of which contains a piece of his soul. The horcruxes are a diary, a ring, a locket, a cup, a crown and a snake. The final vessel of Voldemort's soul is Harry. The horcruxes are not destroyed by Harry alone and appear to be another example of departure from true hero myth narratives. The destruction of the horcruxes is shared: Harry destroys the diary (*Harry Potter and the Chamber of Secrets* ([*Chamber*] 1998); Dumbledore destroys the ring (*Harry Potter and the Half-Blood Prince* [*Prince*], 2005); and in *Hallows*, the locket is destroyed by Ron at Harry's insistence, the cup by Hermione at the urging of Ron and Harry, the crown in a fire set by Crabbe and the snake by Neville. Harry is the final piece of Voldemort's soul, and, reverting to hero myth narratives, is killed by Voldemort during the Ordeal, is Resurrected and defeats Voldemort with Draco's wand.

CHALLENGE TO POWER

Empowered individuals can become agents of change by questioning the status quo and striving to create an environment that brings vision into reality (Kouzes and Posner, 2005). Challenging power is a hallmark of hero myth and a strategic competency for leaders. Heroes slay dragons. Leaders wrestle organizational entrenchment and social injustice.

Empowerment for the students of Hogwarts leads to challenging the power structure of the school, which has been usurped by the Ministry of Magic (*Phoenix*, 2003) and then the minions of Voldemort (*Hallows*, 2007), and "resist[ing] the practice of power over their bodies and minds" (Chappell, 2008, p. 282). Consequently, *Harry Potter* illustrates the paradox of children being both victims and agents during adolescence (Van Praagh, 2005). However, the students are not alone in resisting politically powerful forces, which is atypical for a story in an educational setting (Helfenbein, 2008). The faculty of Hogwarts, parents, disaffected members of the government and the reconvened Order of the Phoenix also work for change. Yet adult efforts within Hogwarts are subtle, within legal boundaries and take form as undetectable support of the resisting students and passive aggression towards Umbridge, Snape and the Carrows. Challenging power in *Harry Potter* is not a revolution, though Neville does characterize it as such (*Hallows*, 2007). In effect, it is bringing order to chaos through resistance.

For Harry, the process of challenging power begins as child resistance. Harry is defiant to his uncle and aunt, sneaks out of the dormitory at night and, as McGonagall says, breaks "a hundred school rules" (*Chamber*, 1998, p. 328). Importantly, there are punishments for breaking rules and Harry frequently serves detentions, culminating in the detention with Umbridge that scars his hand (*Phoenix*, 2003). Indeed, as a literary convention, Harry, Ron and Hermione repeatedly flaunt school rules in their efforts to overcome the obstacles of each year's test.

But breaking rules is not at the core of challenging power in *Harry Potter*. Harry verbally challenges governmental authority because of the Ministry's denial of Voldemort's return. When his outbursts of the truth to Cornelius Fudge (*Harry Potter and the Prisoner of Azkaban*, 1999; *Goblet*, 2000; *Phoenix*, 2003), Umbridge (*Phoenix*, 2003) and Rufus Scrimgeour (*Prince*, 2005; *Hallows*, 2007) are denied and his warnings go unheeded, Harry is compelled to act. Importantly, he acts in collaboration with the students of Dumbledore's Army to break into the Ministry of Magic to liberate Sirius from Voldemort, and, thus, Fudge acknowledges that Voldemort has returned and reinstates Dumbledore at Hogwarts (*Phoenix*, 2003). Harry is once again reluctant to have others be a part of his plan to find Sirius. Neville demonstrates his newfound empowerment and challenges Harry by questioning his virtue and purpose as a leader of Dumbledore's Army: "It was all supposed to be about fighting You-Know-Who, wasn't it? And this is the first chance we've had to do something real – or was that all just a game or something?" (*Phoenix*, 2003, p. 762).

It is truly no game in *Hallows* as the forces of Voldemort have quietly conducted a coup of the government by murdering Scrimgeour and replacing him with a man under a spell to do Voldemort's bidding. Harry's personal transformation as a leader is strengthened and clearly identifies the themes of resistance and social justice in this final book of the series. Harry is determined not to go back to school so he can continue Dumbledore's quest to find the horcruxes. He is adamant about his goal and becomes focused on the eventual defeat of Voldemort and the Death Eaters. However, there are significant ambiguities that Harry, Ron and Hermione must manage. Harry listens to Ron and Hermione voice their differences, but Harry generally ignores their positions. While there is a fine line between being focused on attaining a goal and being inflexible, it appears that Harry has developed the leadership skills to determine the time for discussion is over and the time for action has arrived.

Wizards and witches who are not "purebloods" are in hiding from government agents to escape imprisonment and death. People are uncertain who are friends and who may be an informant to the government. As a consequence of Dumbledore's death, Snape has been installed as the Headmaster of Hogwarts and Voldemort has sent several Death Eaters, notably the Carrows, to enforce discipline and inculcate the students in racist government propaganda. This chaotic environment is where Harry's efforts to empower his peers are culminated and the decisive challenges to power occur.

As Harry, Ron and Hermione return to Hogwarts in search of the final horcruxes, they are met by a battered and gashed Neville Longbottom. Neville has been beaten by the Carrows for disobedience and a "smart mouth," but Neville is undaunted and tells them "it helps when people stand up to them, it gives everyone hope. I used to notice when you did it, Harry" (*Hallows*, 2007, p. 574). Along with Neville, there are several students who are in hiding within the school and who carried out guerrilla attacks on the school administration until one of the students was tortured. Faculty members, such as McGonagall and Flitwick, are still in their posts, but are just as fearful as other adults about the consequences of open criticism of the school administration and government, as resistance could adversely affect the students.

As members of Dumbledore's Army and the Order of the Phoenix begin to arrive at Hogwarts in answer to the news that Harry has returned to the school, it becomes apparent the penultimate challenge to power will occur at Hogwarts. The "Battle of Hogwarts" (*Hallows*, 2007) brings together the forces of Voldemort and the opposing alliance of wizards and magical creatures in a clash over the structure and values of wizarding culture. Underage wizards and witches, along with those who prefer not to fight, are taken away from the school for their own safety. The battle rages as Harry, Ron and Hermione search for the horcruxes. Voldemort's forces are overwhelming and Voldemort is confident he has been victorious.

However, the story reverts to hero myth, as the ultimate challenge to power is the confrontation between Harry and Voldemort—between good and evil. The narrative follows strict mythic elements in that Harry dies in the Ordeal, meets Dumbledore in the limbo of a surreal King's Cross Station and receives the Reward of reconciling an emotional conflict, takes the Road Back by making the choice to return and face Voldemort and endures Resurrection with a second life-or-death moment against Voldemort where Harry prevails. Harry's Elixir is the end of his headaches caused by his duality with Voldemort, not to mention crossing the threshold into adulthood.

The consequence of leadership being thrust upon Harry and how he handles the needs of others is exemplified in the aftermath of the Battle of Hogwarts. The Great Hall is filled with people celebrating their victory and mourning the dead. Harry would simply like to find a place to himself, but:

> They wanted him there with them, their leader and symbol, their saviour and their guide, and that he had not slept, that he craved the company of only a few of them, seemed to occur to no one. He must speak to the bereaved, clasp their hands, witness their tears, receive their thanks, hear the news now creeping in from every quarter. (*Hallows*, 2007, p. 744)

Harry cannot reach the level of transformational leadership without the experiences that form his ethical character, sense of self and relational skills. In terms of these skills, Harry's formation as a leader is indebted to his experiences with the mentorship of Dumbledore. Dumbledore provides Harry with an ethical center, an overarching vision and goal and understanding of self. Dumbledore models virtue, communication, tolerance, empathy, challenging authority, empowerment and supportive guidance. Harry's emotional and relational skills are built through Dumbledore's advocacy of ethical choices as the determinant of self and the power of selfless love.

Additionally, Harry develops the qualities and skills of leadership through the experiential process of being tested and overcoming obstacles each school year. The tests escalate in difficulty and ambiguity, as well as the magnitude of the consequences, until Harry must face the real likelihood of his own death in service to his community. In the course of these tests, Harry develops his moral compass and gains the qualities of integrity, trust, determination, courage, empathy, truthfulness, fairness and self-awareness. Harry uses his self-awareness not simply to identify himself but also to acknowledge his fears and anxieties and use them to inform his decision-making. Other skills that are developed through his experiences include collaboration, communication, learning from others, sharing responsibility and empowering others. Primarily, Harry develops these skills in his relationships with Ron and Hermione, though Dumbledore, Neville, Lupin and the student members of Dumbledore's Army are also key players. The virtuous qualities that Harry ultimately possesses are repeatedly subject to challenge through interactions with others, as well as the annual tests. Harry would be unable to progress into a transformational leader without the challenges that develop these emotional and relational skills.

Experiential learning is a process that can be characterized by blunders and confusion. Harry's process of development suggests the reasonableness of stops and starts, backslides and qualities or skills that lag in improvement while other qualities mature. The important aspect is to learn from experience and understand misjudgments may nevertheless occur and failure is still possible. Harry demonstrates that he learns from his experiences and is undoubtedly aware that failure is very real and consequential as he repeatedly voices caution and concern, if not outright rejection, when his peers insist on being a part of the solution. In this way, Harry attempts to help others and take a leadership role before his personal transformation is complete. Harry's premature efforts, primarily to warn others away and try to solve the problem singularly as a means of protecting others, can be clumsy and cause mistrust and resentment, which in turn creates the conflict necessary to all compelling stories.

In *Hallows*, Harry completes his personal transformation and at last seems to forego his futile preoccupation with protecting others and accepts that others can and will be of benefit in the attainment of destroying Voldemort. This is a key piece of knowledge and self-awareness that Harry must recognize to make the leap in his personal transformation. More importantly, Harry discovers as a part of his personal transformation that others *must* be allowed to make their own choices and present solutions to problems, even if they choose to put themselves in dire circumstances and even if this causes Harry anxiety. This discovery elevates Harry's character from a "protector hero" to a leader working within a power-sharing structure.

Upon analysis, the development process of Harry's leadership style cannot be considered as a linear progression. Harry maintains a reluctance to include others nearly to the end of the story, even though he has repeatedly benefited from and sought the help and advice of others. Even so, leadership theory does not generally suggest a preference for a linear or hierarchical progression of leadership style development. Fletcher's (2004) description of transformational leadership as a process and not a status that can be attained is well matched to the character of Harry Potter proven by the uneven assimilation of leadership qualities and skills. Indeed, in the epilogue of *Hallows* there is no suggestion that Harry has continued a leadership role in his community, although his fame is still evident.

Acknowledging Harry Potter as a post-heroic leader holds significant value to educators and organizational leaders. Readers who have experienced the stories may be attracted to emulating Harry's qualities, as well as those of other major characters, as a consequence of the function of children's literature. Unfortunately, Harry is primarily discussed in terms of heroic qualities and not properly seen as a character that develops into a leader within a shared power structure where resistance is the primary objective. Correctly identifying the post-heroic characteristics of Harry Potter can assist educators and organizational leaders in presenting Harry as a contemporary role model for building shared leadership opportunities as well as demonstrating resistance to coercive social structures. In addition, the negative emotions that Harry experiences, such as fear, reluctance, resentment and anger can be instructive to validate emotional responses to situations and navigating relationships. The positive emotions and qualities, such as determination, courage, inquisitiveness, making moral and ethical choices, respect and listening to others serve the same purposes. Furthermore, the immense popularity of the novels creates a shared experience and an ability to discuss issues of ethics, self-awareness, resistance, leadership and more through the experiences of Harry and his peers.

NOTE

1.   Published in the UK as *Harry Potter and the Philosopher's Stone*.

REFERENCES

Alton, A.H. (2009), "Playing the genre game: Generic fusions of the Harry Potter series," in E.E. Heilman (ed.), *Critical perspectives on Harry Potter* (2nd ed.), New York, NY: Routledge Publishing, pp. 199–223.

Appelbaum, P. (2009), "The great Snape debate," in E.E. Heilman (ed.), *Critical perspectives on Harry Potter* (2nd ed.), New York, NY: Routledge Publishing, pp. 83–100.

Behr, K. (2005), "'Same-as-difference': Narrative transformations and intersecting cultures in Harry Potter," *Journal of Narrative Theory*, **35** (1), 112–32.

Bousquet, M. (2009), "Harry Potter, the war against evil, and the melodramatization of public culture," in E.E. Heilman (ed.), *Critical perspectives on Harry Potter* (2nd ed.), New York, NY: Routledge Publishing, pp. 177–95.

Campbell, J. (1949), *The hero with a thousand faces*, Princeton, NJ: Princeton University Press.

Chappell, D. (2008), "Sneaking out after dark: Resistance, agency, and the postmodern child in J.K. Rowling's Harry Potter series," *Children's Literature in Education*, **39**, 281–93.

Djupedal, K. (1993), "Mass media, esoteric groups, and folklorists," *Journal of Popular Culture*, **26** (4), 69–78.

Douglas, A., J.O. Burtis and L.K. Pond-Burtis (2001), "Myth and leadership vision: Rhetorical manifestations of cultural force," *The Journal of Leadership Studies*, **7** (4), 55–69.

Feldman, M.S. and K. Skoldberg (2002), "Stories and the rhetoric of contrariety: Subtexts of organizing change," *Culture and Organization*, **8** (4), 275–92.

Fletcher, J.K. (2004), "The paradox of postheroic leadership: An essay on gender, power, and transformational change," *Leadership Quarterly*, **15** (3), 647–61.

Gehmann, U. (2003), "Modern myths," *Culture and Organization*, **9** (2), 105–19.

Gooderham, D. (1995), "Children's fantasy literature: Toward an anatomy," *Children's Literature in Education*, **26** (3), 171–83.

Heilman, E.E. (2009), "Fostering insight through multiple critical perspectives," in E.E. Heilman (ed.), *Critical perspectives on Harry Potter* (2nd ed.), New York, NY: Routledge Publishing, pp. 1–9.

Helfenbein, R.J. (2008), "Conjuring curriculum, conjuring control: A reading of resistance in *Harry Potter and the Order of the Phoenix*," *Curriculum Inquiry*, **38** (4), 499–513.

Kidd, D. (2007), "Harry Potter and the functions of popular culture," *The Journal of Popular Culture*, **40** (1), 69–89.

Kouzes, J.M. and B.Z. Posner (1995), *The leadership challenge*, San Francisco, CA: Jossey-Bass.

Ligon, G.S., S.T. Hunter and M.D. Mumford (2008), "Development of outstanding leadership: A life narrative approach," *Leadership Quarterly*, **19** (1), 312–34.

Napierkowski, T.J. (2005), "Beowulf: The heroic, the monstrous, and Anglo-Saxon concepts of leadership," *International Journal of Public Administration*, **28**, 503–16.

Natov, R. (2001), "Harry Potter and the extraordinariness of the ordinary," *The Lion and the Unicorn*, **25**, 310–27.

Nikolajeva, M. (2009), "Harry Potter and the secrets of children's literature," in E.E. Heilman (ed.), *Critical perspectives on Harry Potter* (2nd ed.), New York, NY: Routledge Publishing, pp. 225–41.

Northouse, P.G. (2007), *Leadership theory and practice* (4th ed.), Thousand Oaks, CA: Sage Publications.

Nylund, D. (2007), "Reading Harry Potter: Popular culture, queer theory and the fashioning of youth identity," *Journal of Systemic Therapies*, **26** (2), 13–24.

Rowling, J.K. (1997), *Harry Potter and the Sorcerer's Stone*, New York, NY: Scholastic.

Rowling, J.K. (1998), *Harry Potter and the Chamber of Secrets*, New York, NY: Scholastic.

Rowling, J.K. (1999), *Harry Potter and the prisoner of Azkaban*, New York, NY: Scholastic.

Rowling, J.K. (2000), *Harry Potter and the Goblet of Fire*, New York, NY: Scholastic.

Rowling, J.K. (2003), *Harry Potter and the Order of the Phoenix*, New York, NY: Scholastic.

Rowling, J.K. (2005), *Harry Potter and the Half-Blood Prince*, New York, NY: Scholastic.

Rowling, J.K. (2007), *Harry Potter and the Deathly Hallows*, New York, NY: Scholastic.

Taub, D.J. and H.L. Servaty-Seib (2009), "Controversial content: Is Harry Potter harmful to children?," in E.E. Heilman (ed.), *Critical perspectives on Harry Potter* (2nd ed.), New York, NY: Routledge Publishing, pp. 13–32.

Thomas, M. (2003), "Teaching fantasy: Overcoming the stigma of fluff," *English Journal*, **92** (5), 60–64.

Van Praagh, S. (2005), "Adolescence, autonomy, and Harry Potter: The child as decision maker," *International Journal of Law in Context*, **1** (4), 335–73.

Vogler, C. (1998), *The writer's journey: Mythic structure for writers* (2nd ed.), Studio City, CA: Michael Wiese Productions.

Wolosky, S. (2014), "Foucault at school: Discipline, education and agency in Harry Potter," *Children's Literature in Education*, **45**, 285–97.

PART II

Aural leadership

5. Women troubadours, horizontal leadership and the Mississippi Summer Project of 1964: a missing chapter in Civil Rights Movement history

Susan J. Erenrich

INTRODUCTION

On 2 August 2015, I visited *Folk City: New York and the Folk Music Revival*, a temporary installation at the Museum of the City of New York. The exhibit, on display from 17 June 2015 through 29 January 2016, and the companion book by the same name were years in the making. As I carefully examined the curated scene on that hot Sunday morning in August, I thought about Henrietta Yurchenco and my deep connection to the folk music revivalists. The historic video footage, the listening stations, collectibles, archival photographs, posters and original instruments jarred my memory and touched my heart. For more than 25 years, I produced and chronicled many of the artists on display, so a single image or song would awaken my senses, capture my imagination and overwhelm me with emotion. In particular, the area highlighting music and the Civil Rights Movement caught my eye. Some of the singers-songwriters spotlighted in this section were participants in the Southern Freedom struggle in Mississippi during the summer of 1964 where close to 1,000 college students from the North joined on-the-ground organizers in a dangerous operation to bring about social reforms for Southern blacks, including voting rights, better schools and adequate housing. They were beaten, jailed and murdered; yet they continued their fierce battle for racial and economic equality.

The singers-songwriters who answered the call to serve, many of them featured in the *Folk City* presentation, were involved in a variety of efforts to dismantle the closed society during the dog days of that Mississippi summer more than 50 years ago. One group, the Council of Performing

Artists, donated a week out of their busy schedules to serenade integrated audiences in the Magnolia State. The Artists Civil Rights Assistance Fund, Inc. was also on board. Participants in this organization contributed a day's earnings to the philanthropic effort. A third group, which is the focus of this chapter, the Mississippi Caravan of Music, consisted of approximately 22 artists who went south for varying periods of time. They traveled and sang at the more than 30 projects created by Movement organizers and coordinators. Members included Len Chandler, Bob Cohen, Judy Collins, Jim Crockett, Barbara Dane, Alix Dobkin, The Eastgate Singers, Jim and Jean Glover, Carolyn Hester, Greg Hildebrand, Roger Johnson, Peter La Farge, Phil Ochs, Cordell Reagon, Pete Seeger, Ricky Sherover, Gil Turner, Jackie Washington and Don Windelman. The Caravan was the cultural arm of the Freedom Summer Project and the enlisted folk singers were from all walks of life: male, female, black, white, Native American, young, old and from various religious denominations. In spite of the important role played by these topical composers, there is very little in the literature written about their experiences, and the scholarship that does exist doesn't underscore the contributions made by the women troubadours in the group. This chapter is about them.

The women troubadours were on a mission. They were valiant and determined. It took courage and a collaborative spirit to travel to Mississippi during those dark days to support the battle-fatigued domestic warriors. It was also difficult to be a woman in a predominantly male musical landscape during the pre-women's liberation era. In spite of the anticipated challenges, however, they went. Their efforts helped to abolish the Jim Crow laws in the South and culminated in the passage of the Civil Rights Act of 1964. This chapter hopes to shed light on this missing link of the American history chain.

PORTRAITURE METHODOLOGY

Just like the distinct images accentuated in the *Folk City* exhibition, this chapter will call attention to the salient part the women troubadours played during one of the most quintessential social change initiatives ever undertaken during the twentieth century. The methodology used to complete this task is portraiture, a qualitative approach pioneered by Harvard scholar Sara Lawrence-Lightfoot. Portraiture "combines systematic, empirical description with aesthetic expression, blending art and science, humanistic sensibilities and scientific rigor" (Lawrence-Lightfoot and Davis, 1997, p. 3). It's a form of inquiry referred to by social historian Joseph Featherstone (1989) as a "people's scholarship" because it is transparent and penned for the masses, usually in the form of a first-person narrative. It is also detail-oriented, using a substantial number of adjectives.

Portraiture methodology was chosen for this chapter because it captures the ethos, intricacy and scope of human experience in a social and cultural context, conveying the perspectives of the people who are negotiating their life stories. The portrait is shaped through dialogue between the portrait-ist and the subject, each one participating in the drawing of the picture (Lawrence-Lightfoot and Davis, 1997, p. 3). In this case, it is the written testimony submitted by the women troubadours for a special collection earmarking the 30th anniversary of the Southern Freedom movement in Mississippi, chronicled here. The portrait is also based upon more than 25 years of my personal conversations with the women singers-songwriters.

HIGHLANDER FOLK SCHOOL: A TRAINING GROUND FOR GRASSROOTS LEADERSHIP AND CULTURAL ACTIVISM

Highlander Folk School, launched in Monteagle, Tennessee in 1932 by Myles Horton and Don West, was highlighted in the "Political Activism" section of the *Folk City: New York and the American Folk Music Revival* book written by Stephen Petrus and Ronald D. Cohen. Zilphia Mae Johnson, an accomplished instrumentalist and vocalist, joined the Highlander staff in 1935. She incorporated the arts into every facet of the leadership development adult education program. The daughter of an Arkansas mine owner and a graduate of the College of the Ozarks, she was determined "to use her musical and dramatic abilities in some field of radical activity" (Glen, 1996, p. 43). Zilphia married Myles Horton on 6 March 1935, approximately two months after attending her first labor workshop at this non-traditional training ground for grassroots leaders and organizers (Glen, 1996). From that point forward, she was known as "the singing heart of the folk school" (Dunson, 1965, p. 28).

Zilphia is most closely identified with the song "We Shall Overcome." In 1945, members of the striking food and tobacco workers' union in Charleston, South Carolina changed the lyrics of the old religious spir-itual "I Will Overcome" to "We Will Overcome" while walking the picket line (Glen, 1996). In 1947, when a few of the striking women attended a Highlander Workshop, they taught the latest version of the tune to the assembled group:

When Zilphia heard the new words, "we will organize" and "the Lord will see us through," she knew it was a song with meaning for communities all across the South. She adapted it to her accordion and sang it at union meetings, community gatherings and Highlander workshops. It became a theme song at Highlander throughout the labor period of the 1940s and 1950s. (Carawan, n.d., p. 1)

Shortly thereafter, Zilphia shared the song with Pete Seeger. He slightly altered the arrangement, changing "we will overcome" to "we shall overcome." That same year, Pete published the text in *People's Songs* and incorporated it into his set list during concerts (Winkler, 2009). A few years later, "We Shall Overcome" became the anthem of the Civil Rights Movement.

Zilphia did not live long enough to see this musical creation take hold. She died in 1956. Prior to her passing, she amassed 1,300 songs from unions, progressive organizations, traditional Appalachian culture and the South (Dunson, 1965). These songs played a significant role in the decades ahead. Some of the tunes, like "We Shall Overcome," were sung by the women troubadours during their pilgrimage to Mississippi in the summer of 1964.

Approximately three years after Zilphia Horton's premature death, Guy Carawan, a folk singer from California, joined the Highlander inner circle and reinvigorated the cultural program. Guy originally visited the school during the summer of 1953 with encouragement from Pete Seeger (Carawan and Carawan, 2010). In 1959, after hearing one of Dr King's sermons at a local black church in Boston, Guy was eager to call Myles Horton (Carawan and Carawan, 2010). He offered to volunteer his services at Highlander. Myles asked Guy what he thought he could contribute. Guy answered that he had learned some tunes from the Labor Movement and he could play a guitar and banjo. Myles said "Come on down. We really miss the work that Zilphia did here" (Carawan and Carawan, 2010). Guy accepted the invitation and ushered in the next wave of topical songwriting balladeers.

STANDING ON MY SISTER'S SHOULDERS

While Highlander was busy preparing the next generation of domestic warriors for battle in the South, another campaign was brewing in the North, specifically, in New York City's Greenwich Village scene. At the leading edge of the activity was long-time cultural activist, Sis Cunningham. Sis, whose photograph was on display at the *Folk City* exhibit, co-founded a national topical song magazine, *Broadside*, along with her husband Gordon Friesen.

The two Oklahomans, who were joined in matrimony in 1941, were not strangers to the political and cultural landscape (Cunningham and Friesen,

1999). Decades before the birth of the publication, the couple was intensely absorbed in the social concerns of their day. Sis, a former member of the Almanac Singers, and Gordon, a journalist, were blacklisted during the Joseph McCarthy Red Scare. They persevered and gave birth to *Broadside* magazine in February of 1962, 20 years after the Almanacs split. Others were on the scene to help launch the topical songwriting magazine and catapult it into the national spotlight. Among them were Josh Dunson, Julius Lester, Gil Turner, Gordon's brother Ollie and the Friesen daughters, but "The main contributors, however, were the song writers themselves, known and unknown, who flooded *Broadside* with their creations and then waited more or less patiently to see what would happen to them" (Dunson, 1965; Cunningham and Friesen, 1999, p. 284).

Sis, Gordon and the others helped pave the way for the next generation of topical balladeers. Among them were the women troubadours who ventured South during the sizzling Mississippi summer of 1964.

NORTH AND WEST MEET SOUTH

During the summer of 1960, four years before the woman troubadours traveled to Mississippi, the seeds for the soulful Civil Rights Movement were sown. The Highlander Folk School initiated a series of "Singing for Freedom" cultural workshops, which brought together balladeers from across the country. The first gathering, which took place at the school's headquarters in Monteagle, Tennessee, included musical ambassadors from some of the previous civil rights campaigns in Montgomery and Nashville (Carawan and Carawan, 2007). Topical singers-songwriters from the budding folk revival in the North were also present (Dunson, 1965). Collectively, collaboratively and creatively, they challenged the segregated Southern bastion. Their artistic North/West/South alliance continued through the Freedom Summer Project of 1964 and beyond.

Increasingly, culture acted as a powerful engine in the battle for liberation. By 1964, a potpourri of melodious arrangements had become an integral piece of the country's fabric. Every tune performed a different task. Some numbers headlined the unspeakable repressive conditions endured by African Americans. In the Southern belly of the beast, songs were used as an organizing tool. The lyrics, which were colorfully scored to suit every occasion, evoked a range of responses: courage in the face of danger, hope to ward off despair, humor to poke fun at the ridiculous and joy to deflect the pain. Ditties also helped youthful protesters in their recruitment efforts.

TRAINING FOR THE SUMMER PROJECT IN OXFORD, OHIO

In June 1964, hundreds of essentially white, well-to-do university students descended upon the Western College for Women, a four-year liberal arts institution, for two successive weeklong informational and instructional workshops. The first session, designated for voter registration, took place on 14 June (Bond, 1999). The second session, that occurred shortly thereafter, oriented freedom school volunteers.

Throughout the crash survival course the enlisted young men and women were inundated with data about the Magnolia State's Closed Society. They were tutored in the Movement's non-violent protocol and solemnly listened as countless civil rights warriors emphatically discussed the pending danger awaiting them in Mississippi. Among the realists was SNCC's executive secretary, James Forman, who warned, "I may be killed, you may be killed, the whole staff may go" (Cagin and Dray, 1991, p. 30). John Doar, the deputy chief of the Civil Rights Division of the US Justice Department, also warned the assembled altruists not to expect protection from federal authorities (Cagin and Dray, 1991).

In between the intensive, no-nonsense classes, lectures and simulations, students and staff eased their jitters by participating in vigorous recreational games like volleyball and soccer. Evenings were earmarked for freedom singing: "It was, as one student wrote, 'a strange [combination] of children headed for summer camp and soldiers going off to war'" (Cagin and Dray, 1991; Dittmer, 1995, p. 246).

The women troubadours didn't attend either of the preliminary consultations in Oxford, Ohio, but Bob Cohen, the Director of the Mississippi Caravan of Music, was on hand during the second assembly. The tone of that orientation was dismal. One volunteer from the first contingent of volunteers, Andrew Goodman, had already disappeared along with two other civil rights workers, Michael Schwerner and James Chaney. Everyone knew they were dead even though their bodies weren't found until 4 August.

MISSISSIPPI CARAVAN OF MUSIC

The Mississippi Caravan of Music was the cultural arm of the Freedom Summer initiative. Participating artists, including the women troubadours featured in this chapter, teamed up with the Council of Federated Organizations (COFO), a coalition of Civil Rights Movement groups operating in Mississippi in the early 1960s. They were determined to jam open the closed society. Over the summer, the singers-songwriters journeyed to the Magnolia State for varying periods of time to perform, boost morale and illuminate the problems associated with the segregationist mentality that plagued the region. They were allies in the long struggle for racial equality.

The Caravan's hands-on role during the 1964 summer project did not surprise anyone. Bob Cohen, who coordinated the risky singers-songwriter operation, was the former roommate of Bob Parris Moses. Following the 1960 lunch counter sit-ins, Bob Moses, after forging a relationship with Ella Baker, the mother of the Movement, navigated his way into Amite County, otherwise known as "the Ninth Circle of Hell" (Newfield, 1999, p. 85). After being "beaten twice and jailed thrice" (Newfield, 1999, p. 85), Bob Moses moved to Jackson. Early on, he recruited his friend Bob Cohen to musically support the efforts of the various wings of the Southern Freedom struggle.

Bob Cohen initially traveled to Mississippi with the New World Singers (Gil Turner and Delores Dixon) and Bob Moses in 1963 to conduct one of the freedom songs workshops in Edwards (Cohen, 1999). He was unaware at the time that he would spearhead the Caravan venture approximately one year later. Prior to that pivotal moment in history, Bob and the New World Singers visited Highlander, were Gerde's Folk City regulars, were *Broadside* contributors and raised money for the Student Nonviolent Coordinating Committee, otherwise known as SNCC.

Shortly thereafter, Bob Cohen became the director of the Caravan of Music. His job throughout the summer of 1964 was to coordinate logistics for the visiting artists, which included the women troubadours, and to sing. He and his wife Susan were based in the Jackson office where a telephone, map and calendar were his primary tools (Cohen, 1999). Upon entry into the state, Bob spent a few hours with each singer, orienting him or her to "the unreality of Mississippi—an almost impossible but necessary effort" (Cohen, 1999, p.185). Then he charted their tour and dispatched them throughout the state (Cohen, 1999). Everyone traveled in groups. It was safer.

I'M ON MY WAY AND I WON'T TURN BACK

The women troubadours meticulously prepped for their pilgrimage to the Magnolia State. Judy Collins, Barbara Dane, Alix Dobkin and Carolyn Hester wrote about their experiences for an anthology I edited in 1999. Some of their musings are included below.

Judy Collins signed on to the Summer Project after encouragement from ethnomusicologist Henrietta Yurchenco. She reported for duty in Mississippi on Sunday, August 1st, three days before the decaying bodies of James Chaney, Michael Schwerner, and Andrew Goodman were discovered at the bottom of an earthen dam:

> We arrived in Jackson on the plane at 5 o'clock in the afternoon, after flying in from Newark Airport. There was a purple and deep red sunset that nearly covered the sky of Jackson like a cloak of blood; the light of the sun passed through it to the wet pavements and the thick green grass. The humidity was high. Walking in the air was a little like swimming. Bob and Sue Cohen picked us up at the airport. We drove to the COFO office in their little red car. Driving along, Bob began to talk about what was going on, and the seepage of understanding and fear soaked into my mind. He started with the basic rules about traveling, (never travel integrated, for instance,) no mingling with Negroes in most public spots, with the exception of one or two spots in Jackson that are integrated restaurants. (Collins, 1999, p. 201)

Barbara Dane, a blues and jazz singer, who had lent her voice to the cause of racial and economic justice since 1945, enlisted as soon as she learned about the Caravan of Music. She was one of the older members of the group:

> SNCC workers met us at the plane in Jackson and took us immediately to headquarters. There they briefed us on the frightening situation surrounding the kidnapping of the three volunteers, details of the ongoing search, as well as what security measures we should follow. Clearly, whatever had happened to the three had been done to try to intimidate the rest of the volunteers in the hopes they'd all go home. But one of the key songs on everyone's lips was "We'll Never Turn Back." (Dane, 1999, p. 223)

Alix Dobkin was drafted for the Southern mission by Gil Turner. She did not take much convincing. Gil, one of *Broadside's* editors and a member of the New World Singers, was a mentor to many of the artists involved in the blossoming folk revival. Gil's initial tour to the Magnolia State with the New World Singers was in August 1961 (Dunson, 1965). The group was the first from the North to vigorously participate in the freedom movement in Mississippi. When they returned to New York City, the New World Singers introduced promising topical singer-songwriters like Alix, to the movement repertoire at Hootenannies and SNCC benefit concerts (Dunson, 1965). Alix acknowledged Gil in her written testimony:

> Having spent much of my 24 years in fear of "missing something," there was no way for me to pass up an invitation to join the Folk Music Caravan in 1964 for the Mississippi "Freedom Summer." Besides that, my politically activist Communist parents had named me after a heroic uncle killed fighting Franco in Spain, and had trained me to be a political troublemaker. Some of my folkie friends from Greenwich Village, namely Gil Turner and Len Chandler as I recall, recruited me along with other Gaslight Café regulars like Peter LaFarge, Tom Paxton, Eric Andersen and Carolyn Hester. And of course Pete Seeger

would be there, as he was on behalf of every cause worth singing for. (Dobkin, 1999, p. 195)

Gil Turner also inducted Carolyn Hester into the Freedom Movement. They drove together to Mississippi in August, a few days after the bodies of the three civil rights workers were found. Gil originally contacted Carolyn in the spring of 1964 to request her participation. She agreed. Determined not to worry her parents, however, Carolyn, never disclosed her travel plans. Carolyn and Gil packed their vehicle and left New York City around midnight. Their future was uncertain:

> One small suitcase each, one guitar each, some cash, a few sandwiches and apples. We stopped for water, coffee, soft drinks, and restrooms along the way. Otherwise, we drove nonstop, straight through to Jackson. Certain moments stand out in memory—driving past the Lincoln Memorial, all lit up. Gil let me drive that early morning out of Washington, along the Appalachians past Charlottesville. Gil slept about two hours in two days—I slept about four. (Hester, 1999, p. 191)

A SOUTHERN WELCOME

Mississippi officials vigorously prepared for the summer invasion prior to the start of the 1964 project. In Jackson, the state capital, the police force was enlarged from 390 to 450 (Bond, 1999). City administrators added two horses, six dogs and 200 new shotguns to its armory. They stockpiled tear gas canisters and distributed a mask to every patrolman to shield him from toxic fumes. Three canvas-topped troop transporters, two half-ton searchlight vehicles and three colossal trailer trucks were obtained to haul demonstrators to two spacious detention sites assembled at the state fair-grounds (Bond, 1999). Lastly, a 13,000-pound armored personnel carrier, "Thompson's Tank," named for the incumbent mayor, was amassed at a dollar a pound (Bond, 1999).

The white citizenry of Mississippi was also prepared to extend a "friendly" welcome to the summer guests. For instance, when Carolyn Hester and Alix Dobkin arrived at their hotel in Jackson, they were coldly received by the front desk clerk. Carolyn was born in the South and was no stranger to the segregationist mindset. Alix, on the other hand, was experiencing Black Belt racism for the first time. Carolyn and Alix shared a room on their initial night in the state:

> Late in the afternoon of our arrival, Alix, Gil, and I went to eat dinner, and when we returned to the third floor hotel rooms, we had a message waiting. It

hadn't been there when we'd left an hour or so before. To our astonishment, on the doors of our rooms was scrawled KKK in huge, black letters. "My guitar," I thought—I hoped my guitar was OK. After carefully opening our doors we found all the instruments and our other belongings intact.

The next morning, I jumped when the wake-up call came but realized thankfully that I had fallen asleep after all. Cancel that comforting thought—the voice on the other end of the line said, "OK, nigger lover, time to get up." I hung up quickly, told Alix, and we dressed immediately, fearing that an unfriendly knock on the door would soon follow. Not only had our operator scared the wits out of us, but it was only 5:30 a.m. We woke Gil anyway and made a hasty exit, looking neither right nor left. (Hester, 1999, p. 191)

CONCERTS

By the time the women troubadours entered the scene in 1964, incremental change was on the rise in Mississippi. Integrated events were becoming slightly more commonplace, thanks partly to the creation of the "Tougaloo Cultural and Artistic Committee" (Dittmer, 1995). Due to discriminatory practices, the group launched a major letter-writing campaign encouraging celebrities and artists to stand with the Movement by boycotting whites-only or racially segregated public events in the state (Dittmer, 1995). The majority of luminaries complied, with the exception of Holiday on Ice (Dittmer, 1995).

Following that successful crusade, not only did various members of the Caravan of Music play for mixed audiences, they also sang to support the embattled civil rights warriors. Judy Collins recalled joining a couple hundred people at a freedom house staff party:

All of us went to the staff party at the freedom house. They don't very often get out of the routine of work and eating and sleep, and so it was very festive for everyone. About 200 people were there. The food, [sic] (hot dogs, potato salad) was gone in five minutes and the singing started, in the backyard, with people standing and sprawling on the lawn. Barbara sang the new song, "It Isn't Nice," a rock-and-roll song, with her melody and Malvina Reynolds's words, and the place really rocked. They are so thirsty for music. It was so great, singing, with the sweat just pouring off, and the people just singing out with all their might. That's one thing you see right away; just start a song, and everyone is right there, singing out. The evening finished with all of us singing "We Shall Overcome," and you know, even though you know it is true all the time, when you sing it together, there is something that happens that makes you just as sure as you live that it is going to happen, and happen when you will see it happen. It was very beautiful. (Collins, 1999, p. 203)

FREEDOM SCHOOLS

Following the Supreme Court's unanimous vote to strike down segregation in the public schools on 17 May 1954, Mississippi Senator James Eastland positioned himself for battle: "The South will not abide by nor obey this legislative decision of a political court . . . We will take whatever steps are necessary to retain segregation in education . . . We are about to embark on a great crusade to restore Americanism" (Dittmer, 1995, p. 37). Throughout the early 1960s, the Senator from the Magnolia State managed to thwart the decree. Mississippi's academic institutions remained separate and unequal. Black children did not have a fighting chance.

Movement veterans in the know believed the situation was unconscionable and took matters into their own hands. Prior to the start of the Summer Project they created a freedom school program and curriculum that turned the Mississippi educational system on its head. Myles Horton of the Highlander Center; Septima Clark, a former teacher and SCLC staff member; Norma Becker, a New York educator and United Federation of Teachers activist; Noel Day, who developed a citizenship curriculum in question and answer format and Staughton Lynd, who authored *Guide to Negro History* (as cited in Chilcoat and Ligon, 1999), were delegated the cumbersome task of planning and cultivating the project (Cobb, 1999). Lynd assumed the directorship role once the freedom school model was established.

By the time the Caravan of Music and the women troubadours arrived, freedom schools throughout the state were operating. Bob Cohen described the overall Caravan freedom school experience in a 1964 *Broadside* article:

> A typical Caravan day would begin with the singers participating in a class on Negro history at the freedom school. They showed that freedom songs were sung back in the days of slavery—and how some songs even blueprinted the way to freedom on the underground railroad. The singers demonstrated the important contribution of Negro music in every aspect of American musical and cultural history. For children who have been educated—or rather brainwashed—by the public school system to accept the myth of their own inferiority, this was an exhilarating revelation. For the majority of adults, as well as children, it was the first time they had heard of such great musical artists as Leadbelly and Big Billy Broonzy. For many, the music they had learned to be ashamed of was given new stature by the visiting musicians. (Cohen, 1999, pp. 183–5)

Approximately 2,000 students enrolled in some 40 schools in the face of white opposition (Cobb, 1999). Black ministers welcomed movement personnel and students in spite of being threatened with violence by the local power elite. Black families housed volunteer teachers undeterred by the warnings. The consequences were dire in some cases, like McComb, where a bomb flattened a church that harbored a freedom school (Dittmer, 1995). Determined COFO staff, Freedom Summer recruits and students kept right on learning. Seventy-five students attended class on the lawn outside the smoky building (Dittmer, 1995).

VOTER REGISTRATION

The voter registration drive was one of the signature programs of the 1964 project. Members of the Caravan of Music did not directly participate in the door-to-door canvassing. Instead, they raised their voices in song to provide moral support and spiritual sustenance to their movement brothers and sisters who spent their days trudging on the hot dusty dirt roads of Mississippi. Through their music and informal conversations, the artists also rallied the local troops and encouraged involvement in the democratic process. Alix Dobkin provided a synopsis of her backcountry tour with Carolyn Hester:

> Carolyn and I began our backwoods tour, singing for meetings and rallies, visiting families in one community after another who treated us to spectacular meals consisting of endless courses of home cooked, crispy fried chicken and ham, luscious mashed potatoes, sweet potatoes, biscuits, gravy, corn, black-eyed peas, greens and beans cooked in lots of salt pork, and unfamiliar chitterlings and okra which I sampled and praised politely, coffee with evaporated milk, pies, cookies, jello, fruit and much more. Were we quite sure that we didn't want another helping? My stomach was completely full, but my mouth wanted to eat that southern food forever, and I've been a fan ever since.
>
> Our week was spent driving many miles on two-lane highways and dirt roads, going from churches to schools, from simple, comfortable houses on the outskirts of small towns to isolated, run-down wooden shacks stuck way out in a lonely field. We talked with people about the importance of voting, and how their vote would make a difference. I remember standing in front of a mailbox listening to one resolute, old woman, her eyes glittering as she declared that nothing could keep her from exercising the right to vote on election day. Then she turned and made her painstaking way down the narrow, potholed road, leaning on a cane for support. She was awe-inspiring. (Dobkin, 1999, p. 197)

MASS MEETING WITH FANNIE LOU HAMER

The women troubadours involved with the Caravan of Music sang at mass meetings during their stay in the Magnolia State. The meetings, which were rooted in the sacrosanct traditions of the black church, were a salient part of movement culture. They brought people together, served as a platform to debate strategy and tactics, provided an outlet for sharing news from the front and afforded a framework to confront fear. Music was the glue.

And one local song leader, in particular, who crossed paths with the women troubadours made an indelible impression. Her name was Fannie Lou Hamer. She was a brave, celebrated, local sharecropper from the Mississippi Delta. Barbara Dane wrote about her encounter with this compelling organizer:

> Most of all I remember the power of Fannie Lou Hamer among her people, weaving together song and talk and song again, making the spirits of her weary, sweaty neighbors visibly rise as their hearts connected. She seemed the perfect fulfillment of the concept "singer:" not just one who sings, not only a great voice, but a shaman, preacher, teacher, healer taking responsibility for community and continuity, making sure that life itself will go on with any sense of the reasons for it. As she reminded them again of the rightness of their struggle and led them into the cadences of call and response so old and yet so new, you could almost touch the ties that bound them ever closer into a community with the strength to resist and triumph. (Dane, 1999, p. 225)

Judy Collins distinctly recalled her rendezvous with Fannie Lou Hamer at a voter registration meeting in Drew, Mississippi. She was also cognizant of her disquietude. Drew was a perilous place in the summer of 1964. Judy expected the worst:

> We drove into Drew and into the Negro neighborhood. It is a relatively small town. Strange that it should house such hatred. The home where the meeting was held was owned by a woman whose son was beaten nearly to death only a few months ago by the sheriff, who sat outside the house in his car during the whole time of our meeting—their meeting, for it is not ours.
> Mrs. Fannie Lou Hamer spoke to them, and to us; she who has been beaten and arrested and harassed for saying that she has a right to vote. To vote man. Fired from her job the day after she registered in 1962 in Indianolla in Sunflower County, the lady of dignity who stood up and sang with us "This Little Light of Mine." She led us in singing that song while the police cars roamed the neighborhood and the cars of the Klan circumnavigated the block and the town stood in horror at the gall of 75 Negroes who had come to sing about freedom and listen to a beautiful woman talk about the right of a man to be human. (Collins, 1999, pp. 205–6)

In spite of moments of impassioned exhilarating singing at mass meetings, danger was ever present and it was real. Everyone and everything was a target. By the end of the summer "four project workers had been killed; four people had been critically wounded; 80 workers had been beaten; there had been over 1,000 arrests; 37 churches had been bombed or burned; and 30 Black businesses or homes had been burned" (Bond, 1999, p. 82).

ALLIES IN THE STRUGGLE

The women troubadours were part of the overall cultural arm of the Freedom Summer Project. They toured through the Magnolia State for short stints, supporting the dangerous frontline operation. Their job was to provide sustenance to the troops and draw attention to the racist practices perpetuated by Southern whites throughout the Black Belt region. Following their pilgrimage to Mississippi, the women educated audiences through their lyrics and raised money for SNCC, COFO and other organizations combating segregation. They accompanied the freedom struggle in vital ways.

It was the day-to-day grueling tedious work by local leaders, SNCC, CORE and COFO organizers, however, that broke the back of Jim Crow with assistance from their Northern friends. The indigenous folks and civil rights warriors were the decision makers. They were the planners. They endured the routine harassment and brutality. They were in Mississippi for the long haul.

The women troubadours were not leading change initiatives inside the Magnolia State. They were allies who accompanied the real actors in the freedom struggle. Nevertheless, they played a salient role, and it was dangerous. Even though they were part of the cultural arm of the operation, there were still risks involved with their participation.

First, the women troubadours threatened the social, economic and political status quo. Each close associate of on-the-ground activists entering the Magnolia State was viewed as a menace, and, in the case of the Northern white singers-songwriters, a traitor to their race. The White Citizens Council and the KKK instituted a variety of state-sanctioned methods of terror in order to preserve the Southern segregated way of life. Thrashings, arrests, cross burnings, drive-by shootings, bombings, harassment, loss of employment and murder were the modus operandi to stop the freedom train. Fortunately, the women survived their tours of duty and went home relatively unscathed. The long-term battlefield abolitionists and volunteers did not fare as well. Change eventually came to Mississippi, but the cost of freedom was high.

Second, the women troubadours were not the mobilizers; they were the mobilized. They helped to reinforce the organizing efforts of others. Their job, while in Mississippi, was to support the local black communities and the Movement's domestic warriors. James Forman, the executive secretary of SNCC, accentuated the role of volunteers in his book, *The Making of Black Revolutionaries*:

> We felt that it was high time for the United States as a whole, a White-dominated country, to feel the consequences of its own racism. White people should know

the meaning of the work we were doing—they should feel some of the suffering and terror and deprivation that Black people endured. We could not bring all of White America to Mississippi. But by bringing in some of its children as volunteer workers, a new consciousness would feed back into the homes of thousands of White Americans as they worried about their sons and daughters confronting "the jungle of Mississippi," the bigoted sheriffs, the Klan, the vicious White Citizens' Councils. (Forman, 1985, p. 372)

The women troubadours in particular, and the Caravan of Music in general, successfully provided necessary assistance to the freedom crusade. Through their celebrity, a few of the participants managed to lure white students to movement-sponsored concerts, resulting in integrated audiences. This was a major step forward. When they returned home, most of them composed songs that revealed Mississippi's brutality towards its black populace. They also raised money for the struggle.

Third, the women troubadours assisted with the implementation of new practices and tactics conceived by SNCC, CORE and COFO. The singing that took place in the Freedom Schools, during mass meetings, voter registration drives and Mississippi Freedom Democratic Party events were instituted after endless strategizing sessions at Highlander, the various Movement offices in Mississippi and elsewhere. By the time the summer volunteers and Caravan of Music arrived, they were funneled to the various project sites to lend their support and provide sustenance to the troops.

Fourth, the women troubadours openly expressed the hidden transcripts of opposing views. Every member of the Caravan was a prolific topical songwriter. Their in-your-face confrontational lyrics served as an educational platform, a rallying cry and a recruitment tool for new enlistees. Through their music they managed to focus the nation's attention on the harsh rural conditions endured by black Mississippians and embarrass the perpetrators of the segregated Jim Crow system.

Fifth, the women troubadours helped keep the stories of repressive power alive. Music was the anchor of the Movement. Every song highlighted an aspect of oppression and rallied the troops to keep marching in the face of adversity. Prior to the arrival of the Mississippi Caravan, SNCC song leaders utilized music as an organizing tool. Wazir Peacock, a native Mississippian and SNCC field secretary, captured the essence of how singing was incorporated early on:

One night in February, we held a mass meeting. It was the largest one yet—we had to hold it in the First Christian Church. It was powerful. We couldn't stop singing freedom songs. Those songs had a real message that night: Freedom doesn't come as a gift. It comes through knowledge and power—political power. It comes from the vote. That night I went to bed at the office. That next morning, people started knocking on the door first thing in the morning. They were ready to go down and attempt to register. They kept coming and coming— they knew they probably wouldn't be allowed to register, but it was their right to try. (Peacock as cited in 50th Anniversary of the SNCC Program Booklet, 2010, p. 47)

After the Caravan arrived a new type of lyric was introduced to the communities. Many of the ballads and ditties were hard-hitting and con-frontational. They delighted freedom struggle activists and agitated the segregationists who tried to discredit the Movement and squelch all forms of protest.

The songs have continued to focus attention on Mississippi's sordid past for half a century. The quest for justice persists. The SNCC Freedom Singers, song leaders and Caravan artists have carried their songs into the new millennium. They are performed at concerts, inserted into docu-mentary films and played at demonstrations and large gatherings. The contemporary outlets for the troubadours do not pose the same type of threat as their days trudging the hot dirt roads in the Magnolia State. They have provided inspiration and fodder for other folks who currently carry the torch.

Additionally, the women troubadours assisted ordinary people usually locked out of the political process to write their own scripts. This approach is based on a popular education model. The popular education philoso-phy and method was the centerpiece of the Mississippi Freedom Summer Project of 1964. The Freedom Schools, voter registration, the Mississippi Freedom Democratic Party and the local Movement leadership were grounded in participatory democracy principles, including "Trust in the people's ability to govern themselves" (Jacobs, 2003, p. 185). Each com-ponent was directly related to the black indigenous population's struggle against oppression and was based upon Highlander's doctrine and convic-tion. Myles Horton believed that:

> For people to be really free they must have the power to make decisions about their lives, so that they can acquire knowledge as tools to change society. The people that conceived all the programs held a radical philosophy: the system was bad and had to be changed. They all had a revolutionary purpose. (Jacobs, 2003, p. 184)

Besides Highlander, it was the mother of the movement, Ella Baker, whose indomitable spirit and mentorship that helped shape the bottom-up lead-ership philosophy in the Magnolia State. Miss Baker deserves credit for ushering in the next generation of civil rights activists. It was her behind the scenes coaching and wealth of organizing experience, dating back decades, which helped set the stage for the Summer Project. So when the women troubadours arrived on the scene, they were actually boosting already existing programs. Some of the topical singers-songwriters were already drilled in popular education techniques. Among them were Bob Cohen, Gil Turner, Phil Ochs and Len Chandler. They had attended previous Highlander sponsored events leading up to the summer project of 1964. None of the women troubadours, however, had prior exposure to the model.

Lastly, the women troubadours fell into a previously established bottom-up leadership platform carried out by local SNCC song leaders, like Fannie Lou Hamer, Hollis Watkins, Wazir (Willie) Peacock and Sam Block. They were organizing in the state long before the Mississippi Caravan of Music signed on to the Freedom Summer Project, and they continued to organize in their communities long after the Caravan went home. Wazir Peacock described what it was like to be a SNCC warrior and song leader in the early days of the Movement:

> Everything I've heard about soldiers in combat describes us—the never- ending tension, the exhaustion, the constant danger. We were guerrillas. The difference was we weren't going in to fight and win, we were teaching people who were already there how they could win. You don't liberate people—you teach them how to liberate themselves. (Seeger and Reiser, 1989, p. 181)

Music was the glue. Wazir talked to me on a number of occasions about the power of song. He articulated his thoughts during the session "From Student Activists to Field Organizers" at the SNCC 50th Anniversary Reunion. Much of what he said was documented in Pete Seeger's book, *Everybody Says Freedom: A History of the Civil Rights Movement in Songs and Pictures*:

> When you sing, you can reach deep into yourself and communicate some of what you've got to other people, and you get them to reach inside of themselves. You release your soul force, and they release theirs, until you can all feel like you are part of one great soul. Sometimes when Hollis and I were leading a song, we could feel it. We were together with the people, and they would not let us go, you knew you could not cut the singing short until it reached a conclusion. The singing could go on for hours. (Seeger and Reiser, 1989, p. 180)

When the women troubadours arrived in the summer of 1964, they received their marching orders from seasoned local activists. Bob Cohen, the director of the Caravan, coordinated schedules and provided orientation for the artists, but it was the SNCC Field Secretaries and COFO organizers who were leading the charge. The artists fell in wherever they were needed. No one had authorization from the state. It was an all-out non-violent war against Mississippi's caste system.

The women cultural carriers of the Movement made their mark on Mississippi. Most of them continued to influence, uphold, reinforce and lead other struggles following the Freedom Summer Project of 1964. They get together now and then. When they do, they remember the past, work in the present, and strategize for the future. Most importantly, they sing and sing and sing.

The woman troubadours highlighted in this chapter are still among the living. Sadly, however, many of the Civil Rights Movement veterans are dead and gone. My hope is that this chapter sheds a little light on an underappreciated subject. Additionally, I hope that the contributions of the Mississippi Caravan of Music and the other artists involved in movement activity will find their rightful place in the growing scholarship on that shameful period in this country's past.

No analysis describing leadership roles of women troubadours in the Mississippi Summer Project of 1964 have been conducted. It's an episode that has been left out of Civil Rights Movement history. The leadership experience of these particular women has also been overlooked. This piece, not only highlights the role the women played, it also places the women in proper context. The Mississippi Movement was a grassroots transformational social change initiative. Leadership was based on a bottom-up model. This narrative, coming on the heels of the 50th anniversary commemorative events, is an opportunity to help illuminate another side of this consequential period of time.

REFERENCES

50th Anniversary of the Student Nonviolent Coordinating Committee (SNCC) (2010, April 15–18), [Program Booklet]. Raleigh, North Carolina: Author.

Bond, J. (1999), "1964 Mississippi Freedom Summer," in S. Erenrich (ed.), *Freedom is a constant struggle: An anthology of the Mississippi Civil Rights Movement*, Montgomery, AL: Black Belt Press, pp. 78–83.

Broadside (1964, November 20), [Mimeograph Copy]. New York, NY.

Cagin, S. and P. Dray (1991), *We are not afraid: The story of Goodman, Schwerner, and Chaney and the Civil Rights Campaign for Mississippi*, New York, NY: Bantam Books.

Carawan, C. (n.d.), *Zilphia Horton: A profile*, unpublished manuscript, New Market, TN: Highlander Research and Education Center.

Carawan, G. and C. Carawan (1963), *We shall overcome: Songs of the Southern Freedom Movement*, New York, NY: Oak.

Carawan, G. and C. Carawan (1999), "Carry it on: Roots of the singing Civil Rights Movement," in S. Erenrich (ed.), *Freedom is a constant struggle: An anthology of the Mississippi Civil Rights Movement*, Montgomery, AL: Black Belt Press, pp. 143–51.

Carawan, G. and C. Carawan (2007), *Sing for freedom: The story of the Civil Rights Movement through its songs*, Montgomery, AL: New South Books.

Carawan, G. and C. Carawan (2010), [Unpublished Manuscript Notes].

Chilcoat, G. and J. Ligon (1999), "Developing democratic citizens: The Mississippi freedom schools," in S. Erenrich (ed.), *Freedom is a constant struggle: An anthology of the Mississippi Civil Rights Movement*, Montgomery, AL: Black Belt Press, p. 129.

Cobb, C. (1999), "Organizing freedom schools," in S. Erenrich (ed.), *Freedom is a constant struggle: An anthology of the Mississippi Civil Rights Movement*, Montgomery, AL: Black Belt Press, pp. 134–7.

Cohen, B. (1999), "Sorrow songs, faith songs, freedom songs: The Mississippi Caravan of Music in the summer of '64," in S. Erenrich (ed.), *Freedom is a constant struggle: An anthology of the Mississippi Civil Rights Movement*, Montgomery, AL: Black Belt Press, pp. 177–89.

Collins, J. (1999), "Mississippi," in S. Erenrich (ed.), *Freedom is a constant struggle: An anthology of the Mississippi Civil Rights Movement*, Montgomery, AL: Black Belt Press, pp. 201–7.

Cunningham, A. and G. Friesen (1999), *Red dust and broadsides: A joint autobiography*, edited by R.D. Cohen, Amherst, MA: University of Massachusetts Press.

Dane, B. (1999), "Michigan to Mississippi: A journey," in S. Erenrich (ed.), *Freedom is a constant struggle: An anthology of the Mississippi Civil Rights Movement*, Montgomery, AL: Black Belt Press, pp. 222–7.

Dittmer, J. (1995), *Local people: The struggle for civil rights in Mississippi*, Urbana, IL: University of Illinois Press.

Dobkin, A. (1999), "Pages from Mississippi," in S. Erenrich (ed.), *Freedom is a constant struggle: An anthology of the Mississippi Civil Rights Movement*, Montgomery, AL: Black Belt Press, pp. 195–9.

Dunson, J. (1965), *Freedom in the air: Song movements of the 60s*, New York, NY: International.

Erenrich, S. (1999), *Freedom is a constant struggle: An anthology of the Mississippi civil rights movement*, Montgomery, AL: Black Belt Press.

Featherstone, J. (1989), "To make the wounded whole," *Harvard Educational Review*, **59**, 367–8.

Forman, J. (1985), *The making of Black revolutionaries*, Seattle, WA: Open Hand.

Glen, J. (1996), *Highlander: No ordinary school*, Knoxville, TN: University of Tennessee Press.

Hester, C. (1999), "August 1964 in Mississippi," in S. Erenrich (ed.), *Freedom is a constant struggle: An anthology of the Mississippi Civil Rights Movement*, Montgomery, AL: Black Belt Press, pp. 190–93.

Jacobs, D. (2003), *The Myles Horton reader: Education for social change*, Knoxville, TN: University of Tennessee Press.

Lawrence-Lightfoot, S. and J.H. Davis (1997), *The art and science of portraiture*, San Francisco, CA: Jossey-Bass.

Miller, M. (1999), "The Mississippi Freedom Democratic Party," in S. Erenrich (ed.), *Freedom is a constant struggle: An anthology of the Mississippi Civil Rights Movement*, Montgomery, AL: Black Belt Press, pp. 295–303.

Newfield, J. (1999), "Amite county," in S. Erenrich (ed.), *Freedom is a constant struggle: An anthology of the Mississippi Civil Rights Movement*, Montgomery, AL: Black Belt Press, pp. 85–99.

Petrus, S. and R.D. Cohen (2015), *Folk City: New York and the American Folk Music Revival*, Oxford: Oxford University Press.

Seeger, P. and B. Reiser (1989), *Everybody says freedom: A history of the Civil Rights Movement in songs and pictures*, New York, NY: W.W. Norton.

Winkler, A. (2009), *To everything there is a season: Pete Seeger and the power of song*, New York, NY: Oxford University Press.

6. El Chapo for *presidente*: an examination of leadership through Mexico's *narcoculture*

Patricia D. Catoira and Virginia K. Bratton

Just hours after Mexican drug lord Luis Guzmán Loera was again apprehended on 8 January 2016, artists were rushing to compose new songs telling the latest episode in the life of the world's most powerful kingpin. Since his ascendance to the top of the *narco* world in 2003, "El Chapo" (Spanish nickname for "shorty") has been the subject of *corridos*, traditional folk lyric-based ballads. The analysis of *narcocorridos* contained in this chapter contributes to the cross-cultural leadership literature responding to House et al.'s (1997) advocacy of qualitative investigations of leadership, especially in the context of cultural artifacts that are difficult if not impossible to quantify. As Morgan (1998) observes, "Scholarship that contributes to an understanding of the way music enters into the question of political agency, cultural appropriation and hegemony, and taboos and conceptions of morality has given new perspectives to 'practical' problems" (p. 29). The overwhelming celebratory characterization of El Chapo in the so-called *narcocorridos* highlights his popularity among the Mexican people despite all the violence he is responsible for. An article from *The New York Times*, addressing El Chapo's latest capture, points to this paradox:

> As the head of the Sinaloa cartel, Mr. Guzmán is the embodiment of an identity the country has fought to shed for decades. To some, the uneducated farm boy turned cartel magnate is a Robin Hood figure for modern times, revered for his fight against the government and generosity to the poor. For others, he is a heartless criminal who floods America's streets with narcotics and leaves streets strewn with bodies. Either way, Mr. Guzmán represents a deep crisis for Mexico's leaders as they struggle to define the country's image. (Ahmed, 2016, p. 15)

The popularity of El Chapo and the draw to the lavish consumer-driven *narco* lifestyle has left the Mexican government baffled. Their celebration of *narco* figures and lifestyle is problematic, but, in the Mexican context, it responds to an endemic frustration with a failed State and leadership. Acknowledging the power of popular culture, especially among the disenfranchised, less educated and traditionally oppressed lower classes, Mexican authorities have attempted to curtail the spread of *narcocorridos* through censorship.

As advocated by House et al. (1997) in their cultural congruence proposition, the cultural context in which a leader performs typically determines the success of that leader. Examinations of leadership in Latin America (see Behrens, 2010) similarly find paternalistic leadership approaches that emphasize both "personal and social relationships" (Davila and Elvira, 2012, p. 548) as most effective. Using a qualitative approach in this chapter, we investigate Guzmán's manifestation of paternalistic charisma, his relationship with his followers as expressed in *narcocorridos* and the political and cultural context that has given rise to his leadership success in Mexico against the violent backdrop of the illicit narcotics industry.

We begin with a brief discussion of House et al.'s (1997) cultural congruence proposition and an examination of the culture and context surrounding Guzmán's leadership in Mexico. We further review cross-cultural leadership research to construct a normative profile of effective leadership in this context. Through a qualitative analysis of folk songs, *corridos*, we investigate the romanticized portrayal of El Chapo's leadership against the juxtaposition of traditional and modern influences in Mexican culture. Finally, we examine the mechanisms by which this outlet of popular culture has provided a space to both inscribe and legitimize models of *narco* leadership through their widespread popularity.

THEORETICAL FRAMEWORK

The cultural congruence proposition suggests leader behaviors that are consistent with the values within a given culture are more likely to be accepted by and effective among that population (House et al., 1997). From this perspective, leadership success can be explained by an individual's understanding and exhibition of behaviors that are consistent with the values inherent within the cultural context of his or her leadership. By exploring this proposition in a culturally specific leadership setting, we can develop a deeper understanding of the elements that contributed to the rise and success of Guzmán's leadership in Mexico.

The cross-cultural organizational leadership literature traditionally defines culture normatively. House et al. (1997) define normative culture as "modal patterns of shared psychological properties among members of collectives that result in compelling common affective, cognitive, and behavioral orientations that are transmitted across generations and that differentiate collectives from each other" (p. 7). However, they also acknowledge that the literature treats culture experientially where common values and behaviors are the result of shared experiences within a shared environment. Both approaches to culture are useful when examining Guzmán. His leadership context is defined by the cultural norms of Mexico as well as the shared experiences and environment of the Mexican people. These depictions of culture help us to define preferred leader behavior within the context of modern day Mexico.

ANTECEDENTS TO LEADERSHIP

Hofstede's (2001) work examining cultural norms and variations world-wide reveals that Mexican culture is defined by high levels of masculinity, power distance and collectivism, as well as a short-term, rather than long-term, orientation toward time (Hofstede et al., 2010). Hofstede's cultural dimensions illuminate the context of Guzmán's leadership. In their review of cross-cultural leadership research, House et al. (1997) identify six antecedents to "preferred leader behavior" (pp. 26–30) that further delineate the circumstances giving rise to Guzmán's leadership success in Mexico.

The first antecedent, *dominant norms and religion*, is derived from the cultural congruence proposition. These define a culture's values and norms and include Hofstede's cultural profile as well as religious beliefs. According to a recent Pew Research survey, the vast majority of Mexican respondents self-identified as Catholic and adhere to traditional practices thereof (Donoso, 2014). Additional norms include having strong family attachments and a sense of despair, as well as expectations that their organization will take care of employees and their family members (Dickson et al., 2003).

The second antecedent, *the dominant elite*, tends to serve as models for would-be leaders particularly if the elite are respected and trusted. However, if the elite do not enjoy positive regard by the masses, they may model the antithesis of leadership. How the elite are viewed within a culture is largely dependent on the third antecedent, *historical leaders*. In cultures where power is allocated unevenly by class, historical leaders can be respected and emulated. However, if historical leaders are known for violating strong cultural norms, the opposite holds true—particularly in cultures previously dominated by charismatic dictators (House et al., 2004).

The fourth antecedent, *modernization*, also shapes a culture's expectations and preferences for leader behavior. Modern countries tend to value achievement, organization, reliability, logic and improvement (Bass, 2008;

House et al., 1997). Leaders from traditional countries are more likely to tolerate bribery and place women in lower-level positions (Davis et al., 1986). Although Mexico has made substantial progress using conventional indices of modernization (for example, literacy rates, electric power consumption, GDP) (International Energy Agency, 2014; UNESCO Institute for Statistics, 2012), the pronounced power distance between the elite and the lower classes has limited the distribution of economic benefits to the upper echelons of the population.

The fifth antecedent, *unique role demands of leaders*, refers to idiosyncratic forces within a leader's cultural and organizational context that shapes expected leader behaviors and performance. As discussed previously, Mexico is a collectivist, masculine culture with high power distance and a short-term time orientation. Each of these characteristics influences the role expectations of leaders in this country.

The last antecedent is *cultural convergence*, which suggests that as Western research and media spread across the world, cultures will evolve to incorporate the principles, conventions and procedures of Western culture (House et al., 1997). This is a gradual process and many traditional cultural norms endure while new values and practices come into being. We examine one instance of cultural convergence by exploring the current struggles of the impoverished to increase the quantity and quality of their consumption in Mexico (Sinclair and Pertierra, 2012).

LEADERSHIP IN MEXICO—A NORMATIVE PROFILE

Traditionally, a successful Mexican leader is benevolently paternalistic and demanding (Littrell and Barba, 2013). Dickson et al. (2003) describe this paternalistic style as "a highly directive leadership style that is also high on status-orientation, support and involvement in nonwork lives" (p. 739). Littrell and Barba (2013) compare this style to an "old stern father encouraging subordinates to work hard" (p. 645). Effective leaders in Mexico grant power to their followers and reward achievements (Littrell and Barba, 2013). Some also describe the leadership style as a form of culturally specific charisma, which stems from the role of the father figure in this context (Behrens, 2010).

The successful Mexican leader exhibits a leadership style consistent with a culture that is highly masculine—assertive, forceful, generally male (Hofstede, 2001). Effective leader behavior is also influenced by Mexico's history of collectivist values, where leaders provide for their followers out of a sense of duty and loyalty (Hofstede, 2001). Typically, when a culture has high power distances, coercive and autocratic leadership approaches are effective (Bass, 2008). The impact of power distance on leadership success in Mexico is equivocal. Cross-cultural leadership research indicates that countries, like Mexico, that were previously dominated by charismatic dictators view authoritarian leadership approaches with strong suspicion and aversion (House et al., 2004). However, in recent years, a growing sense of disillusionment with democracy (as it has manifested during the last century) among the people of Mexico (Paller, 2013) suggests that the culture may be more receptive to authoritarian leadership behaviors today than in the past.

Finally, Mexican leaders exhibit a sense of fatalism consistent with Hofstede's (2010) short-term cultural orientation and Schwartz's (1992, 1994) Hedonism cultural dimension. In this respect, leaders emphasize "pleasure and sensuous gratification for oneself" (Littrell and Barba, 2013, p. 638) and focus on living in the moment.

House et al. (1997) recognize that qualitative research approach may yield valuable insights in cross-cultural leadership research. They further acknowledge that cultural artifacts, which are not easily quantified, can inform our understanding of leadership across cultures (p. 79). Our analytical approach builds on this view. First, we develop a narrative analysis of the roles of *corridos*, and *narcocorridos* in particular, and the context that gave rise to these expressions of popular culture. Second, we examine lyrics from a selection of exemplar *narcocorridos* and consider the leadership style, follower relationships and leadership context of Guzmán.

We conducted a search of newspaper and magazine outlets for articles on the *narco* industry published in the last 15 years. We used these to identify *narcocorridos* that mention or allude to El Chapo. We supplemented this effort with additional searches on Internet video repositories (for example, YouTube) and using search engines (for example, Google and Yahoo). Combined, we identified more than 100 *narcocorridos*. We narrowed this list to ten *narcocorridos* based on two factors: (1) how widely discussed the songs are in the media and (2) the popularity and recognition of the songs among the Mexican people. The first author, a native Spanish speaker, translated the lyrics of these *narcocorridos* into English. Then, drawing on the cultural and leadership profiles discussed earlier, we analyzed and categorized excerpts from the lyrics into themes based on the (1) context of leadership, (2) the attributes and behaviors of Guzmán and (3) his reputation among the Mexican people.

CORRIDOS AS A CULTURAL ARTIFACT

The existence of *corridos* in Mexico dates back as far as the seventeenth century. They were influenced by Spanish *romances* but began showing signs of an autochthonous tradition by mid-nineteenth century at a time when Mexico was enjoying the fruits of its independence from Spain. With a simple rhyme-based, three-step narrative structure and the accompaniment of a guitar, the songs were composed and disseminated by nomadic singers. These modern-day troubadours became de facto beacons of news and information, especially for the large uneducated and impoverished portion of the population. Frazer (2006) suggests that "[A]n analysis of *corridos* shows that the rural and urban poor were less concerned about their own readiness for citizenship and more interested in asserting lower-class notions of justice that often defied the authority of the state" (p. 131). In this sense, *corridos* document the shared cultural experiences of the lower echelons of the Mexican people; this function frequently places *corridos* at odds with the government.

The genre escalated during the Mexican Revolution (1910–20) as scores of *corridos* were composed chronicling the national upheaval. Most significantly, *corridos* cemented their subversive undertone during this period as they focused on the rebels and praised the heroic feats of leaders such as Pancho Villa and Emiliano Zapata in their battles against government forces. The ballads expressed the rebels' fight for issues such as agrarian reform and social justice.

There are many *corridos* about love and non-political themes, as well, but, even then, the protagonists are from the lower classes. The Mexican poor could identify with the content of the songs while also learning about the events taking place around the country. *Corridos* thus had a great influence in informing and shaping public opinion until the coming of mass media. It is this association of *corridos* as a source of information from and for the underprivileged layers of society that casts the genre as a popular and potential opponent of government authority.

NARCOCORRIDOS AND THE MEXICAN NARCOTICS INDUSTRY

The *narcocorrido* carries on the tradition of producing songs that arise from the fringes of mainstream Mexican society, but, interestingly, became widely popular in recent years. The emergence since the 1980s of popular culture outlets such as telenovelas celebrating the world of drugs created the controversial cultural phenomenon of *narcoculture*, praising kingpins and their lavish Hollywood-like lifestyle on one hand and showing the government as inept at best and corrupt at worst on the other. This characterization places *narco* popular culture at odds with the Mexican government and other sectors of civil society. Originally a marginal cultural aesthetic, *narcoculture* has become embraced as a cultural institution associated with wealth and prosperity in Mexico, helping to shape national consumption patterns (Mondaca Cota, 2014). For instance, the sale of extravagant goods such as Hummers, whiskey and luxury brands, such as Louis Vuitton, has skyrocketed in the past ten years (Segovia, 2011). *Narcocorridos* in particular reached wide popularity, especially in the northern states of Mexico where cartels dispute territory for moving drugs along the US border.

The close connection between composers/singers and the cartels creates a dangerous win-win situation for both the artists and drug lords. Cartels fund the artists' careers in exchange for songs that will make them and their narcotic enterprise popular in the eyes of the people (McGirk and Schwarz, 2010). Singers, eager to acquire fame and notoriety, are quick to enter into these deals that have the added bonus of financial wealth.

Prominent *narcocorrido* singer Edgar Quintero acknowledges that he is commissioned to write songs in exchange for large sums of money. However, he is unapologetic about his singing about this infamous underworld: "They're the Mexican Robin Hoods. They're the ones that these kids in Mexico are looking up to, because they're the ones that are helping out their community when the government is not doing [anything] about it" (Arcos, 2013, p.11). Still, this relationship is a risky livelihood for the artists. Many have been murdered by rival cartels or even their own benefactors for performing at the wrong private party or falling out of favor (Arcos, 2013).

Violence in Mexico has been steadily on the rise since the 1990s, making it one of the most violent countries in the world (Ángel, 2016). Widespread corruption among security forces and government officials has perpetuated crime impunity and public mistrust of authorities (Ahmed and Schmitt, 2016). Growing up in this environment, young Mexicans feel hopeless about their future prospects and trapped in a life of poverty (Spiller, 2011). For young Mexicans, in particular, *narcocorridos* act as advertisements for a materialistic and dangerous life. These songs promote a consumerist lifestyle that values materialism over ideology and successfully recruit the youth into the *narco* industry by using the lure of financial stability.

Whereas the *corrido* of the Mexican Revolution offered a medium through which to spread ideas about improving the lives of the poor and the masses with free education, health care and agrarian reform, among others, the *narcocorrido* promotes a life of crime and self-indulgence to escape hardship. The situation highlights the failure of the State to provide a state of law, as well as opportunities and conditions for social mobility (Levin, 2015). Violence and poverty are issues political leaders have started to acknowledge. For example, at the start of his term in 2012, President Enrique Peña Nieto promised to enact sweeping reforms across the board that would politically modernize Mexico and bring about economic prosperity in what became known by names such as "the Mexican miracle" or "the Mexican hour" (Cabañas Díaz, 2015). There was a wave of optimism in the first two years of Peña Nieto's six-year term that was propelled by several structural reforms and more than 50 amendments to the constitution (Cabañas Díaz, 2015).

However, by the end of 2014 that optimism had come to a sharp halt. The outcry over two highly publicized massacres, in which institutional forces were presumably involved, plus continued cases of public officials' corruption and scandals renewed the feeling of mistrust and disgust with the Mexican government. Many analysts argued Peña Nieto had gone back to the old and familiar authoritarian tactics of his political party, *Partido Revolucionario Institucional*, which has been the dominant ruling party for nearly a century in Mexico, and engaged in increasing censorship and repression: "What was supposed to be the 'Mexican hour', a new era of transparency and reforms, in reality became a time of violence and corruption" ([translated from Spanish] Cabañas Díaz, 2015, p. 4162). In this context, popular culture such as *narcocorridos* offers a forum—albeit imperfect—in which to discuss topics the government would like to silence.

Beyond the war being fought between the State and the cartels regarding crime, both sides are also engaged in a cultural war. Whereas the former is localized mostly in the northern border states, the latter is fought in the collective, in the minds of all Mexicans. As critics have pointed out, "the government is facing a new cultural phenomenon: the search for easy money" (Beltrán del Río, 2015). The ubiquitous *narco* slogan, *Mas vale vivir cinco años de rey y no cincuenta de buey* (translated: "It's better to live five years as a king than 50 as an ox"), foreshadows a short life for most in this world. However, the Mexican government has not been able to counteract the appeal of this message with real alternatives. Instead, the solution from the State has been to censor or ban *narcocorridos* for inciting crime in order to prevent the encouragement of "bad behavior among the young" (Ponce, 2016).

The economics of the *narco* industry have infiltrated the most marginalized sectors of Mexican society. At the same time, the cultural expression of the *narco* industry has become normalized across all sectors of Mexican society. This level of conformity that Mexicans and civil society have adopted towards *narcoculture* and the violence thereof indicates that the State has lost this cultural war (Beltrán del Río, 2015). Guzmán's reputation and the portrayal of El Chapo in *narcocorridos* is a symbol of this defeat.

ANALYSIS OF LEADERSHIP THEMES IN SELECTED *NARCOCORRIDOS*

In Table 6.1, we present a thematic analysis of Guzmán's leadership traits and behaviors, his reputation and the context of his leadership against the violent backdrop of the *narco* industry and dissatisfaction with the State.

The *narcocorridos* illustrate several dominant cultural norms. Lyrics describing El Chapo's virtues use masculine imagery. For example, in *"El hijo de la tuna"* (p. 7) Guzmán is described as short, but brave, and in *"El encuentro"* (p. 4) Guzmán is depicted in the lyrics as a forceful and violent person: "You get out of our way because we will go through either way." This also demonstrates a readiness to accept authoritarian leadership tactics as is typical in a high power distance culture. In *"El rey de la sierra"* (p. 3), the lyrics portray Guzmán as a member of the lower strata who climbed to the top. In the two *narcocorridos* entitled, *"La captura del Chapo"* (pp. 8–9), Guzmán depicts collectivist values in his loyalty to the people of Mexico, "I prevented poverty, kidnappings, thefts because I wanted that way [. . .] I always wanted to help, never to harm."

The dominant elite are portrayed as the antithesis of leadership in *"La captura del Chapo"* (p. 8) and *"La captura del Chapo como la revolucion"* (p. 10). In the latter *narcocorrido*, Guzmán compares himself to a revered historical leader, Pancho Villa, and claims to be his modern day successor: "If Villa gave them hell with his rifle and runnings, just imagine what Guzmán would do."

Mexico's resistance to modernization is represented in *"Chapón, cuerno, y cachucha"* (p. 6), *"La captura del Chapo"* (p. 8), and *"La captura del Chapo como la revolucion"* (p. 10). These three *narcocorridos* allude to Guzmán's bribery of government officials as a regular practice.

Several *narcocorridos* illuminate the unique role demands of Guzmán as a leader. In *"La captura del Chapo"* (p. 9), Guzmán "gives jobs to people" and "puts an end to bad things." Additionally, in *"El encuentro"* (p. 4) he warns his enemies, "better not to make me use violence."

"El M16" (p. 1) illustrates a desire among the people to acquire quantity and quality of goods to consume. Guzmán represents a success story to the impoverished in that he, "started from the bottom" (*"El rey de la sierra"* [p. 3]) "selling oranges in the mountains" (*"El hijo de la tuna"* [p. 7]) but now he enjoys many "pleasures" and "people admire [him]" (*"Chapón, cuerno, y cachucha"* [p. 6]).

Overall, Guzmán is depicted by *narcocorridos* as a highly paternalistic leader who provides for the people out of a sense of loyalty and benevolence: "my people depend on [me]" (*"Chapón, cuerno, y cachucha"* [p. 6]).

Table 6.1 Analysis of narco leadership themes in a sample of ten narcocorridos

| | | Narcocorridos | | | Leadership Themes | |
				Traits and Behavior	Relationship with Followers	Context
Song Title	Performer	Source	Lyric*			
1. El M16	Los Buknas de Culiacán	Armas y Billetes. La Disco Music, 2012	In their BMWs, Escalades or Cheyennes people see him around with his people on the look black cars and dressing fashionably.			The narco life, consumption, luxury
2. El señor de la montaña	Los Canelos de Durango	Los últimos corridos del compa Pepe. Hyphy Music, 2013	Wherever he goes Colombia and Mexico admire him [. . .] he is like an animal up there in the mountains [. . .] he protects and captures when needed.	Masculine, strong, brave, protector	Widely admired	
3. El rey de la sierra	Los Gavilleros de la Sierra	El rey de la sierra. Viva Music Group, 2014	His ability to manage so many people under him draws envy [. . .] How does he do it so that they continue working for him? Must be because he started from the bottom. [. . .] He is respected by everybody because of his great wisdom.	Hard working, smart, good manager	Of the people, respected	
4. El encuen-tro	Los Alegres del Barranco	Corridos pa' la Clika. Titan Records/Hyphy Music, 2010	[. . .] and with an R15 told them I am who you are looking for. You get out of our way because we will go through either way [. . .] better not to make me use violence.	Strong, violent when necessary, feared	Reputation for strength	

				Values		
5. *El Chapa-rrito*	Los Alegres del Barranco	*El Chaparrito.* RH Music, 2015	Now the government has really screwed up [. . .] I am talking about my brain and knowing how to make things work. I have lots of friends [. . .] A friend can do more even open the earth for you. That is true gentlemen. [. . .] There's work and deals many things I need to align.	friendship, loyalties, integrity, smart, work ethic		Disillusionment with government, consumption/money
6. *Chapón, cuerno, y cachu-cha*	Los Buknas de Culiacán	*Los corridos más pisteables del año.* La Disco Music, 2013	I know it is your job but I also have mine and it will never come down. My people depend on it. I don't tolerate failure [. . .] I am Chapo Guzmán. I know the name scares you. I am a noble and simple man [. . .] I am an expert for work. People admire me. If you catch me I will escape.	Feared but reasonable, noble, work ethic, resourceful	Of the people, respected, benevolent outlaw	Corruption— government officials take bribes
7. *El hijo de la tuna*	Los Gatos de Sinaloa	*De qué color es la suerte.* Reca Music Inc, 2010	As a child he sold oranges in the mountains so he could eat. He is never ashamed of it, on the contrary, he is proud of it [. . .] I am brave from my origin. I am also a good friend that's how we the Guzmán are.	Not ashamed of his origins; short but brave; values friendship		

Table 6.1 (continued)

	Narcocorridos			Leadership Themes		
Song Title	Performer	Source	Lyric*	Traits and Behavior	Relationship with Followers	Context
8. *La Captura Del Chapo*	Anonymous	http://www.musica.com/letras.asp?letra=2205936	[. . .] the rich getting richer and the poor getting poorer. We don't see any improvements. [. . .] Don't make me compare myself to the president that you have now. I prevented poverty, kidnappings, thefts because I wanted it that way. [. . .] I always wanted to help never to harm unlike this government.	Helping the people, honest, integrity		Government is the enemy and ignores the poor; poverty and violence by government
9. *La captura del Chapo*	Los Alegres del Barranco	*El terror.* Hyphy Music, 2014	They accuse of being a delinquent. I give jobs to people. I put an end to bad things. [. . .] I will come back to La Tuna [the Guzmán family ranch] and will escape again. That's what the people want.	Provider for people; brings justice and prosperity	Benevolent outlaw	Escaping imprisonment
10. *La captura del Chapo Como La Revolucion*	El Potro de Sinaloa	https://www.youtube.com/watch?v=3aktEPI2360	If Villa gave them [government leadership] hell with his rifle and runnings, just imagine what Guzmán would do. [. . .] I think that if they catch the old man and hand him over to the gringos then you will have to find somebody else to feed you.	Provider for people	Comparison to esteemed historical leader of the people, Pancho Villa	Government corruption

* All lyrics have been translated into English from Spanish by coauthor.

Like a stern father, Guzmán demands a lot from his followers: "I don't tolerate failure" (*"Chapón, cuerno, y cachucha"* [p. 6]). As discussed previously, lyrics portray him as assertive and forceful. He is highly charismatic and admired by his followers, "he is respected by everybody" (*"El rey de la sierra"* [p. 3]) and this respect transcends national borders (*"El señor de la montaña"* [p. 2]). Much of Guzmán's reputation is attributed to his wisdom (*"El rey de la sierra"* [p. 3]), expertise (*"Chapón, cuerno, y cachucha"* [p. 6]) and work ethic as demonstrated by his reluctance to retire and end his sustained efforts on behalf of the people.

Finally, the *narcocorridos* reveal a hedonistic attention to momentary pleasures such as BMWs and Escalades and fashionable clothing (*"El M16"* [p. 1]). Such indulging may be informed by the theme of fatalism, revealed by casual references to violence and taking lives as a matter of business in the *narco* industry.

This holistic exploration of Guzmán sheds light on the cultural context of *followers* as well as the cultural context *giving rise to* the leader. Rather than obscuring details in order to focus on commonalities of leaders across contexts (an etic approach), this chapter demonstrates, in ways that only an emic approach can, the path-dependent history that unfolds as leaders and followers interact to create a cultural leadership icon.

The history of the Mexican people, as well as Guzmán's followers and leadership context all play a role in his rise to power, his influence and the willingness of the public to embrace and accept his behaviors. The *narcocorridos* further suggest the public's willingness to excuse the violence and illicitness of Guzmán's trade as a necessary evil that brings protection and care to the impoverished people of Mexico. Given the corruption and violence perpetuated by the government in the past century, the impoverished people of this country prefer Guzmán's benevolent paternalism, peppered with occasional acts of "warranted" violence.

The *narcocorridos* intimate that it is not Guzmán's intention to usurp the government, but rather to achieve and maintain his business success in the *narco* industry. Nonetheless, the celebration of Guzmán's success in *narcocorridos* deeply threatens the State. These songs illustrate and legitimize his success while highlighting his virulent paternalism against the stark absence of State support for the Mexican people. Irrespective of political and social commentary, *narcocorridos* are an especially popular form of entertainment and widely appeal to the people of Mexico on the basis of entertainment value and artistic merit (Hastings, 2013).

One wonders if Guzmán's latest capture and extradition to the United States will lead to a new model of leadership. With Trump's ascendency to power in the United States and antagonistic policy toward Mexico, will the State and Peña Nieto enjoy a resurgence of patriotic unity from the populace (for example, Kahn, 2017)? Or will Peña Nieto be unable to capitalize on anti-Trump fueled nationalism due to his long history of troubled relations with the populace? Will another player in the *narco* world step up to fill Guzmán's void? Will the government attempt to address the needs of all strata of the Mexican people? No doubt that the *corridos* will be there to chronicle these events.

REFERENCES

Ahmed, A. (2016), "How El Chapo was finally captured, again," *The New York Times*, 17 January, p. A1.

Ahmed, A. and E. Schmitt (2016), "Mexican military runs up body count in drug war," *The New York Times*, 27 May, p. A1.

Ángel, A. (2016), "Rising homicide rate in Mexico wiping out recent gains," *Insight Crime*, 5 April, accessed 25 May 2016 at http://www.insightcrime.org.

Arcos, B. (2013), "Drug lords pay this Mexican-American singer to write their ballads," *PRI's The World*, accessed 8 June 2016 at http://www.pri.org/stories/2013-12-11/drug-lords-pay-mexican-american-singer-write-their-ballads.

Bass, B.M. (2008), *The Bass Handbook of Leadership: Theory, Research and Managerial Applications*, 4th ed., New York, NY: Free Press.

Behrens, A. (2010), "Charisma, paternalism, and business leadership in Latin America," *Thunderbird International Business Review*, **52** (1), 21–9.

Beltrán del Rio, P. (2015), "El Santo Chapo," *el Circulo Rojo*, 13 October, accessed 28 May 2016 at http://www.elcirculorojo.com.mx/gasparin/el-santo-chapo-pascal-beltran-del-rio/.

Cabañas Díaz, P. (2015), "Pacto por México: Corrupción y autoritarismo," *Proceedings of XXVII AMIC, Queretaro Mexico 2015*, pp. 4160–79, accessed 10 May 2016 at http://amic2015.uaq.mx/docs/memorias/GI_14_PDF/GI_14_PACTO_POR_MEXICO.pdf.

Davila, A. and M.M. Elvira (2012), "Humanistic leadership: Lessons from Latin America," *Journal of World Business*, **47**, 548–54.

Davis, H.J., L.W. Ming and T.F. Brosnan (1986), "The Farmer-Richman model: A bibliographic essay emphasizing applicability to Singapore and Indonesia," Paper, Academy of Management, Chicago.

Dickson, M.W., D.N. Den Hartog and J.K. Mitchelson (2003), "Research on leadership in a cross-cultural context: Making progress, and raising new questions," *The Leadership Quarterly*, **14**, 729–68.

Donoso, J.C. (2014), "On religion, Mexicans are more Catholic and often more traditional than Mexican Americans," *Fact Tank: New in the Numbers*. Pew Research Center. Accessed 15 May 2016 at http://www.pewresearch.org/fact-tank/2014/12/08/on-religion-mexicans-are-more-catholic-and-often-more-traditional-than-mexican-americans/.

Frazer, C. (2006), *Bandit Nation: A History of Outlaws and Cultural Struggle in Mexico, 1810–1920,* Lincoln, NE: University of Nebraska Press.

Hastings, D. (2013), "Bloody 'narcocorrido' ballads are most popular Latin music," *New York Daily News*, 17 December, accessed 28 April 2016 at http://www.nydaily news.com/news/world/performers-narcocorridos-sell-arenas-u-s-mexico-generate-

millions-sales-songs-romanticizing-drug-lords-beheadings-violent-drug-ballads-w
in-grammys-article-1.1536307.

Hofstede, G. (2001), *Culture's Consequences: Comparing Values, Behaviors, Institutions, and Organizations Across Nations*, 2nd ed., Thousand Oaks, CA: Sage Publications.

Hofstede, G., G.J. Hofstede and M. Minkov (2010), *Cultures and Organizations: Software of the Mind*, 3rd ed., New York, NY: McGraw-Hill.

Holzinger, I., T. Medcof and R.B. Dunham (2006), "Leader and follower prototypes in an international context: An exploratory study of Asia and South America," *Proceedings of the 34th Annual Meeting of the Administrative Sciences Association of Canada*, Banff, AB, 3–6 June, accessed 28 April 2016 at: www.schulich.yorku.ca/SSB-Extra/Faculty.nsf/d3344026438b8e3885256b1800688b5c/251ccdd5c97f6c7785256c1600712614/$FILE/ASAC%202006%20Holzinger_Medcof_Dunham.pdf.

House, R.J., P.J. Hanges, M. Javidan, P.W. Dorfman, V. Gupta and Globe Associates (2004), *Leadership, Culture and Organizations: The GLOBE Study of 62 Societies*. Thousand Oaks, CA: Sage Publications.

House, R.J., N.S. Wright and R.N. Aditya (1997), "Cross-cultural research on organizational leadership: A critical analysis and a proposed theory" [prepublication manuscript], in P.C. Earley and M. Erez (eds), *New Perspectives on International Industrial/Organizational Psychology*, San Francisco, CA: Jossey-Bass, pp. 535–625.

Howell, J.P., J.M. DelaCerdab, S.M. Prietod, J. Leonel Bautista, J. Arnoldo Ortiz, P. Dorfman and M.J. Méndez (2007), "Leadership and culture in Mexico," *Journal of World Business*, **42** (4), 449–62.

International Energy Agency (2014), "Mexico: Indicators," *Statistics Search*, accessed 30 July 2016 at http://www.iea.org/statistics/.

Kahn, C. (2017), "Anti-Trump protesters take to the streets across Mexico," *NPR*, 13 February, accessed 15 February 2017 at http://www.npr.org/2017/02/13/515043679/anti-trump-protesters-take-to-the-streets-across-mexico.

Levin, M. (2015), "'El Chapo' is a beloved folk hero in his Mexican homeland," *Houston Chronicle*, 15 July, accessed 25 June 2016 at http://www.chron.com/crime/article/El-Chapo-is-a-beloved-folk-hero-in-his-Mexican-6386265.php.

Littrell, R.F. and E.C. Barba (2013), "North and South Latin America: Influence of values on preferred leader behavior in Chile and Mexico," *Journal of Management Development*, **32** (6), 629–56.

McGirk, T. and S. Schwarz (2010), "Ballads for the bad guys", *Time*, 1 November, **176** (18), 66–70.

Mondaca Cota, A. (2014), "Narrativa de la narcocultura. Estética y consume," *Ciencia desde el Occidente*, **1** (2), 29–38.

Morgan, B.M. (1998), "From Fierro to Farándula: Music and archival fictions in Spanish American literature" (Doctoral dissertation), retrieved from Proquest Dissertations and Theses.

Paller, J.W. (2013), "Political struggle to political sting: A theory of democratic disillusionment," *Polity*, **45** (4), 580–603.

Ponce, A. (2016), "Coahuila analiza prohibir narco corridos," *Laguna*, 3 March, accessed 15 April 2006 at http://www.milenio.com/politica/Narco_corridos_en_Coahuila-Congreso_de_Coahuila-Ruben_Moreira-seguridad_en_Coahuila_0_694130680.html.

Schwartz, S.H. (1992), "Universals in the content and structure of values:

Theoretical advances and empirical tests in 20 countries," in M. Zanna (ed.), *Advances in Experimental Social Psychology*, vol. 25, New York, NY: Academic Press, pp. 1–65.

Schwartz, S.H. (1994), "Beyond individualism/collectivism: New cultural dimensions of values," in U. Kim, H.C. Triandis, C. Kagitcibasi, S.C. Choi and G. Yoon, (eds), *Individualism and Collectivism: Theory, Method and Applications*, Thousand Oaks, CA: Sage, pp. 85–119.

Segovia, F. (2011), "Mexico: Cultura y violencia," *Ñ*, 30 September, accessed 10 July 2017 at http://www.revistaenie.clarin.com/edicion-impresa/Narcotrafico_y_corrupcion_0_564543551.html.

Sinclair, J. and A.C. Pertierra (2012), "Understanding consumer culture in Latin America: An introduction," in J. Sinclair and A.C. Pertierra (eds), *Consumer Culture in Latin America*, New York, NY: Palgrave Macmillan, pp. 1–13.

Spiller, A. (2011), "La ilusión del narco," *Replicante: Cultura crítica y periodismo digital*, 10 July, accessed 28 June 2016 at http://revistareplicante.com/la-ilusion-del-narco/.

UNESCO Institute for Statistics (2012), "Mexico: Literacy rate," *UNESCO eAtlas of Literacy*, accessed 30 July 2016 at http://uis.unesco.org/country/mx.

7. An idol leader: David Bowie, self-representation, otherness and sexual identity

Shawna Guenther

INTRODUCTION

Sadly, 2016 began with the loss of the most influential musician of the past 50 years, David Bowie (born David Robert Jones in Brixton, United Kingdom, on 8 January 1947). Bowie died in Manhattan, New York, on 10 January 2016 of liver cancer. Bowie's incredible musical and artistic abilities made him a legendary: "a vocalist of extraordinary technical ability" (Schinder and Schwartz cited on "David Bowie," n.d.). His stylistic range is exceptional: "hard rock and heavy metal, soul, psychedelic folk and pop" ("David Bowie," n.d.), and, of course, glam. He is an idol's idol. Bowie's modes of cultural production changed (and continue to change) the way we see, hear, construct, and interpret our world. His prolific and eclectic creative output breaches diverse cultural, political, and individual boundaries—apocalypse and messianic cultism, futurity and intergalactic life, authoritarianism and revolution, identity and sexual ambiguity, fanaticism and celebrity—while suggesting the temporal solution of wild escapism, through sex, drugs, and rock and roll. A more permanent solution, suggested by Bowie's determination to continually strive for the new and unique, is Art. And it is through artistic production that Bowie brilliantly fashioned himself as rock god with the power to create and destroy his various personae, and, significantly, to effect social change. Bowie's charisma, in all its strange manifestations, and his visionary expressions of humanity empower his followers, not as legions of passive fans behind him, but as active participants in fantasy, and of change, *with* him.

While other musicians have employed their celebrity status itself as a means of empowerment, Bowie uses the myriad facets of his creative production, and the establishment of his own microcosmic presence, as the sources of his influencing power. Here, I mean the Bowie universe, or "Bowieverse," in which every aspect of his artistic production and presentation is under his aesthetic control. In addition, Bowie's iconoclastic lyrics are expressive of the despairing *zeitgeist* of his various times. Bowie affirms, "Everything that contributes to stagnation is evil. When it has familiarity, it's no longer rock-'n'-roll" (Crowe, 1976a [2005], p. 280). Thus, unlike many musicians of his generation who tour their old worn-out hits, Bowie continued to create and innovate new music and art—his final album *Blackstar* being released two days before his death, on his 69th birthday. As Wells and Barclay (2016) attest, the "release of *Blackstar* was the final masterstroke from a genius of self-creation . . . Blackstar sounds not much like anything else Bowie had done." And Bowie stunningly transformed himself again and again, in what many have called a chameleon-like career. Although Bowie changed characters frequently, and even "his voice change[d] dramatically" (Campbell, 2008, p. 284), to refer to him as a chameleon is not quite correct. The purpose of the chameleon's change is to blend into his background. Bowie certainly has never done that as an artist. However, one might consider that if the chameleon's objective is to hide, this may be a relevant metonym such that the changes hide the real person, David Bowie, from the prying eye, as will be discussed further on. Using all aspects of the Bowieverse, Bowie influenced social attitudes, fabulously, across the five decades of his cultural production, and his creative legacy will continue to do so into the future.

Three main performative aspects illuminate Bowie's central cultural impact. First, within the icon that is David Bowie, the aforementioned microcosm, constructed by the artist, rather than the human being David Bowie, exist many personae, each part of a consciously constructed self-representation that both reveals and conceals man, artist and meaning. Second, in his repeated emphases on alienation, loneliness and despair, Bowie empathizes with, and cleaves to, that which is socially othered, projecting an accepting atmosphere for all the freaks, the non-conformists and the marginalized. This is particularly effective when Bowie transforms himself into the otherest of them all. Third, the sexual ambiguity of several personae (and early on, Bowie himself) enables Bowie's foregrounding of considerations of sexual identity through his cultural practices, making unconventional sexual and gender identities (what we might now refer to as sexual and gender spectra) bold spectacles rather than closeted shadows. What is considered dangerous, questionable and inappropriate finds its place of free experimentation within the Bowieverse.

SELF-REPRESENTATION

Who is David Bowie? This is an important question when we consider this particular cultural icon given the numerous characters in his repertoire. Perhaps we should also ask what is David Bowie? Cinque and Redmond (2013) attest Bowie is "one who reinvents himself in and across the media and art platforms in which he is found" (p. 377). Hawkins (2009) sees him as a classic British dandy "voyeuristically offering himself up as an object" (p. 4). We might ask when is David Bowie? Whenever he wants. He "has proven himself to be perhaps the rock star least affected by age" (Perone, 2002, p. 88). In every decade, Bowie contributes to cultural production and garners new generations of fans. *What* David Bowie is is a unique (re)construction of things past, present and future. Finally, how is David Bowie David Bowie, that Bowieverse, the complete package presented to the world—the music, images, quotations, actions *in toto*? And how can this package be created and used? Ultimately, we may find the answer to *why* is David Bowie.

Initially, I am most interested in who is David Bowie, beginning with the man who is a solid, biological being. As with any celebrity, fans are often sure they know the *real* person, the living entity. But despite being outlandish, loud and anything but a shrinking violet in his public image, David Bowie, the person, was extremely covetous of his privacy. However, who the *real* David Bowie was, need not enter into our account because that David Bowie, the man, was no different than any other human—Bowie, the person, was a man, a husband, a father, a grandfather, who did all the things that other men do, outside of his celebrity and the Bowieverse—in terms of that to which we (fans, critics, the public) respond. The David Bowie with which we are concerned here is a self-fashioned construction, the inner core of rock idol. Extending from that core are the myriad personae enacted on stage, in the music and in the limelight. These David Bowie-bred characters have fascinated the western world, particularly with the arrival of the infamous, (im)mortal Ziggy Stardust.

Having begun in a somewhat lacklustre way, both as a band member and a solo artist, David Bowie reinvents the rock idol with his drug-addled, sexually ambiguous, outrageous persona Ziggy Stardust, introduced in 1972. With stark, pointy, red hair, androgynous make-up derived from Japanese Kabuki theatre (Tawa, 2005, p. 250) and groovy jumpsuits, Ziggy is the fictional leader of what Hoffmann (2008) calls "sci-fi glitter rock" (p. 254), in the guise of the fictional band called The Spiders from Mars. Bowie describes the purpose of the character thusly:

> What I did with my Ziggy Stardust was package a totally credible, plastic rock-'n'-roll singer . . . my plastic rock-'n'-roller was much more plastic than

anybody's. And that was what was needed at the time. And it still is. Most people still want their idols and gods to be shallow, like cheap toys. (Crowe, 1976a [2005], p. 279)

If we are to believe Bowie (remembering that the Bowie being interviewed is a consciously staged representation), then we must believe that Bowie (in retrospect perhaps) shames us for believing such an obvious illusion, while he revels in the fact that the illusion works. Ziggy made Bowie a superstar and initiated his career-long tying of musical performance to theatrical spectacle in such an obvious way as to force spectators to totally escape into his world of make-believe.

Bowie even claims to have fallen too deep into the illusion himself: "I became convinced I was a messiah" (Crowe, 1976a [2005], p. 280). With the extent of his cocaine use during his Ziggy days, this is not surprising. Wilcken (2005) reveals that Bowie's (possible) cocaine psychosis "highly distorted perceptions of reality, hallucinations, affectlessness and a marked tendency towards magical thinking" with paranoid delusions (p. 9). But is Bowie's claim an identity confusion (enabled or disabled by drug use) or merely a continuation of the theatrical? Bowie's narcissistic messianic persona is a priori; he defines Ziggy as such in the song's lyrics *before* the character is introduced to the world: "Making love with his ego . . . like a leper messiah" (Bowie, 1972). Bowie offers a completely (and obviously) artificial persona with the power of a god who can lead us to happiness, until we admit we believe the hype. Then Bowie shoots us back down into reality, claiming that we have sacrificed him through idolatry and imitation: "When the kids had killed the man I had to break up the band" (Bowie, 1972). The lesson here, at least in part, is not to follow the leader blindly. Cinque and Redmond (2013) note that in constantly changing personae, Bowie effectively "constantly kills himself" (p. 377). Perhaps this plays into Bowie's conception of his own godhood—he ably resurrects himself time and time again, retreating, as if dead, to reconstruct himself.

What follows is a series of bizarre personae and lyric narrators corresponding to new songs and new albums. Bowie's 1973 persona, Aladdin Sane, with a lightning bolt across his whitened face, according to Bowie, is "a crossover out of Ziggy and not really knowing where I was going" (Loder, 1992, p. 141)—a lad insane. That is, Aladdin Sane is the perfect representative of a generation that cannot define itself. In 1975, as Garofalo (2002) indicates, Bowie makes "another unexpected turn, swapping the 'sci-fi future' of his glam period 'for the rising form of white soul boy'" (p. 248 citing Chambers, 2008, p. 133) as the Thin White Duke, a character extrapolated from the extraterrestrial Thomas Jerome Newton ("David Bowie," n.d.), the character Bowie played in *The Man Who Fell to*

Earth (1976). Bowie is yet another alien. But the music is no longer glam or rock or pop. It is white soul—music that mocks hegemonic white power by combining markers of white privilege (a duke) with those of conventionally black music (soul). Major Tom from "Space oddity," is Bowie's 1969 heroic astronaut persona, signaling (and timed to correspond with) the hopeful age of space exploration. By 1980's "Ashes to ashes," this figure morphs into free-floating drug addict, "adrift from humanity" (Doggett, 2012, p. 1), when the dream of man's defiance of gravity by escaping the confines of the earth becomes defeated by his physical and moral weaknesses. And the list goes on, all the way to the Lazarus character of his off-Broadway play of the same name (Bowie and Walsh, 2015) and his final album, *Blackstar* (Bowie, 2016), a chilling construction of a man approaching his actual physical death. Both play and album tease us with another potential biblical return.

Now we come to why. Why is David Bowie all of these self-constructed personae? Why does Bowie take "style to absurd extremes" (Hawkins, 2009, p. 16)? Why does Bowie "flaunt the constructedness" (Hawkins, 2009, p. 18) of his personae? Why is David Bowie real, but not real? The proposed answers are as disparate as his personae. Rüther (2004) claims that "Bowie is never concerned with identity, only roles" (p. 21), while Perone (2002) argues that the roles are "really as much about identity" (p. 89) as they are characterizations. In his dandifying of Bowie, Hawkins (2009) insists that the personae provide "a platform on which to stand" (p. 5), explaining that, through the personae, Bowie

> can be demure, sensual, sexually naïve, or bold, cock-sure, rough and vulgar, or even passive, regressive and a psycho-case. And mocking his own self-loathing … exhibits an outward expression of superiority, an embodiment of the [Oscar] Wildean idea of the self as a work of art. (p. 5)

Alternatively, Cinque and Redmond (2013) claim that Bowie creates "a figure who constantly seems to be artificial or constructed and yet whose work asks us to look for his real self behind the mask" (p. 377). But is this "real self" the rock star, the person, the artist or the microcosm to which I have previously referred? There is another valid possibility. Is this "real self" a David Bowie that is beyond the man's construction, the messiah or alien or *Homo superior* (Bowie, 1971b), the approaching character in "Oh! You pretty things"? Bowie quips, "I always had a repulsive sort of need to be something more than human. I felt very, very puny as a human. I thought, 'Fuck that. I want to be a superman'" (Crowe, 1976b). Is Bowie projecting larger-than-life characters to escape being merely human? Or is he playing the game of cat and mouse with us again?

For Bowie, as artist, the creation of various personae is part of the package of a changing style that anticipates musical, and, more widely, cultural change. He asserts that rock is "changing its vocabulary continually . . . Because it is social currency; it actually has a place in society. It's a living art, and it is undergoing constant reevaluation and change" (Loder, 1992, p. 141). Furthermore, Bowie anticipates the need to continually push the limits of art: "The minute you know you are on safe ground you're dead. You're finished" (Crowe, 1976a [2005], p. 280). As a cultural and social leader, Bowie's musical, artistic and identity change-ability translates into his ability to manipulate and take control of his production and his influence. And just as Bowie's personae borrow from and reimagine pervious cultural markers, his personae empower other performance artists, opening avenues of risk-taking in their own practices of cultural production. Star and Waterman (2007) attest, "Bowie's unique ability to create quasi-fictional stage personae, and to change when every new album, was a precedent for the image manipulation of 1980s stars like Michael Jackson, Prince, and Madonna" (p. 331). Musicians, actors and other artists continue to draw inspiration from the array of Bowies. Nevertheless, Bowie "typically remain[ed] one step ahead of prevailing cultural trends" (Hoffmann, 2008, p. 254). Importantly, these identity and style transformations also contribute to the commercial viability of all that is Bowie. Frith et al. (2001) confirm that Bowie was "the first musician to appreciate the pop importance of artist as brand" (p. 196). The unexpected, the outrageous, and the dangerous are all critical lures in a competitive industry that changes rapidly with successive generations of fans and anticipates consumer tastes.

In addition to being both brilliant marketing strategies and self-aggrandizing artistic extravaganzas, the personae of the Bowieverse are, in part, a method of self-protection for the person behind the fame. Bowie states, "Being famous helps put off the problems of discovering myself" (Crowe, 1976a [2005], p. 279). Perone (2002) suggests that Bowie's (intentional) lack of self-recognition is resultant of privileging the public over private image (p. 88). I would argue that Bowie is very much aware of himself, protecting his private image through careful use of his public one, albeit one that often changes. Bowie others *himself*, by separating the man from the idol and the idol from mainstream culture. Doggett (2012) concurs, stating that "By becoming something *other*, [Bowie] would refuse to be enclosed by gender, by race, by style, or by reality" (p. 18). Furthermore, the iconic Ziggy Stardust character remains "an eternal outsider who could act as a beacon for anyone who felt ostracized from the world around them" (Doggett, 2012, p. 3). Thus, by becoming something other (alien, god, *Homo superior*), Bowie transcends limitations of cultural modes (and earth-boundedness) and forces mainstream culture to accept, or at least consider, the Other. And as he croons, we willingly follow him, much to his own delight: "I've got believers, believing me" (Bowie, 1979). Then, in an astounding reversal, Bowie lets his fans lead him: "[H]e invited fans to call a hot line and tell him which songs to perform on the [Sound and Vision] tour. After years of setting his own agenda, is Bowie now letting fans dictate what he does? 'Totally and completely. Absolutely'" (Christensen, 1990, quoting Bowie). The fans incorporate him into themselves and take their lead.

OTHERNESS

Let us turn and face the changes that Bowie's lyrics bring to those who identify with him as champion of otherness. Despite Bowie's insistence that he has "no message whatsoever" (Crowe, 1976a [2005], p. 279), he affirms that he wanted to make a mark artistically (Crowe, 1976a [2005], p. 279). Astutely, Bowie realizes that the unveiling of Ziggy Stardust on tour placed him in a precarious, yet powerful, position. He comments, "There was quite a bit of antagonism . . . the first couple of months were not easy. I mean, it was 'Aw, a bunch of poofters' . . . we played it up . . . Because it was the most rebellious thing that was happening at the time" (Loder, 1992, p. 141). Through this strange extraterrestrial characterization, Bowie's music enables the dissemination of his lyrics and music to a public that understands his alienated, non-conformist Other, in a way that traditional popular musical genres do not. From the beginning of his career, Bowie's cultural production has been suffused with such alienation (for Bowie, "alien" has many definitions—something unfamiliar, something non-human, something non-earthly, something out of sync with mainstream acceptance). Furthermore, Doggett (2012) suggests, "Through Ziggy, Bowie was also able to access themes that preoccupied the wider culture: the ominous hum of apocalypse, the fear of decay, the compulsive attraction to power and leadership, the search of renewed belief in a time of disillusion" (p. 5), a globally recurring theme.

Bowie's songs, with their recurrent themes of non-earthly existence and space travel, totalitarian subjugation, the generation gap and "disconnected images" (Perone, 2002, p. 90), along with Bowie's overt denial of standardized cultural codes, confirm that, in fact, Bowie does have a meaning that is very much connected with making his mark in art. He comments,

All the papers wrote volumes about how sick I was, how I was helping to kill off true art . . . I want to know why they wasted all that time and effort and paper on my clothes and my pose. Why? Because I was a dangerous statement. (Crowe, 1976a [2005], p. 278)

And being a dangerous statement is exactly how Bowie enables his artistic expression: danger is alluring. Therefore, "[p]laying out narcissism and alienation from everyday life to extremes" (Hawkins, 2009, p. 18), Bowie, again, provides an avenue of wild escapism and social experimentation. Perone (2002) agrees, stating that "Bowie had turned time and time again to depicting various social outcasts who fit in only within their own sub-cultures" (p. 96). For example, in the song, "Join the gang," Bowie attests to the universal human desire to avoid loneliness, but destroys the image of belonging by pointing out that within the group one must conform to its codes: "This is how to spend now that you've joined the gang" (Bowie, 1967a). Poignantly, Bowie lifts the mask to show the futility of individu-alism within a defined society: "It's a big illusion but at least you're in" (Bowie, 1967a). Bowie invites us to partake of society, but urges us not to lose ourselves in its codified terms.

The overt alienation in Bowie's lyrics are further emphasized by recur-ring political destabilization. From themes of totalitarianism reminiscent of Hitler to those of post-colonialism throughout the world, Bowie's lyrics are effective tools in communicating his concern for oppressed others. For example, Bowie famously expresses his defiance of East German social-ism in his song "Heroes" (Bowie, 1977) in which the narrator and his lover kiss at the Berlin Wall. In 1967's "We are hungry men," Bowie's narrator becomes a dictator as part of a "master race" (Perone, 2002, p. 89), who rations air and enacts mandatory infanticide and, potentially, the apoca-lypse: "Show you how I'll save the world / or let it die within the year" (Bowie, 1967b). The awful extremism of this master race is metaphorically struck down in the chorus in which drunken men eat, drink and burp. A bar patron (perhaps a delusional or sarcastic man, perhaps a real but ineffective savior) whines, "Who will buy a drink for me, your messiah?" (Bowie, 1967b). Regarding Bowie's reaction to 1980s post-colonialism, Hisama (2003) puts forth an argument that "China Girl" (1983) places the Asian women in danger of corruption from the powerful (white) western world: "Rather than evoking jasmine, perfume and oriental exoticism, she, as an inhabitant of the Third World, lacks blues eyes and television – epitomized here to be the destructive, ruinous forces of the west" (p. 333). Hisama (2003) claims that Bowie turns the "tranquil and simple" ste-reotypical Asian woman into an "angry and garish" one, positioning the Asian woman in power (p. 334). In various ways, therefore, Bowie mocks political power, and destroys that power by fragmenting and distorting its cultural representations.

To remain relevant through 50 years of music and culture, and to continue to resist social conformity, however, Bowie needs to appeal to generations of what is the most rebellious portion of society, young adults and teenagers. As Perone (2002) explains, Bowie "describ[ed] the generational changeover and the desire of each generation that life be better for the next" (p. 89). This is evident in the song "Oh! You pretty things" (Bowie, 1971b) in which Bowie empowers the younger generation dubbing them *Homo superior*: "they're the start of the coming race" (Bowie, 1971b). "Golden years" bears a similar supportive essence: "Nothing's gonna touch you in these golden years" (Bowie, 1976). In "Changes," Bowie chastises his own generation for their failure to realize the potential of the next generation: "And these children that you spit on as they try to change their world are immune to your consultations" (Bowie, 1971a). Frith (1992) states that musical engagement provides an important avenue of social maturation, teenagers "choosing from, operating with (and perhaps subverting) musical practices that carry wider cultural messages" (p. 177), such as those that Bowie promotes in his myriad artistic productions. Bowie's championing of youth and the coming generations is an extension of his belief that to keep creative power one must continue to change, evolve, innovate, because artistic stagnation is fatal.

Closely connected to generational change and artistic innovation is Bowie's position as countercultural icon. Coates (2005) avers that, since its beginnings in the 1950s, "[r]ock has been represented as a site of opposition to dominant cultural formations" (p. 57). Indeed, various forms of popular music (glam, punk and heavy metal, for example), have thrived on non-conformist ideologies, challenging the status quo and shifting what is socially acceptable. As we have seen, Bowie uses diverse means to accomplish this. Having done so, Bowie takes us one step further, by "heap[ing] scorn on those who set out to form a counterculture to be fashionable" (Hawkins, 2009, p. 159). This is beautifully apparent in his megahit "Fashion" (Bowie, 1980b) in which he satirically directs people's actions (literally and metaphorically) as counterculture becomes part of the automatic, unquestioned cultural mainstream, losing its power to effect change and represent the social Other—again, don't follow the leader blindly. Bowie is also critical of art as a tool for celebrity as the song appropriately entitled "Fame" demonstrates: "Fame puts you there where things are hollow . . . what you get is no tomorrow" (Bowie, 1975). Celebrity is an illusion in which people assume personae and success is temporary and shallow—unless you are David Bowie.

SEXUAL IDENTITY

Problems associated with the "ambivalent sexuality of David Bowie" (Frith and McRobbie, 1978 [1990], p. 382) have been of media interest since the late 1960s. And after the presentation of the androgynous Ziggy Stardust, that interest dramatically increased. Hawkins (2009) claims that the "Ziggy Stardust character must be the ultimate example of the flaunted queer identity" (p. 96). However, Ziggy is not an openly homosexual construction. There is a clouding of sexual identity that does not confirm a specific sexual preference but does suggest that there is more to one's sexual identity than what the homosexual/heterosexual binary implies. Bowie explains that, in America, "Nobody understood the European way of dressing and adopting the asexual, androgynous, everyman pose" (Crowe, 1976a [2005], p. 278), despite the fact that cross-dressing (specifically men dressing as women) has a very long history in British performance. Hawkins (2009) declares that "the celebration of androgyny would call into question patriarchy and conservative attitudes" (p. 18), by denying traditional masculine heteronormative sexuality. Bowie's emasculation of the rock idol was seen as revolutionary, inflammatory and dangerous. In the second half of the twentieth century, as Oakes (2009) attests, "in almost every instance, popular music is continually and compulsively bound up with the interrogation of gender" (p. 221). However, different genera of popular music have different sets of gendered codes. Rock, for example, "has depended upon the reiteration of a stable representation of heterosexual" (Coates, 2005, p. 58), and has, until relatively recently, positioned the female in the roles of sexual object or of the subjected desiring spectator rather than musical creator. Frith and McRobbie (1978 [1990]) contend, "Rock, as an ideological and cultural form, has a crucial role to play in the process by which its users constitute their sexuality" (p. 372); sexual identity is a construction rather than an inherent quality of rock or rock idols. David Bowie created, for rock, what Coates (2005) refers to as "fictive masculinity" (p. 52), a self-consciously performed alternative masculinity that may or may not exist offstage. And not surprisingly, Bowie was the best at doing it: "No artist marketed sexual ambiguity more successfully than Bowie did" (Garofalo, 2002, p. 247). However, as Hawkins (2009) claims, "Resurrecting androgyny and transvestitism through intellectual stylishness, Bowie not only rejected heteronormative constructs, but also heaped scorn on the machismo that typified the rock music of the day" (p. 18). With his small stature, light frame and effeminate affectations, Bowie would not have been convincing in the guise of macho man, and so leads the way for alternative representations of rock star.

Then Bowie brings in glam (or glitter rock), which immediately raises questions of identity and gender because of its visually androgynous aspects: make-up, clothing and actions all crossing into the traditionally feminine (but, again, reminiscent of the English theatrical cross-dressing tradition). Hawkins (2009) claims that "glam-rock was modelled on a Warholian aesthetic that had a profound effect on how young people started exploring sexuality" (p. 31). Much more accessible than Warhol, his art and his circle, Bowie has a wider influence, opening a space for people who are unsure of their sexuality, a space for experimenting beyond socially acceptable heteronormative codes. The sexual ambiguity of Bowie's personae enables Bowie to "challenge . . . the gender norms of American and European societies in the early 1970s" (Auslander, 2009, p. 307). Eventually, others follow, or join him, until "ambiguity of gender and sexual preference became the common attribute of a pop star, rather than an unmentionable secret" (Doggett, 2012, p. 12) in the 1980s. Today, sexual ambiguity is everywhere as the binary definitions of homo- and heterosexual collapse in western society.

Although Bowie was labelled "gay" early in his glam days, he insists in 1972 *Melody Maker* and 1976 *Playboy* interviews that he is bisexual (Hoffmann, 2008, p. 321; Crowe, 1976a [2005], p. 277). In 1973, the Gay Liberation Organization asks Bowie to pen a national gay anthem, which Bowie declines on the grounds that he does not represent "gay" (Hoffmann, 2008, p. 339). However, Bowie uses the public's curiosity with his sexual identity very well: "Someone asked me in an interview once if I were gay. I said, 'No, I'm bisexual' . . . Seventy-one was a good American year. Sex was still shocking. Everybody wanted to see the freak" (Crowe, 1976a [2005], pp. 277–8). That freak foregrounds and challenges the very definition of male by blurring the lines of heteronormative binaries and revealing potential alternative gender and sexual identities and practices. Bowie

> ably captures the key contradictions in which masculinity is trapped—on the one hand, the artistic mindset, the work-ethic and the behind-the-scene stamp of an auteur . . . and, on the other, the apparently natural, effortless and emotionally inexpressive qualities that are likewise associated with masculinity. (Oakes, 2009, p. 229)

Oakes (2009) says Bowie puts "masculinity in crisis" (p. 221). However, this crisis (especially in the twenty-first century with its increasing awareness of LGBT+ culture) enables positive social change—acceptance, understanding and candidness. As Hawkins (2009) puts it, there is "a masking of gender through a process of pluralizing" (p. 158). Again, Bowie multiplies rather than divides. The Bowieverse has room for all of society's freaks.

CONCLUSION

Bowie's artistic expression follows the literary tradition of intercourse and intertextuality: Bowie pays attention to his literary (and musical) predecessors, his lyrics frequently alluding to others' cultural productions. Yet, Bowie takes himself, his personae, his music and his fans past the art to which he alludes and beyond the cultural paradigms upon which he builds his microcosm. Bowie employs every facet of his encompassing artistic production to invent new concepts of self-representation, Otherness and sexual identity to make his artistic mark, to become more than just man and to empower the freaky, the non-conformist and everyone in between. Menon et al. (2010) assert that "the association between social and physical position might reflect a cultural schema" (p. 51), explaining that a leader who stands behind the people rather than in front of them allows the leader to protect those people and focus on their needs. While Menon et al. (2010) mean this literally, in comparing American leaders with their Asian counterparts, I think this metaphorically delineates Bowie's relationship with his "followers." Although Bowie and his personae, on stage, literally stand in front of the fans, they invite, as I have discussed, the fans, en masse and individually, to stand with him/them as acceptable Others and to sanction self-leadership and the destabilization of social codes. Furthermore, Graham (1987) indicates that "fostering follower *autonomy* is the hallmark of effective leadership" (p. 73). Such leadership is derived from a charismatic leader who encourages individuality and free choice (Graham, 1987, pp. 73–6). Although I take this concept out of its original context of business leadership, the underlying premise applies to Bowie whose changeability and mock narcissistic messianic role-playing signals individual defiance of all forms of social oppression and exclusion.

Furthermore, Bowie's cultural leadership continues beyond his own production practices. Within the music industry, others use Bowie's work as influences on their own music and styles, as fragments of their own songs and as important pieces that deserve homage as inspiration. Bowie's past influence on this world remains and the end of his influence is nowhere in sight. In a move that must have absolutely delighted Bowie, fulfilling his fantasy of other-worldliness, Canadian astronaut Chris Hadfield made a recording of "Space oddity" at the International Space Station. According to Hadfield's webpage (2016), "22 million people have watched his famous cover of David Bowie's 'Space Oddity,' which he filmed to mark his departure from his final mission" in 2013. After Bowie's death, Hadfield (2016) writes, "When David Bowie wrote and recorded Space Oddity in 1969, I wonder if he ever imagined it being played in orbit?" I would argue that all that is Bowie has been launched into orbit by Bowie himself, as part of that extraordinary Bowieverse, and will continue to lead us in stellar directions.

REFERENCES

Auslander, P. (2009), "Musical persona: the physical performance of popular music," in D.B. Scott (ed.), *The Ashgate research companion to popular musicology*, Surrey, UK: Ashgate, pp. 303–15.

Bowie, D. (1967a), "Join the gang," by D. Bowie, recorded November 1966–February 1967, *David Bowie* [Studio Album], London, UK: Deram.

Bowie, D. (1967b), "We are hungry men," by D. Bowie, recorded November 1966–February 1967, *David Bowie* [Studio Album], London, UK: Deram.

Bowie, D. (1969), "Space oddity," by D. Bowie, recorded June 1969, *Space oddity* [Studio Album], United States: Mercury.

Bowie, D. (1971a), "Changes," by D. Bowie, recorded June–August 1971, *Hunky dory* [Studio Album], New York, NY: RCA.

Bowie, D. (1971b), "Oh! You pretty things," by D. Bowie, recorded June–August 1971, *Hunky dory* [Studio Album], New York, NY: RCA.

Bowie, D. (1972), "Ziggy Stardust," by D. Bowie, recorded November 1971, *The rise and fall of Ziggy Stardust and the Spiders from Mars* [Studio Album], New York, NY: RCA.

Bowie, D. (1973), "Aladdin Sane," by D. Bowie, recorded October–December 1971, *Aladdin Sane* [Studio Album], New York, NY: RCA.

Bowie, D. (1975), "Fame," by D. Bowie, C. Alomar and J. Lennon, recorded January 1975, *Young Americans* [Studio Album], New York, NY: RCA.

Bowie, D. (1976), "Golden years," by D. Bowie, recorded September–November 1975, *Station to station* [Studio Album], New York, NY: RCA.

Bowie, D. (1977), "Heroes," by D. Bowie and B. Eno, recorded July–August 1976, *Heroes* [Studio Album], New York, NY: RCA.

Bowie, D. (1979), "DJ," by D. Bowie, B. Eno and C. Alomar, recorded March 1979, *Lodger* [Studio Album], New York, NY: RCA.

Bowie, D. (1980a), "Ashes to ashes," by D. Bowie, recorded April 1980, *Scary monsters (and super creeps)* [Studio Album], New York, NY: RCA.

Bowie, D. (1980b), "Fashion," by D. Bowie, recorded February–April 1980, *Scary monsters (and super creeps)* [Studio Album], New York, NY: RCA.

Bowie, D. (1983), "China girl," by D. Bowie and I. Pop, recorded December 1982, *Let's dance* [Studio Album], London, UK: EMI.

Bowie, D. (2016), *Blackstar*, D. Bowie et al., recorded 2014–15 [Studio Album], ISO RCA Columbia Sony.

Bowie, D. and E. Walsh (2015), *Lazarus,* Ivo van Hove, dir. New York Theatre Workshop, Manhattan, NY, December 2015–January 2016.

Campbell, M. (2008), *Popular music in America: and the beat goes on*, New York, NY: Schirmer.

Christensen, T. (1990), "Stardust memories: after years of chameleon-like behavior, Bowie will revisit his past for one last fling," *Milwaukee Journal*, 8 June, accessed 23 July 2016 from Proquest.

Cinque, T. and S. Redmond (2013), "Who is he now? The unearthly David Bowie," *Celebrity Studies*, **4** (3), 377–9, accessed 23 July 2016 from Proquest.

Coates, N. (2005), "(R)evolution now? Rock and the political potential of gender" in S. Whiteley (ed.), *Sexing the groove: popular music and gender*, London, UK: Routledge, pp. 50–64.

Crowe, C. (1976a), "David Bowie interview," *Playboy*, September 1976, reprinted in D. Brackett (ed.) (2005), *The pop, rock, and soul reader: histories and debates*, New York, NY: Oxford University Press, pp. 277–82.

Crowe, C. (1976b), "Ground control to Davey Jones," *Rolling Stone*, February 1976, accessed 23 July 2016 at http://www.rollingstone.com/music/features/gro und-control-to-davy-jones-19760212.

"David Bowie" (n.d.), International Movie Database, accessed 13 July 2016 at http://www.imdb.com/name/nm0000309/?ref_=fn_al_nm_1.

Doggett, P. (2012), *The man who sold the world: David Bowie and the 1970s*, New York, NY: Harper.

Frith, S. (1992), "The cultural study of popular music," in L. Grossberg, C. Nelson and P. Treichler (eds), *Cultural studies*, New York, NY: Routledge, pp. 174–82.

Frith, S. and A. McRobbie (1978), "Rock and sexuality," *Screen education* **29**, reprinted in S. Frith and A. Goodeon (eds) (1990), *On record: rock, pop, and the written word*, New York, NY: Routledge, pp. 371–89.

Frith, S., S. Straw and J. Street (2001), "Star profiles II" in S. Frith, S. Straw and J. Street (eds), *The Cambridge companion to pop and rock*, Cambridge, UK: Cambridge University Press, pp. 193–210.

Garofalo, R. (2002), *Rockin' out: music in the USA*, 2nd ed., Upper Saddle River, NJ: Pearson.

Graham, J.W. (1987), "Chapter 3 commentary: transformational leadership: fostering follower autonomy not automatic followership," in J.G. Hunt, B.R. Baliga, H.P. Dachler and C.A. Schriesheim (eds), *Emerging leadership vistas*, Lexington, MA: International Leadership Symposia Series, pp. 73–9.

Hadfield, C. (2016), "Chris Hadfield," accessed 1 August 2016 at www.chrishadfield.ca.

Hawkins, S. (2009), *The British pop dandy: masculinity, popular music and culture*, Surrey, UK: Ashgate.

Hisama, E.M. (2003), "Postcolonialism on the make: the music of John Mellencamp, David Bowie, and John Zorn" in R. Middleton (ed.), *Reading pop: approaches to textual analysis in popular music*, Oxford, UK: Oxford University Press, pp. 329–46.

Hoffmann, F. (2008), *Chronology of American popular music, 1900–2000*, New York, NY: Routledge.

Loder, K. (1992), "David Bowie," *Rolling Stone*, vol. 641, 15 October, p. 141, accessed 23 July 2016 from Proquest.

The Man who fell to Earth (1976), [Film] Nicolas Roeg, dir., London, UK: British Lion Films.

Menon, T., J. Sim, J.H.-Y. Fu, C. Chiu and Y. Hong (2010), "Blazing the trail versus trailing the group: culture and perceptions of the leader's position," *Organizational Behavior and Human Decision Processes*, **113** (1), 51–61.

Oakes, J.L. (2009), "'I'm a Man': masculinities in popular music" in D.B. Scott (ed.), *The Ashgate research companion to popular musicology*, Surrey, UK: Ashgate, pp. 221–39.

Perone, E.J. (2002), "David Bowie: *Hunky Dory* (1971)" in J.E. Perone (ed.), *The album: a guide to pop music's most provocative, influential, and important creations*, vol. 2, Santa Barbara, CA: Praeger, pp. 87–95.

Rüther, T. (2004), *Heroes: David Bowie and Berlin*, London, UK: Reaktion.

Star, L. and C. Waterman (2007), *American popular music: from minstrelsy to MP3*, 2nd ed., New York, NY: Oxford University Press.

Tawa, N. (2005), *Supremely American popular songs in the 20th century: styles and singers and what they said about America*, Lanham, MD: Scarecrow.

Wells, P. and M. Barclay (2016), "It's confusing these days," *Maclean's*, 25 January, accessed 23 July 2016 from Proquest.

Wilcken, H. (2005), *Low: 33 ⅓*, New York, NY: Continuum.

PART III

Visual leadership

8. A two-way street: the leader-follower dynamic in *Glory* and *Twelve O'Clock High*

Nicholas O. Warner

> "Leadership is a two-way street, loyalty up and loyalty down."
> – Rear Admiral Grace Murray Hopper
> *60 Minutes* interview, 6 March 1983

INTRODUCTION

The intersection of leadership with American popular culture is nowhere more apparent than in cinema. And more than any other cinematic genre, it is the war film that shows leadership at its most intense, as the leader-follower dynamic in combat plays out for the highest possible stakes—life or death. While this intensity accounts, in part, for the wide appeal of war films, another important factor appears to be even more deeply rooted in the psyche of moviegoers: "the celebration of the leader hero and the yearning for the heroic seem somehow ingrained in our DNA" (Cronin and Genovese, 2012, p. 229).

In light of this yearning, it is understandable that many war films highlight the traits or behavior of the individual leader hero. In this way, Hollywood has often perpetuated something akin to the "great man" or "great woman" approach, treating leadership as a special set of qualities that reside in the singular figure of the leader. But such one-sided portrayals, even if entertaining or insightful, can too easily reduce leadership to a mere synonym for a powerful position or a powerful person. This oversimplification, in turn, can short change the understanding of leadership as a relational process in which leaders and followers alike play essential and sometimes overlapping roles (Eberly et al., 2013).

By contrast to this pattern, two of Hollywood's most compelling war movies widen the spotlight beyond the leader to take in the seemingly more mundane but crucial contributions of followers. In *Twelve O'Clock High* (Henry King, 1949), set in World War II, and the Civil War film *Glory*

(Edward Zwick, 1989), leadership is not a unidirectional system wherein all change and impetus come *from* official leaders and *toward* official followers. Rather, each film shows how even within the inherently hierarchical structure of a wartime army, leaders can effect social change within their organization by empowering their followers and, at times, becoming followers themselves. Such change in *Twelve O'Clock High* remains very much within the limited world of a single Air Force bombing group, the "918." In the case of *Glory*, however, the leader-follower relationship has broader ramifications for American society as a whole, given that the film depicts the gradual acceptance and empowerment (albeit limited) of African American soldiers during the Civil War.

Both films stress the necessity to an organization not only of inclusive, empowering leaders, but also of proactive, committed followers, the kind of followers who demonstrate "enthusiastic, intelligent, and self-reliant participation—without star billing—in the pursuit of an organizational goal" (Kelley, 1995, p. 195). Thus, *Twelve O'Clock High* and *Glory* vividly dramatize successful, ethical leadership as a two-way street of mutual loyalty and guidance between leaders and followers. Although these films' immediate frame of reference is war, their relevance to leadership, and their portrayal of both leaders and followers as agents of change, extends far beyond the confines of their specific historical contexts and military settings.

Different as *Glory* and *Twelve O'Clock High* are in tone, visual style and historical period, each film presents a similar initial leader-follower situation: a commander steps into a new leadership role in which he must overcome a wide gap between himself and his followers. In *Glory*, Colonel Robert Gould Shaw (Matthew Broderick) struggles to bridge the social and racial chasm between himself as an elite white officer and his regiment of untrained freedmen and former slaves. In *Twelve O'Clock High*, General Frank Savage (Gregory Peck) assumes command of a demoralized Air Force bombing unit from a subordinate but much more popular officer, and must find a way quickly to overcome his fliers' hostile resistance and to transform the unit's culture of lackadaisical performance and inertia into one of high achievement and initiative. Despite their different temperaments and circumstances, Colonel Shaw and General Savage gain credibility and authority largely through their empowerment of, and reliance on, followers. These followers in turn become subleaders, partaking of the leader's own authority and advancing his cause—indeed, making his cause their own.

In their exploration of leader-follower dynamics, each of these films reveals thought-provoking implications for leadership's relation to social change. Social change in *Glory* appears most obviously in the film's subject matter: how military leadership in the 54th Massachusetts Regiment led to greater social acceptance of black Americans as soldiers and even as leaders in the United States Army, and thus helped to pave the way for greater acceptance of African Americans in society at large. A second significant aspect of the film's relation to social change has to do with the marketing and screening campaign that recuperated a largely ignored aspect of the history of social justice in America; presented that aspect to the American public not just through the film itself but also through ancillary activities and publications; and helped to foster greater awareness of black Americans' contributions to the Civil War. In *Twelve O'Clock High*, the theme of social change is much less overt, having less to do with social justice or broader social situations than with the leadership problems faced within the enclosed world of a single Air Force bomb unit during World War II.

Both *Twelve O'Clock High* and *Glory* enjoyed critical and commercial success, garnering Best Supporting Actor Oscars for, respectively, Dean Jagger and Denzel Washington, the latter of whom saw his career soar to stardom on the strength of his performance as the ex-slave, Trip. (It is perhaps a reflection not only of Jagger's and Washington's superb acting abilities, but also of the strength and significance of the characters they played, that in each film the actor playing a follower, rather than a leader, won an Academy Award.) *Twelve O'Clock High*, a pet project of Hollywood mogul and one-time pilot Darryl F. Zanuck, opened to great fanfare at its Los Angeles and New York premieres; shortly thereafter, its star, Gregory Peck, graced the cover of *Life* magazine in connection with a story on the popular film, then enjoying wide circulation in American theaters. *Twelve O'Clock High* received highly positive reviews for its realism, attention to character, and moral seriousness (McAdams, 2002, p. 110; Duffin and Matheis, 2005, pp. 84–5, 89–90; Jeansonne and Luhrssen, 2014, p. 53). Although it is difficult to gauge the impact of any single film on public attitudes, *Twelve O'Clock High* did draw attention in its own time to combat fatigue, and anticipated our current understanding of PTSD. It joined several other films of the late 1940s and early 1950s in de-emphasizing combat heroics and focusing instead on the psychological dimensions of war and on war's physical and emotional toll—for example, *The Story of G.I. Joe* (1945), *The Best Years of Our Lives* (1946), *Battleground* (1949) and *The Men* (1950). It is likely, however, that all of these films, with their wide national distribution and acclaim, played some role in changing social perceptions of war's impact on its participants. Of these, however, *Twelve O'Clock High* is the film most explicitly concerned with leadership. Still widely referenced in military and business leadership settings (Landon, 1999, p. 320; Jeansonne and Luhrssen, 2014, p. 57), the film inspired a mid-1960s television series of the same name, influenced the air combat scenes in George Lucas's *Star Wars*, and provided inspiration for director Rian Johnson's movie *Star Wars VIII* (2017) (Suid, 2002, pp. 3; Call, 2002, pp. 59–62, 104; Grimsley, 2014; and Jagernauth, 2014); these examples all point to the film's subtle but ongoing influence.

The social impact of *Glory* is easier to discern: the film rediscovered and popularized earlier historical texts about the 54th Massachusetts Regiment, raised public awareness about the role of black soldiers in the Civil War, and gave rise to extensive movie-themed philanthropic campaigns, museum exhibits and community programs devoted to themes of racial equality and harmony (Blatt, 2001, p. 215). The extent of this impact, of course, was closely related to the film's popularity and commercial success. *Glory's* box-office profits during its initial release in December 1989, far exceeded expectations. After a trial run at only three theaters in New York, Los Angeles and Toronto, *Glory* was soon playing on some 900 screens across North America (AFI Catalog of Feature Films, 2016). The film's themes of prejudice, racial equality and social justice, as well as its fore-grounding of African American contributions to the Union cause, made the famed Apollo Theater in Harlem an appropriate venue for a benefit screening shortly after the movie's premiere. Equally appropriate was the choice of the event's beneficiary—the Boys Choir of Harlem, also featured on the film's soundtrack. The popularity of *Glory* sent sales soaring for the historical texts on which the movie was chiefly based—Lincoln Kirstein's *Lay this Laurel* (1973) and Peter Burchard's *One Gallant Rush* (1965). Such firms as Pepsi-Cola and Eastman Kodak tied some of their philanthropic activities to the film, distributing "hundreds of thousands" of educational kits, videocassettes, posters and other *Glory*-related materials to schools and community groups (AFI Catalog of Feature Films, 2016). Long after its theatrical run came to an end, the film continued to inspire various museum exhibits, documentaries, 54th Regiment-themed toys, National Park programs and the like (Blatt, 2001).

From this review of the marketing and reception of these films, it is clear that both *Twelve O'Clock High* and *Glory* in some measure contributed to or reflected social change, with *Glory* in particular dealing explicitly with actual social change and its intersection with leadership.[1] In addition, each of these films takes a broad view of leadership, exploring the crucial contributions of followers to the leadership process and to the social or cultural transformations that result from that process. In these ways, *Glory* and *Twelve O'Clock High* inadvertently anticipated the recent turn toward the theme of followership in leadership studies.

While long acknowledged as important by students of leadership, the role of followers has still lagged behind the attention to leaders as a scholarly topic. As recently as 2007, Barbara Kellerman could write that "Good leadership is the stuff of countless courses, workshops, books, and articles . . . Good followership, by contrast, is the stuff of nearly nothing" (Kellerman, 2007, p. 84). A more recent assessment similarly concludes that "The study of followers as key components of the leadership process . . . has largely been missed in the leadership literature"; still needed is an "approach that views both leaders and followers as co-producers of leadership and its outcomes" (Uhl-Bien et al., 2014, p. 83).[2]

As noted earlier, a parallel emphasis on leaders has dominated film (as well as fiction and drama). This is to be expected, given the colorful characterizations that are possible with heroic leaders—or, for that matter, with diabolical leaders who, though reprehensible, often exert their own fascination, whether Richard III or Darth Vader, Captain Ahab or Tony Soprano. All the more reason, then, to examine the ways that films like *Glory* and *Twelve O'Clock High* present leadership as a relational process shared fully by leaders and followers. The two films discussed here implicitly confirm the view that "Leadership is not something that inheres in the person of the leader . . . *One cannot have leaders without followers, but going further, one cannot understand leadership without understanding followership*" (Fiorina and Shepsle, 1989, p. 36, emphasis added). And in its own distinct way, each of these movies emerges as an outstanding example of filmmaking and as a substantive, even profound, statement on the nature of leadership and the leader-follower relationship.

GLORY: TRUTH AND IRONY

In selecting his film's title, Edward Zwick considered various options until "one day it came to me, in all of its truth and irony," and the movie was called *Glory* (Zwick, 2004). The phrase "truth and irony" is an apt one. There is truth in the title's fidelity to nineteenth-century America's elevated rhetoric of war and abolition alike, as in Julia Ward Howe's "Battle-Hymn of the Republic." There is, as well, truth in the 54th's courageous contributions to the struggle for freedom. But there is also the irony of the carnage that that struggle entailed, graphically presented from the film's opening scene at the Battle of Antietam to the final, futile assault on Fort Wagner. And both truth and irony apply to the unlikely partnership between Shaw and his men, as a callow, sheltered Boston Brahmin and his motley group of first-time black soldiers forged one of the most remarkable leader-follower relationships ever seen in history or film.[3]

After briefly establishing Colonel Shaw's background as the scion of a prominent abolitionist Boston family, the movie turns to his inauspicious first encounter with the newly formed 54th Regiment. Though well-intentioned, Shaw comes across as hesitant and inexperienced, addressing his wary new charges in stilted, high-sounding generalities. This brief scene provides an important contrastive backdrop to Shaw's subsequent evolution into a truly transforming leader. That change becomes possible, however, only after Shaw turns to his followers for guidance, and makes them his partners in the process of leadership.

Before that partnership occurs, Shaw reaches the nadir of his faltering leadership when, in one of the most famous scenes in the film, he authorizes the whipping of a soldier, the insolent Trip (Denzel Washington), for going AWOL. Although the event is completely fictitious (flogging was forbidden in the Union army, and no such incident took place in the 54th), the scene has undeniable emotional power, as well as psychological, if not factual, truth about the power relations between white commanders and black soldiers (Brode, 1997, p. 85), and about the historical Shaw's tendency to use legal but harsh, sometimes demeaning forms of punishment (Duncan, 1999, p. 73).

Still trying to find his footing as a leader, the young colonel agrees to have the hard-driving, stereotypically tough Sergeant Mulcahy punish Trip by flogging. And then comes one of the most memorable leadership dilemmas ever shown on screen. Preparing to administer the whipping, Mulcahy tears off Trip's shirt, only to recoil from the sight of his hideously scarred back, a horrifying record of former floggings. For all of his ostentatious toughness in earlier scenes, Mulcahy balks at whipping a man who has been so severely beaten before. The sergeant jerks his head violently around, looking to Shaw for guidance (see Figure 8.1). And now the somewhat complacent, idealistic young leader must choose between two awful alternatives. He can back down from his order and appear weak, or proceed and appear no different from the Southern slave masters with whom he is at war. It is the latter option that Shaw, his face contorted with anguish, chooses.[4]

In the night-time scene that follows the whipping, despair hangs over the 54th's encampment. Shaw, more distant than ever from his soldiers, hesitantly appeals to the older black recruit, John Rawlins (Morgan Freeman): "Mr. Rawlins . . . this morning, I . . . it would be a great help to me if I could talk to you from time to time about the men." Better late than never, Shaw here demonstrates what Martin Chemers identifies as the first of the "key elements of effective leadership," namely, that "leaders must enlist the help of others" (Chemers, 2001, p. 378). Originally too reticent and unsure either of himself or his followers to enlist that help from the 54th, Shaw now realizes the need for guidance that comes upward, from the followers toward him as the leader, instead of only downward, from his own

Figure 8.1   Trip and Sergeant Mulcahy, both looking at Colonel Shaw: Will he rescind the flogging order? A scar from previous beatings is just visible on Trip's left shoulder (Photofest)

position as commanding officer.[5] Difficult as it is, this moment leads to the breakthrough in Shaw's relationship with his followers. In response to Shaw, Rawlins respectfully but candidly insists that the troops desperately need shoes, and that they need them "now"—they cannot wait for Shaw to proceed through sluggish bureaucratic channels. In the next scene, the camp's somber mood gives way to a new energy as Shaw and his men, in a low-angle shot that emphasizes their unity and resolve, briskly stride toward the army supply office. Once there, the soldiers form a phalanx-like blockade outside the office door, preventing any interruption as their leader confronts the racist quartermaster who has been withholding supplies. For the first time, these men act with assertiveness and confidence as they have become, instead of passive subordinates, active partners with their leader, a change emphasized by the camera's attention to their erect carriage and proud expressions (see Figure 8.2). Inside the office, Shaw demonstrates similar newfound authority as he transforms himself from passive observer of protocol to dauntless champion for his troops, and succeeds in obtaining shoes, clothes and other supplies.

In this scene, Shaw embodies Burns's famous concept of transforming leadership, which entails the "mutual stimulation and elevation that converts followers into leaders and may convert leaders into moral agents" (Burns, 1978, p. 4). And Shaw does this by first becoming a follower himself, seeking out his men's guidance and acting on it. This process of

Figure 8.2   *The men of the 54th Massachusetts forming a barrier outside the quartermaster's office, so that their leader, Colonel Shaw, can obtain necessary supplies for the regiment (Photofest)*

a leader learning from and, in a sense, following his followers, continues when the 54th learns of the government's plan to reduce black soldiers' pay (a bait-and-switch that actually did occur). Enraged, the recruits tear up their pay vouchers in protest, with Trip at their lead. As their angry cries swell into a defiant crescendo ("tear it up, tear it up!"), the fragile leadership edifice that Shaw has struggled so hard to build seems about to crumble. But from this low point, Shaw again manages to grow in leadership as he finds common ground with his men by following *their* lead. In a dramatic symbolic gesture, Shaw holds his own voucher aloft and rips it in half, declaring, "If you men will take no pay, then none of us will." Through this charismatic act of solidarity between white officers and black rank and file, Shaw is simultaneously following and leading his troops. And in so doing, he affirms the validity of their dismay over the pay cut, and channels the regiment's anger into an affirmation of support, as the men's threats turn to cheers for their colonel.

Both of these scenes testify as well to the importance of balancing what Burns calls the lower level needs of transactional leadership with the higher level needs of transforming leadership. For Burns, while the narrowly transactional leader appeals only to followers' more material, lower-level needs, and limits followers' potential for reaching more noble ends, the transforming leader seeks to "satisfy higher needs" for esteem and moral purpose, and "taps the needs and raises the aspirations and helps shape the values—and hence mobilizes the potential—of followers" (Burns, 1978, p. 4, 455). Appeals to such higher level needs, however, will ring hollow without satisfying essential lower level needs. Only by, first, acknowledging the legitimacy of his men's lower level needs (proper clothing, equipment, weapons and pay) and by acting to satisfy those needs can Shaw lay the groundwork for achieving the higher, nobler goals associated with transforming leadership. In fact, as the film makes clear, to the men of the 54th, seemingly "lower" level items, such as rifles, shoes and the "blue suits" worn by white soldiers, had more than material value; for these black soldiers, such objects were not only practically useful tools but also important symbolic validations of their own soldierly status.

In subsequent scenes, Shaw further empowers his followers through promotions and awards. Unlike the inauthentic, "bogus" empowerment justly derided by Joanne Ciulla (2014), these forms of recognition involve authentic empowerment and genuine responsibility, and are dispensed solely on merit. Shaw scrupulously withholds them from those who have not yet proved their worth, including his close personal friend, Thomas. In one instance, Shaw offers the honor of bearing the regimental colors to Trip, who, though he at first refuses, will later pick up the colors and lead the troops after Shaw is killed at Fort Wagner. Another scene depicts Rawlins's promotion to sergeant-major (a position in the 54th actually held by Frederick Douglass's son, Lewis Douglass). Shaw's promotion of Rawlins establishes a parallel between the two men's roles as leaders, so that leadership here appears not as an exclusive category but as a continuum on which leaders and followers occupy overlapping roles.[6] The new connection between Rawlins and Shaw becomes even stronger in the touching scene where the newly promoted sergeant whispers, "I ain't sure if I want this, Colonel," and Shaw replies, "I know exactly how you feel."

The hard-won unity between leader and follower in *Glory* receives eloquent visual expression in the film's final scene. Here, in keeping with historical fact, we see the bodies of Shaw and his dead troops being tossed into a common grave. The scene is perhaps overly sentimental in its slow-motion shots of dead soldiers' bodies sliding gently into a vast pit, and in the contrived arrangement by which the once-defiant Trip comes to lie in docile repose beneath the arm of his white commanding officer. But for all that, the film's ending fits both logically and emotionally with the entire thrust of *Glory*, as it reminds us of the ultimate bond between Shaw and the followers who made him a leader.[7]

Various scenes throughout *Glory* point to the larger social changes that result from the growth of the 54th into a cohesive, well-trained unit. The regiment's parade through the streets of Boston, an event that actually occurred, illustrates society's changing attitude toward black participation in the Union army, as the onlookers, white and black alike, enthusiastically cheer the 54th. Later in the film, the regiment's first (and successful) military encounter with the Confederate enemy gradually helps transform the initial distrust and racism of white Union soldiers into acceptance and grudging admiration. The promotion of Rawlins, mentioned earlier, to sergeant-major—and thus to a position of authority over even white soldiers of lower rank—marks another social change, important enough for Colonel Shaw to tell the journalist covering the activities of the 54th to take special note of it. But perhaps the most touching and explicit sign of how the leadership dynamics of the 54th contributed to social change appears in the scene where Sergeant-Major Rawlins, with the stripes of his newly earned rank vividly displayed on his arm, speaks to a group of Southern black children. As the children stare wonderingly at what, for them, was a hitherto unimaginable sight—hundreds of armed, uniformed black men marching in military formation on Southern soil—Rawlins leans down and says, smiling, "That's right. Ain't no dream. We runaway slaves, but we come back fightin' men." And as he rejoins the troop vigorously marching forward, Rawlins looks back over his shoulder, triumphantly crying out, "Go tell your folks how kingdom come in the year of jubilee!"—a pithy expression of just how significant a social change had been wrought by the mutually reinforcing leader-follower dynamic of the 54th Regiment.

TWELVE O'CLOCK HIGH: "LEAD A MULE TO WATER"

Where the title of *Glory* is abstract, lofty and inspirational, that of *Twelve O'Clock High* is concrete, technical matter-of-fact. In air combat parlance, the phrase "Twelve o'clock high" indicates an attack that is coming head-on and from above; figuratively, the phrase "became a synonym, among airmen, for potential danger" (Rubin, 1981, p. 121). Thus the title fits in well with the film's Air Force setting and with its atmosphere of tension and crisis.

Unlike Shaw, who is his troops' first leader, General Savage replaces another officer, Colonel Keith Davenport, beloved by the pilots in the 918 bomb group, but handicapped by what Savage labels his "overidentification with his men." That Davenport is Savage's personal friend only complicates the new commander's feelings about his assignment, as he attempts to overcome his pilots' hostility, raise their morale and improve their performance—all in a matter of days that may prove critical to the course of the war in Europe.

In meeting these challenges, Savage cannot afford the luxury of developing personal relationships with the fliers or winning them over through inspirational appeals. As he explains, "there just isn't time" for that. Similarly, Savage does not "have any patience with this what-are-we-fighting-for stuff. We're in a war, a shooting war. We've *got* to fight." Consequently, he behaves as a resolutely task-oriented as opposed to relationship-oriented leader—all efforts are bent on the task of getting more planes into the air and hitting more targets with greater precision.

Savage approaches his task through blatantly transactional, even negatively transactional methods—a carrot-and-stick approach without the carrot. He begins by imposing stricter standards of discipline and doling out punishments, but his chief tactic is the creation of the "Leper Colony," a plane reserved for the lowest performers and shirkers in the unit. Through this ever-present threat of humiliation, Savage hopes to instill in his followers a level of performance that will build up their pride—the very opposite of humiliation. Savage also tries to foster a sense of group identity in his followers. This is not simply *esprit de corps*, but also rigid adherence to a moral calculus whereby the interest of the bomb group always supersedes that of the individual. Hence Savage's brutal berating of the pilot who takes a flight detour to rescue an endangered fellow flier, his roommate. This ostensibly noble act lands the pilot in the Leper Colony for putting personal feelings ahead of concern for the group as a whole. In this way, Savage exemplifies the "collective ethos of the military" (Jennings and Hannah, 2014, p. 149), an ethos sorely lacking in the 918 when Savage assumes command, but very much in evidence by the end of the film.

In all of these situations, Savage demonstrates charisma in his boldness, risk-taking and freedom from convention—all qualities that often mark charismatic leaders (Bognar, 1998; Conger and Kanungo, 1987). Charisma appears as well in Savage's speaking ability (superbly conveyed by Gregory Peck at his sonorous best), and in the dramatic actions whereby Savage focuses his followers' attention on his own person as a source of authority (stripping an improperly attired sergeant of his stripes, tongue-lashing a lackadaisical guard, peremptorily closing the airmen's bar).[8]

But perhaps most significant, and certainly most risky among Savage's charismatic actions, is his offer of a transfer out of the group to any pilot who wishes one. He wants no one under his command who does not want to be there. This offer almost dooms Savage's leadership when every single pilot, including a Medal of Honor recipient, requests a transfer. Up against the pilots' obvious resentment, and severely shaken by news of the impending transfers, the forlorn general stares out his window at a rain-soaked, deserted airfield (see Figure 8.3); as the screenplay directions state, "This has been much worse than he expected, and for the moment he is lost" (Lay and Bartlett, 1949, p. 62). But it is here that a truly proactive follower, Major Harvey Stovall (Dean Jagger), approaches Savage and helps

*Figure 8.3   A leader with no followers: General Savage, alone, facing a
             leadership crisis in the wake of his pilots' unanimous decision
             to transfer out of his unit (Photofest)*

him to achieve a positive, and eventually transforming, leader-follower
relationship with his fliers.

In a pivotal scene, Major Stovall first engages his isolated general by
simply offering him some coffee. But their small talk proves inconclu-
sive, and Savage, preoccupied and disappointed, thanks Stovall for the
coffee and starts to leave. At the last minute, however, Stovall stops him,
shares his own perspective on the situation and formulates a plan to get
Savage time to change the fliers' minds about transferring. With mock
punctiliousness—a detail that humanizes the interaction between the two
men and provides one of the few comic touches in the film—a deadpan
Stovall starts enumerating the bureaucratic steps that will delay the
transfer requests for ten days. This tactic will give Savage the momentary
reprieve he needs. Before leaving Stovall's office, the visibly relieved and
even amused general calls Stovall by his first name, engages in some brief
banter and playfully slaps him on the arm—concrete signs of a new personal connection between them. One of the most significant things about
this connection is its source—not Stovall's desire to placate the leader, but
his dedication to the 918 flying group. As Stovall, a lawyer in civilian life,
tells Savage, he wants to help his current "client," the 918, "win its case"
with the general. By standing up for his leader through assisting him with

the transfers, Stovall is actually standing up for his own unit. But there is no contradiction here, either in Stovall's motivations, or in his relationship to the general; in fact, Stovall's concern for the 918 accords with Savage's own repeated insistence on the primacy of "group integrity."

What is especially striking about this scene is the quietly powerful way that it reveals the complex web of motivations, loyalties and values that can inform a leader-follower relationship. There are no impassioned calls to action here, no swelling music or heated exchanges. All we see are two men drinking coffee together on a rainy afternoon. Yet the scene is as important and insightful as any other in the film, as it shows the cluster of emotions and thoughts at work in each of these men, and traces the arc of their interaction from guarded formality to open communication, trust and even a modest camaraderie. In their exchange of views, cooperative dialogue and shared decision-making, both the general and the major simultaneously play "the complicated dual roles of follower and leader" (Matthews, 2008, p. 233), thus demonstrating that even within the supposedly inflexible hierarchies of military command, leadership and followership are not opposites, but complementary components of a larger whole. (See Figures 8.4, 8.5 and

Figure 8.4   *Bridging the gap—Major Stovall (seated) and General Savage get to know each other over coffee provided by the major to his isolated leader (Photofest)*

Figure 8.5   *Having risen from his desk, Major Stovall proactively ap-*
proaches General Savage so as to help him improve relations
with the general's followers—the pilots of the 918 bomb group
(Photofest)

8.6 for the stages of rapprochement that develop between the two men in
this scene.)

While the pilots' transfer requests languish in Stovall's office, more missions succeed, safety improves and group morale and loyalty to Savage
increase to the point that all the pilots withdraw their transfer requests. But
Savage, like Shaw, is not content with mere compliance from his followers.
Instead, he actively seeks to turn even the least promising of them into
leaders. As he instructs Stovall and Cobb (a top flier in the unit), "I want
this group combed for every man who shows signs of being able to lead a
mule to water, and I want every one of them to have a crack at it." Both the
humor of the comment (with the proverbial horse being downgraded to a
mere mule) and its content (even the smallest leadership aptitude needs to
be tapped) speak to two other sides of Savage's leadership. These are, first,
his belief that in its raw form, leadership potential is widely disbursed and
can be identified and developed; and second, his commitment to create
yet other leaders besides himself. He follows through on these principles

Figure 8.6   As a bemused General Savage listens, Major Stovall, back at his desk, lays out a shrewd plan to stall the pilots' en masse transfer from their unit (Photofest)

in asking individual pilots to lead missions and in seeking a commendation for his pilots that will not mention his own leadership. After his initial strictly punitive mode, he starts to bolster follower morale by rewarding excellence as readily as he has penalized incompetence: he removes better-performing pilots out of the Leper Colony, reinstates a demoted sergeant and sincerely, if awkwardly, reaches out to Colonel Gately, the former pariah whom Savage had first assigned to the Leper Colony but who has since redeemed himself by flying successful missions even while injured.

As the film progresses, General Savage moves to a middle position between transactional and transforming leadership. While he retains some of the directive and authoritarian style that marked his first days as a commander, he has built troop confidence and morale through his own competence, dedication and professionalism, apparent in the high standards to which he holds himself, as he flies with his men—significantly, on his very first mission, in the Leper Colony plane.[9] As a result, leadership in the 918 bomb group is far from being a one-man show; while Savage remains in command, such subordinates as Stovall, Davenport, pilots

Cobb and Bishop, and even the once-ostracized Gately have taken on more responsible and vocal roles in the group. In fact, Savage names Gately to a crucial leadership position—leading the pilots in their most important mission after Savage's own mental and physical collapse. In his emphasis on developing leaders out of his men—even if they have only the capacity to "lead a mule to water"—Savage has begun to exemplify that elevation of followers into leaders, which, as we saw earlier, is a hallmark of transforming leadership (Burns, 1978, p. 4).

Twelve O'Clock High is not a film about how leadership change within the military may translate to civilian society. But it does present the 918 bomb group and General Savage's relation to it as a cinematic microcosm of any social organization where leadership entails not simply different attitudes on the part of the official leader, but also a more profound social transformation within the group itself. As we have seen, various factors contribute to that transformation. But none is as significant as General Savage's commitment to turning even the least promising members of the 918—those who can only "lead a mule to water"—into leaders. That said, part of this film's achievement is that it avoids offering Savage's approach as a simplistic blueprint for either leadership success or organizational change. The film's treatment of leadership's relation to change is all the more compelling for its complexity and realism, as it shows the general's own doubts, his initial failures, the need for him to learn from his followers, and, ironically, his own susceptibility to the same emotional identification with his men that he at first criticized in his friend, Davenport. *Twelve O'Clock High* never presents General Savage as some Carlylean "great man" to be adoringly obeyed by passive followers. Instead, the general serves as a social catalyst whose admittedly over-the-top words and actions serve at first as a wake-up call to his followers, and whose eventual willingness to modify his own draconian approach, and to be guided by others, transforms the disaffected, demoralized members of the 918 bomb group into a highly motivated, cohesive unit. And the general's greatest contribution to this transformation occurs because he allows—indeed, demands—that his followers assume greater authority and, eventually, that they become leaders themselves.

CONCLUSION

As in *Twelve O'Clock High*, so too in *Glory*, a military commander's willingness to grant autonomy and authority to his soldiers helps to transform them from passive instruments into active agents, from followers into leaders. In each film, the leader's ultimate goal is an inner transformation of the follower, not the elicitation of perfunctory obedience motivated by external means, whether coercive or mercenary. It is not enough, then, that the troops merely do what the commander wants them to do—they must start to want to do that on their own. So, instead of being equated with rank or official position, or with a fixed skill confined to a single individual, leadership in each film emerges as a fluid, organic process of reciprocal empowerment.

In the context of war, however, that powerful and empowering process can come at a terrible cost, for leaders and followers alike. An awareness of this cost is a sobering part of the vision in both *Glory* and *Twelve O'Clock High*. "Ain't nobody clean," declares Trip, as he describes his feelings of contamination to Colonel Shaw after their first experience of combat together, and as he questions whether the war will truly make any difference—whether it will, in the end, produce any meaningful social change. In *Twelve O'Clock High*, Savage's star pilot, Jesse Bishop, similarly questions the seeming purposelessness of combat missions; another pilot, Zimmerman, commits suicide out of misplaced feelings of guilt about letting Colonel Davenport down and the mounting toll on General Savage plunges him into a nearly catatonic state, as his own "overidentification with his men" exceeds even that of his predecessor, Davenport. It remains true, of course, that *Glory* is a celebratory film, paying tribute to the men of the 54th Regiment. Similarly, *Twelve O'Clock High* honors the American Air Force pilots who paved the way for victory in World War II. These affirmative, uplifting qualities are essential components of each film. At the same time, such affirmations coexist and even merge with darker currents of irony, moral ambiguity and violence. And it is, above all, this interplay of disparate perspectives that testifies to the two films' integrity as works of art, as studies in leadership and as realistic reminders of the values, and the costs, of social change.

NOTES

1. Both films are based on historical events. Apart from a few inventions and modifications, *Glory* relies heavily on letters, scholarship and historical records pertaining to the 54th Massachusetts Regiment. Similarly, *Twelve O'Clock High* reflects the World War II experiences of its screenwriters, former combat pilots Beirne Lay, Jr and Sy Bartlett. Unlike *Glory*, however, which explicitly presents itself as history on the screen, *Twelve O'Clock High* is clearly a "could-have happened" fictional narrative. The film uses only fictitious names for its characters, who are composites of actual people with a strong admixture of authorial imagination, and its plot is likewise an amalgam of the fictive and the factual (see Duffin and Matheis, 2005, pp. 6–7).
2. Since her 2007 lament over the dearth of followership studies, Kellerman has produced two books on this topic (Kellerman, 2008 and 2012); see also Riggio et al. (2008),

for collected papers from a conference devoted entirely to followership. Publications addressing less-specialized audiences have echoed the scholarly call for more attention to followers, for example, Bennis (1989), Keohane (2010) and Grint (2010). Nevertheless, leader-centric approaches still far outweigh studies of followers.

3. Rarely has a film with such popular impact garnered extensive scholarly respect as well. For example, James McPherson, the dean of American Civil War historians, praised the film's blend of historical accuracy and dramatic license, calling *Glory* "the most powerful and historically accurate movie about that war ever made" (McPherson, 1990, p. 22). Gerald Horne, another leading Civil War scholar, wrote that despite his misgivings about the story being told from the perspective of the regiment's white commander (a concern shared by, among others, the distinguished film critic Roger Ebert), "*Glory* merits the plaudits it has garnered and deserves much, much more" (Horne, 1990, p. 1443). For a useful summary of the generally positive response to the film, see Chadwick (2001, pp. 283–5).

4. The screenplay directions for actor Matthew Broderick's response to the flogging pithily summarize Shaw's dilemma: "Shaw's face is wracked with pain. Has he become what he most despises? Yet he must command" (Jarre, 1989, p. 63). On screen, Broderick's tense, ashamed expression and nervous biting of his lips convey Shaw's inner turmoil as Trip, under the lash, stoically and defiantly meets the leader's gaze.

5. For a brief, cogent discussion of "upward influence," whereby followers "can exert influence, especially through information, on a leader," see Hollander (2004, p. 1605).

6. Apropos here is Joseph Rost's disarmingly simple observation that "leaders and followers form one relationship that is leadership" (Rost, 1991, p. 109).

7. One of the 54th's most astute scholars has succinctly described how Shaw's men elevated him as a leader, and how this change led to yet broader change in social perceptions of black Americans: "Fortunate in birth and in war, Shaw grew stronger and developed a richer personal character after he accepted an unwanted position at the head of a black regiment and struggled with his own preconceptions of black inferiority. The men of the fifty-fourth lifted him to a higher plane and educated him even as their efforts caused others to reexamine their own prejudices" (Duncan, 1999, p. 126). Duncan's point here indicates the way that the experiences of the 54th helped to effect broader social change by chipping away at demeaning racial stereotypes.

8. For a thoughtful discussion of *Twelve O'Clock High* in relation to charismatic military leadership, see Bognar (1998). In a series of "leadership vignettes," Bognar lists various examples of General Savage's charismatic qualities, some of which have been touched on in this chapter. In some ways, however, Savage does not exhibit charismatic behavior: neither he nor his followers act as if he has the "divine grace" or inherently special qualities seen in charismatic leaders, and as noted earlier, Savage lacks and even avoids the emotional, inspirational appeals that are often associated with charisma. Just as Savage's approach lies somewhere between the transactional and the transforming, so too his leadership is in some ways charismatic, but in others not—as in his insistent refusal to let "any one man" become relied on too exclusively in the group, including himself. Consistent with this, Savage orders his top pilots to alternate in leading missions, so as to avoid follower over-dependence on, or emotional over-investment in, any one leader. As in other areas, so too with the depiction of Savage, the film resists any totalizing account of leadership, whether in general or in its constituent parts.

9. In contrast to Savage's repeated mission flights, General Frank Armstrong, the real-life prototype for much of Savage's character and behavior, flew only one mission with the bomb group on which the film's 918 unit was based. But like Savage, his leadership style could change, depending on the nature of his circumstances and his followers. With a group known for weak performance, drunkenness and rowdy behavior, Armstrong's approach aptly earned him the nickname of "The Butcher." But with the highly competent, professional, but demoralized unit that served as the model for the 918, Armstrong "was less directive and more supportive than he had been" with the prior group. In addition, with the more professional group, Armstrong—as Savage does in

the film—"sought . . . to show the group's leadership that they could do it themselves" (Gravatt and Ayers, 1988, pp. 205, 207).

REFERENCES

American Film Institute (AFI) Catalog of Feature Films (2016), accessed 21 July 2016 at http://www.afi.com/members/catalog/.

Bennis, W. (1989), "Good followers make good leaders good," *The New York Times*, 31 December 1989, accessed 29 June 2016 at http://www.nytimes.com/1989/12/31/business/the-dilemma-at-the-top-followers-make-good-leaders-good.html.

Blatt, M.H. (2001), "*Glory*: Hollywood history, popular culture, and the fifty-fourth Massachusetts regiment," in M.H. Blatt, T.J. Brown and D. Yacovone (eds), *Hope and Glory: Essays on the Legacy of the Fifty-fourth Massachusetts Regiment*, Amherst, MA: University of Massachusetts Press, pp. 215–35.

Bognar, A. (1998), "Tales from *Twelve O'Clock High*: Leadership lessons for the 21st century," *Military Review*, **78** (1), 94–100.

Brode, D. (1997), *Denzel Washington: His Films and Career*, Secaucus, NJ: Birch Lane Press.

Burns, J.M. (1978), *Leadership*, New York, NY: Harper & Row.

Burns, J.M. (2003), *Transforming Leadership*, New York, NY: Grove Press.

Call, S. (2009), *Selling Air Power: Military Aviation and American Popular Culture after World War II*, College Station, TX: Texas A&M University Press.

Chadwick, B. (2001), *The Reel Civil War: Mythmaking in American Film*, New York, NY: Knopf.

Chemers, M. (2001), "Leadership effectiveness: An integrative review," in M.A. Hogg and R.S. Tindale (eds), *Blackwell Handbook of Social Psychology: Group Processes*, Oxford: Blackwell, pp. 376–99.

Ciulla, J.B. (2014), "Leadership and the problem of bogus empowerment," in J.B. Ciulla (ed.), *Ethics: The Heart of Leadership*, third edition, Santa Barbara, CA: ABC-Clio/Praeger, pp. 82–103.

Conger, J.A. and R.N. Kanungo (1987), "Toward a behavioral theory of charismatic leadership in organizational settings," *The Academy of Management Review*, **12** (4), 637–47.

Cronin, T.E. and M.A. Genovese (2012), *Leadership Matters: Unleashing the Power of Paradox*, Boulder, CO, and London: Paradigm Publishers.

Doherty, T. (1999), *Pre-Code Hollywood: Sex, Immorality, and Insurrection in American Cinema, 1930–1934*, New York, NY: Columbia University Press.

Duffin, A.T. and P. Matheis (2005), *The '12 O'Clock High' Logbook*, Boalsburg, PA: Bear Manor Media.

Duncan, R. (1999), *Where Death and Glory Meet: Colonel Robert Gould Shaw and the 54th Massachusetts Infantry*, Athens, GA: University of Georgia Press.

Eberly, M.B., M.D. Johnson, M. Hernandez and B.J. Avolio (2013), "An integrative process model of leadership: Examining loci, mechanisms, and event cycles," *American Psychologist*, **68** (6), 427–43.

Fiorina, M.P. and K.A. Shepsle (1989), "Formal theories of leadership: Agents, agenda setters, and entrepreneurs," in B.D. Jones (ed.), *Leadership and Politics: New Perspectives in Political Science*, Lawrence, KS: University Press of Kansas, pp. 17–40.

Gravatt, B.L. and F.H. Ayers, Jr. (1988), "The fireman: *Twelve O'Clock High* revisited," *Aerospace Historian*, **35** (3), 204–8.

Grimsley, M. (2014), "The moral world of *Twelve O'Clock High*," *World War II Magazine*, **28** (6), 75–6.

Grint, K. (2010), *Leadership: A Very Short Introduction*, Oxford: Oxford University Press.

Hollander, E.P. (2004), "Upward influence," in G.R. Goethals, G.J. Sorenson and J.M. Burns (eds), *Encyclopedia of Leadership*, vol. IV, Thousand Oaks, CA, and London: Sage Publications, pp. 1605–9.

Horne, G. (1990), "*Glory*," *American Historical Review*, **95** (4), 1141–3.

Jagernauth, K. (2014), "Rian Johnson cites *Twelve O'Clock High* and *Letter Never Sent* among inspirations for *Star Wars: Episode VIII*," accessed 18 July 2016 at www.indiewire.com/2014/07/rian-johnson-cites-twelve-oclock-high-letter-never-sent-among- inspirations-for-star-wars-episode-viii-274007/.

Jarre, K. (1989), *Glory* screenplay, Tristar Pictures.

Jeansonne, G. and D. Luhrssen (2014), *War on the Silver Screen: Shaping America's Perception of History*, Lincoln, NE: University of Nebraska Press.

Jennings, P.L. and S.T. Hannah (2014), "Leader ethos: How character contributes to the social influence of the leader" in R.E. Riggio and S.J. Tan (eds), *Leader Interpersonal and Influence Skills: The Soft Skills of Leadership*, New York, NY, and London: Routledge, pp. 141–72.

Kellerman, B. (2007), "What every leader needs to know about followers," *Harvard Business Review*, **85** (12), 84–91.

Kellerman, B. (2008), *Followership: How Followers are Creating Change and Changing Leaders*, Cambridge, MA: Harvard Business Review Press.

Kellerman, B. (2012), *The End of Leadership*, New York, NY: HarperCollins.

Kelley, R. (1995), "In praise of followers," in J.T. Wren (ed.), *The Leader's Companion*, New York, NY: The Free Press, pp. 193–204.

Keohane, N.O. (2010), *Thinking about Leadership*, Princeton, NJ: Princeton University Press.

Landon, P.J. (1999), "*Twelve O'Clock High* (novel-film-television series)," in M.P. Holsinger (ed.), *War and American Popular Culture: A Historical Encyclopedia*, Westport, CT: Greenwood, pp. 319–20.

Lay, B. and S. Bartlett (1949), *Twelve O'Clock High* screenplay, Twentieth-Century Fox.

Matthews, J.J. (2008), "Exemplary followership: Colin L. Powell," in H.S. Laver and J.J. Matthews (eds), *The Art of Command: Military Leadership from George Washington to Colin Powell*, Lexington, KY: University of Kentucky Press, pp. 231–64.

McAdams, F. (2002), *The American War Film: History and Hollywood*, Westport, CT: Praeger.

McPherson, J. (1990), "The *Glory* story," *New Republic*, **202** (8 January), 22–7.

Meindl, J.R. (1995), "The romance of leadership as a follower-centric theory: A social constructionist approach," *The Leadership Quarterly*, **6** (3), 329–41.

Riggio, R.E., I. Chaleff and J. Lipman-Blumen (eds) (2008), *The Art of Followership: How Great Followers Create Great Leaders and Organizations*, San Francisco, CA: Josey-Bass.

Rost, J.C. (1991), *Leadership for the Twenty-First Century*, Westport, CT: Praeger.

Rubin, S.J. (1981), *Combat Films, American Realism: 1945–1970*, Jefferson, NC: McFarland.

Suid, L.H. (2002), *Guts and Glory: The Making of the American Military Image in Film*, Lexington, KY: University of Kentucky Press.

Uhl-Bien, M., R.E. Riggio, K.B. Lowe and M.K. Carsten (2014), "Followership theory: A review and research agenda," *The Leadership Quarterly*, **25** (1), 83–104.

Wong, L., P. Bliese and D. McGurk (2003), "Military leadership: A context-specific review," *The Leadership Quarterly*, **14** (6), 657–92.

Zwick, E. (2004), "Director's audio commentary," *Glory* special edition DVD, Tristar Pictures.

9. Becoming Other: self-transformation and social change in Neill Blomkamp films

Kimberly Yost

Science fiction films offer imaginative and often sobering narratives of the unexpected ways protagonists become leaders and change agents in their societies. In particular, the films of South African filmmaker Neill Blomkamp, *District 9* (2009), *Elysium* (2013) and *Chappie* (2015), represent a vision of the future in which the possibility of social change is revealed through the transformation of the protagonists into emergent leaders, but also their becoming a literal embodiment of Other. Blomkamp explores contemporary social, economic and political marginalization through the depiction of self-transformation and the consequent subversion of the interests of the powerful. These films also consider the desires of the marginalized to be included in the privileged spheres of society and the often destructive consequences of trying to achieve that goal. They allow us to reflect upon and discuss the dynamic complexities of leadership, the porous nature of identity and ways of supporting inclusionary practices toward social change.

Each of the films follows a male character who is generally reconciled to his current situation, but still yearns for a nobler life. In *District 9*, we meet Wikus van der Merwe (Sharlto Copley), a rather socially awkward administrator for the private military-industrial firm Multinational United (MNU), who is put in charge of gaining consent from aliens being forcibly relocated from a Johannesburg slum. He enjoys his job and seeks a more successful career to provide for his wife, the daughter of his boss. *Elysium* (2013) introduces Max Da Costa (Matt Damon), an ex-offender living on a depleted Earth in Los Angeles circa 2154, striving to maintain his dignity and hope while contending with workplace exploitation, bureaucratic negligence, recidivism and abject poverty. Deon Wilson (Dev Patel), in *Chappie* (2015), is an engineer for weapons manufacturer Tetravaal, who created a highly successful robot police force for Johannesburg and has now developed software to enable the police robots to think and learn independently, but is stymied in his efforts to test the AI program by his supervisor and a jealous colleague.

Each character is vested in maintaining the status quo of their social and economic position: Wikus for human superiority over the aliens and his privileged management position; Max for preserving his conditional freedom (he wears an ankle monitor due to a previous criminal conviction) and his job on the assembly line for Armadyne, a weapons manufacturer; Deon for being on the cutting edge of robotic technology and heralded for the financial success of the company where he works. As viewers, we witness the inequities, corruption, neglect, greed and ostracism of the social system inhabitants in these films and may wonder why the protagonists appear to be complicit in supporting such a deficient society.

An answer may come from social justification theory, which suggests "people are motivated to justify and rationalize the way things are, so that existing social, economic, and political arrangements tend to be perceived as fair and legitimate" (Jost and Hunyady, 2005, p. 260). These arrangements can include accepting, and thus legitimizing, the ideologies of work ethic and meritocracy, fair-market forces and economic inequality, belief in a just world where one gets what they deserve, comfort with power distance and socially dominant groups, authoritarianism and political conservatism (Jost and Hunyady, 2005). These ideologies provide a strong force for the disadvantaged to rationalize their socio-economic position and feelings of uncertainty or safety concerns, but also to desire and work toward attainment of a privileged socio-economic position and greater stability, thus further justifying the status quo.

Of particular note within the connection of social justification theory and science fiction narratives are the concepts of the perception of a dangerous world and mortality salience. When aliens attack or violent crime is rampant, the world is a dangerous place and death can come at any moment. Sustaining a perceptually secure, but ultimately authoritarian and inequitable society that swiftly manages threats from aliens, terrorists and criminals, as well as the despicable poor, is seen to be preferable to the imagined alternative of chaos, violence and engaging in personal and communal duty. Unsurprisingly, Blomkamp features weapons manufacturers granted government responsibilities for peacekeeping as the establishment authorities in his films, but they also serve as the primary antagonists.

Interpretively, the absence of a sturdy and independent democratic government leads to the tragic conflict of the narratives. In Blomkamp's films, the use of power by authorities no longer serves the interests of society, but serves those who hold the power—usually in the not-so-subtle form of a weapon. We see this in MNU's quest to discover the secret of alien weapon technology for their own financial and military dominance through horrific experimentations on and executions of aliens (*District 9*, 2009). In *Elysium* (2013), Defense Secretary Delacourt (Jodie Foster) repeatedly raises the specter of social collapse and loss of privilege in her public justifications for use of force against the Earth's poor who try to reach the orbiting Elysium space station. When a spacecraft eludes her unauthorized destruction order and crashes into a residential district of the station, she is ready to seize control of the government during the crisis and exercise even greater personal power. The theme is pointedly expressed in *Chappie* (2015) as Tetravaal engineer Vincent Moore (Hugh Jackman) puts his competing robot model into the field and indiscriminately uses excessive weaponized force with exceeding joy at the monstrous superiority of his creation.

Not only does the misuse of power create tragic situations of destruction and death, it also sparks the eventual radicalization of the protagonists to social change agents. Although Wikus uses derogatory language about and to the aliens, when he is injured by alien technology and essentially tortured by MNU scientists as they attempt to extract his compromised DNA, his relationship with the company is shattered. This is exacerbated further when he discovers other, more gruesome experimentations being conducted on the aliens by MNU. This break enables him to justify helping the alien Christopher Johnson (Jason Cope) in his efforts to leave Earth (*District 9*, 2009).

For Max, the apathetic negligence of Armadyne when he is exposed to lethal doses of radiation in an industrial accident causes an existential shift in his justification of the status quo. A robot medic dispassionately tells him he has five days to live and tosses a bottle of pills at him. Armadyne's CEO remarks that he wants Max out of the facility as soon as possible. Facing imminent death, Max embraces his criminal past once again and volunteers to steal information from Armadyne for a human smuggler in exchange for passage to Elysium and medical treatment in a Med-Bay machine that cures all sickness and injury, but is not available to the non-citizens who live on Earth (*Elysium*, 2013).

For much of *Chappie* (2015), Deon remains dissatisfied with the progress of his research and fearful his successful sentient robot experiment, Chappie, will be discovered, but he does not reject the social structure of a near-future Johannesburg with a robot police force that keeps the peace. Nevertheless, when the entire robot force is shut down through sabotage by Vincent and criminals are wreaking havoc, Deon's creations are compromised, his reputation is ruined, and he breaks his ties with Tetravaal to protect Chappie against Vincent's robot with tragic results. Importantly, the full radicalization of the protagonists occurs by both the breaking of interpersonal relationships brought about by new and troubling awareness of ethical failures of authorities as noted earlier and through physical transformation.

Contempt and obliteration of the socially excluded body—alien, non-citizen poor, criminal—by the powerful and privileged infuses the narratives of Blomkamp's films. Aliens are arbitrarily blasted by the MNU security forces at the slightest hint of resistance during the canvassing to get their consent to be relocated. Wikus and his team find a shed housing the embryos of alien offspring. As Wikus yanks the nutrient hoses from the embryos, he explains these embryos are illegal and must be destroyed, which they achieve by setting fire to the shed with a flame-thrower. Later, Christopher Johnson is asked if he has a legal permit for his young son. Alien prisoners are straightforwardly exploded to pieces by scientists trying to test alien technology (*District 9*, 2009).

In *Elysium* (2013), the poor are left on Earth and considered non-citizens by the elites who built the space station, Elysium, to escape the pollution, overcrowding, crime, disease and scarce resources of the planet. They protect their economic and social privilege through the exploitation of workers on Earth and destroying human smuggler spaceships attempting to enter Elysium. The government in Elysium appears to have some authority on the planet, but their representatives are mechanized police and parole officers. In a telling scene, Max must visit his parole officer who is nothing more than a mechanized head and torso who can monitor, but not effectively interpret, human bodies and emotions. The mechanized parole officer's solution to Max's emotional frustration at being unfairly stopped and frisked by the mechanized police is to offer a pill. Ostensibly, keeping the poor drugged will make them acquiescent and, thus, useful for further exploitation. Human representation is supplied by the weapons conglomerate Armadyne with the condescending CEO John Carlyle (William Fichtner) and the callous plant foreman who orders Max into the radiation area to fix a problem or lose his job.

The bodies of the poor are without value and expendable. Disease is rampant on Earth, and a doctor remarks to a desperate mother that he cannot simply cure her child because "This isn't Elysium." There is advanced medical equipment on Elysium called Med-Bays, which look somewhat like transparent MRI machines that can cure disease, regenerate body parts and reverse aging almost instantaneously. But the machines are programmed to serve only Elysium citizens. The non-citizens of Earth who are terminally ill or disabled must find an illegal way to be registered as a citizen, get smuggled to the space station and hope their ship is not destroyed by Elysium defense forces, break into a citizen's home, find the Med-Bay and then anxiously wait to see if the dangers were worthwhile and their bodies are made whole before they are discovered and arrested or killed (*Elysium*, 2013). The medical care citizens of Elysium take for granted, the non-citizens of Earth will risk everything to acquire.

Chappie (2015) depicts an attitude toward the socially excluded bodies of criminals in much the same way as aliens and the poor. Criminals are "marked" as different through extensive body tattoos and the non-conventional way they dress. But this film displays another level of socially excluded body through the sentient mechanized body of Chappie (Sharlto Copley). Prior to Chappie's incarnation as a conscious being, the robot body of Scout 22 is damaged during a police raid and deemed to be irreparable. A "reject" label is placed on the robot and it is destined for the scrap heap. Deon steals the parts to surreptitiously test his AI software and is kidnapped by petty criminals who demand he program a police robot to help them steal enough money to pay a large debt to a gangster. Deon is forced to agree and his test on the rejected robot is successful. Scout 22 becomes Chappie, but is still damaged and destined to "die" when his battery fails in just a few days. His consciousness seeks answers and his mortality salience is initially disregarded by Deon, so Chappie turns away from his creator and embraces his newfound criminal identity.

As Chappie learns and assimilates into the criminal life of Mommy/ Yolandi (Yolandi Visser), Ninja (Watkin Tudor Jones aka Ninja) and Amerika (Jose Pablo Cantillo), he is marked with spray painted tattoos, adorned with large gold necklaces and taught the proper speech and body posture of criminals (*Chappie*, 2015). Thus, Chappie embodies the socially excluded criminal, as well as the feared police officer and the maligned conscious robot.

Indeed, Chappie is stoned and set on fire by young men who are distrustful of police robots and see Chappie as a harmless aberration upon which they can take revenge. When Vincent Moore discovers Chappie and realizes Deon tested his AI program against the wishes of their boss, he seeks an opportunity to destroy the body, including "teaching him a lesson" by cutting off Chappie's left arm. Chappie escapes before Vincent can completely disassemble him, returns home to Mommy and is repaired and given a spare arm by Amerika. This causes Chappie to consider his damaged body and imminent death with even greater intensity (*Chappie*, 2015).

Chappie is not the only character to experience body impairment and existential anxiety. Max, Deon and Wikus all transform into an Other due to a life-threatening physical injury. Their self-transformation allows for the nascent interpersonal radicalization against authority to develop and extend to the more fully realized intrapersonal awareness and radicalization which permits actions for creating social change.

As noted above, Max receives a lethal dose of radiation and has only days to live. Yet it is his surgical transformation at the hands of the smuggler Spider (Wagner Moura) into a mech hybrid capable of downloading information directly into his brain that creates the physical Otherness capable of sparking action for social change. Spider is seeking financial information protectively carried by Carlyle in his brain, and Max is the only person desperate enough to undergo the excruciating surgery to attach an exoskeleton and neural implant to transfer the huge amounts of data. This is a self-serving act on Max's part as an exchange for being smuggled to Elysium and finding a Med-Bay to remove the radiation poisoning from his body.

The information they steal is discovered to be the codes for rebooting the entire Elysium computer system; a treasonous plot concocted by Carlyle and Delacourt to enable her to ascend to the presidency. In addition, the codes are able to automatically grant citizenship to all Earth residents. Clearly this information is of the greatest importance to Delacourt, who orders a lockdown of Earth airspace and reactivates her sleeper agent, Kruger (Sharlto Copley), ordering him to retrieve the information and kill Max. When he is found, Max bargains with Kruger to be taken to Elysium and Spider's team also launches as the lockdown is lifted (*Elysium*, 2013).

At the end of the film, Spider and Max are at the computer core of the Elysium station when Spider realizes uploading the information Max carries will kill him. Max accepts this with equanimity and activates the program, understanding that his death subverts the purposes of the rich and powerful and will make life better for the billions of inhabitants on Earth. After the reboot concludes, Elysium security forces refuse to take action against Spider as they register him as a citizen. Furthermore, medical shuttles are seen launching for Earth to care for the sick, old and disabled who are now listed as citizens (*Elysium*, 2013). The social, economic and political privileges of citizenship, medical care and protection against police threat have been achieved through the transformation and body sacrifice of Max.

Deon's transformation to Other comes near the end of *Chappie* (2015) after the violent encounter with Vincent's heavy weapons robot model. Yolandi is killed and Deon is mortally wounded. Chappie rushes him back to the Tetravaal lab in an attempt to save his consciousness. Previously, Chappie had researched the meaning of consciousness and discovered, through testing with Yolandi, that he could download consciousness to a computer by re-engineering the same type of helmet Vincent uses to remotely control his robot and thus be able to put himself into a new body when his battery ceases. Chappie intends to download Deon's consciousness into a new body. But when they get to the lab, there is only one spare Scout robot body and Chappie's battery is nearly spent. Deon insists Chappie save himself, but Chappie quickly places the helmet on Deon and uploads Deon's consciousness to the robot body just before his battery fails. The now bodily transformed Deon finds the "guard key" that can control all the currently non-functioning Scout robots and locates one nearby to transfer Chappie's consciousness. They reunite and escape from the Tetravaal and Johannesburg security forces trying to capture them. The denouement shows Ninja finding the flash drive with Yolandi's consciousness, used by Chappie during his test, and Chappie hacking into Tetravaal's assembly plant to download her consciousness into a new robotic body, while Deon looks on (*Chappie*, 2015).

Deon's radicalization in terms of interpersonal and intrapersonal experiences may not seem momentously epistemological for leading social change, but we can see both Deon's and Chappie's ability and success in enacting social change through self-transformation as counter-intuitive, in that robotic police forces are disbanded in favor of returning to human police. When Vincent vengefully shuts down the robot forces, Johannesburg calls up thousands of reserve human officers to deal with the chaos in the streets. In effect, Deon's efforts to create a sentient robot, Chappie's refusal to accept death and the rampage of Vincent's robot model brings clarity to Johannesburg's civic authorities to no longer outsource and thus abdicate responsibility for the safety of its citizens to a private corporation and weaponized non-humans. The presumed social justification for a mechanized police force has been exposed as ineffectual when authoritative power is misused and reverting to traditional institutions managed by humans/elected officials for the good of the whole society is now seen as preferable.

Much like Deon's complete physical transformation, Wikus transforms from human to alien in *District 9* (2009). During the incursion in the Johannesburg slum inhabited by the aliens, Wikus and his team are also searching for weapons and other contraband. He finds a canister and inadvertently causes it to spray alien fluid used for powering their ship into his face. He begins to show symptoms of vomiting, black mucus seeping from his nose, his fingernails bleed and fall off. Desperately, he bandages his left hand and heads home. His wife has planned a surprise party to celebrate his promotion in managing the relocation and Wikus tries to remain conscious and sociable, but eventually vomits and passes out while trying to serve cake. At the hospital, an emergency room doctor unwraps the improvised bandage and they discover his left arm has morphed into an alien claw.

Wikus is next seen in an MNU lab being examined by scientists. They discover his alien arm is capable of operating alien weapon technology. The scientists, with detached objectivity, compel Wikus to test his alien arm in the execution of livestock and then alien prisoners. His boss and father-in-law, Piet Smit (Louis Minnaar), immediately realizes the immense financial and military value of the alien/human DNA. Smit orders Wikus's DNA is harvested, but Wikus escapes. MNU puts out a report that Wikus is dangerous and smears him by saying he has been having sex with aliens and contracted an alien sexually transmitted disease (*District 9*, 2009).

Wikus finds himself back in District 9 seeking Christopher Johnson for answers and discovers the missing alien command module that controls the mothership under Christopher's shack. Christopher is furious with Wikus that 20 years of gathering fluid to return home has been confiscated. They hatch a plan to steal the fluid back from MNU and Christopher promises to get Wikus's help in reversing the effects of his mutation. As they infiltrate MNU and retrieve the canister, Christopher sees the grotesque experimentation that has been performed on his species and determines to get help in rescuing his people from the planet. Christopher tells Wikus he must go for help and that it will take years to return. Wikus is desperate and tries to steal the command module but is shot down by pursuing MNU forces. Nigerian gang members, also interested in alien technology, join the fight. Wikus, in an armored body of alien technology, shoots down the soldiers and gang members and saves Christopher. Christopher and his son successfully power up the mothership and leave Earth and television reports show crowds cheering the departure. Reports also show Smit being arrested when the illegal experimentation program is revealed. The aliens are moved from District 9 to District 10, though it is still a segregated camp. Wikus's wife is interviewed about his possible whereabouts and talks about how she received a flower. The final image is Wikus, fully transformed to an alien body, sitting on a junk heap crafting a metal flower (*District 9*, 2009).

The transformation of Wikus from human to alien is more problematic than in the other films because he does not willingly consent to becoming Other, it is an accident caused by his own arrogance. Even though Max and Deon had a difficult choice to make, Wikus appears to have no choice. The fascinating element becomes not the choice to embrace Otherness, but the terrifying journey of becoming Other. While he cannot be faulted for wanting to remain human, his transformation sets social change in motion. Because he collaborates with Christopher in retrieving the fluid, defending against MNU and the Nigerians and escaping Earth, the status quo and social justification regarding the aliens is broken. The aliens are moved to relatively better housing. The experimentation ends and the MNU conglomerate is placed in check.

What we find in each of these films are three protagonists who are essentially saving their souls and their humanity in the face of personal and social crises. Indeed, they appear to find greater humanity and connectedness to others as their physical body transforms. Each of them are in various stages of dying/becoming when they make the fateful choices leading to social change. Max sacrifices himself for the betterment of those on Earth, Deon doesn't die and extends his consciousness in a rebellion against the constraints of what it means to be alive, and Wikus puts his own life on the line to help a comrade. Their ability to secure justice for the poor, the robots and the aliens can only be accomplished through shunning the existing social order and the physical/emotional self-transformation of becoming Other. There is a transcendence of the human through the body of the Other.

We need our Other to help us understand our Self. Kearney (2003) offers us a hermeneutic approach to the understanding of the Other as "less in opposition to selfhood than as a partner engaged in the constitution of its intrinsic meaning" (p. 80). Kearney's (2003) key is to "imagine other possibilities of existence which challenge the status quo and embrace peace and justice" (p. 41). Blomkamp's films propose an imagined possibility where emergent leaders challenge the status quo in support of those who are socially excluded and ultimately advocates for justice. However, leaders must also demonstrate principled actions as "transformation is not in itself a guarantee of ethical improvement" (Kearney, 2003, p. 223). Inclusion is readily apparent in the embracing of the Other by becoming Other, which is not only a physical transformation but also an interpersonal and intrapersonal relational process demonstrated in these films.

Love is another principled action at the heart of Blomkamp's films. Oord's (2010) definition "To love is to act intentionally, in sympathetic response to others (including God), to promote overall well-being" (p. 15) seems most appropriate. Love is characterized as a deliberate or intentional decision with a noble purpose and taken freely, along with the acceptance of responsibility for the choices made. Love is relational and requires an empathy "internally influenced by the other such that one's own experience is partially constituted by the one or ones perceived" (Oord, 2010, p. 20). Max intentionally sacrifices himself to make life better for the poor because of his love for Frey and her daughter. Deon uploads Chappie's consciousness and helps in uploading Yolandi's not as an engineering research activity, but an act of love formed from his relational experiences with them. Wikus, however begrudgingly, understands his actions to fight on the side of Christopher are sympathetic actions that will lead to the well-being of aliens and humans alike. In addition, Wikus grasps his humanity and retains the romantic love of and for his wife by creating little gifts anonymously left on her doorstep.

Indeed, these intentional acts of love could also be interpreted as seeking redemption. "Redemption is salvation from the states or circumstances that destroy the value of human existence" (Clark, 2003, p. 76) and a process that moves relationships from estrangement to reconciliation.

Caldwell et al. (2011) identify repentance as a "behavior that incorporates an ongoing desire to improve one's life by honoring duties owed to oneself and to others . . . [with] an integrated change in one's actions or way of life that seeks to improve relationships with others, either individually or as members of a group" (p. 474). Redemption is an intentional action that comes from self-awareness and a sense of humility in the restoration of relationships and "can potentially enhance the ability of leaders and other individuals within the social system to reach their full human potential" (Yost, 2012, p. 62). We can interpret the actions of the protagonists as seeking redemption for previous injuries and attempting to restore relationships through duty to others. Max disappointed Frey and her daughter when they needed his help earlier, and caused harm to others when he was a car thief, but redeems himself through activating the computer program that kills him. Deon rejected Chappie's existential concerns and disparaged Yolandi for her lifestyle and treatment of Chappie, but redeems himself through transferring their consciousnesses to other bodies. Wikus spent much of his life denigrating the aliens, working for a company intent on exploiting their technology and killing their children, but redeems himself by fighting for Christopher's escape. In addition, each develops a greater self-awareness and understanding of the larger societal forces influencing their previous behaviors and rationalizations, which were a detriment to their relationships with others, and make choices to subvert the interests of the powerful and bring about social justice.

Blomkamp's films are not content with simply telling stories of emergent leaders overcoming obstacles to bring about social justice. He meets the viewer's belief in a just world head on and challenges us to reconsider our ingrained notions of justice on social and personal levels. Appel (2008) contends fictional narratives cultivate a belief in a just world and states "their endings typically include a resolution that brings together unconnected story lines, thus restoring balance and, ultimately, justice" (p. 64). We want to believe in a just world because we have been conditioned by stories told to us since we were in our cradles that this is so. Good people live happily ever after and bad people are punished. Intellectually and through our life experiences, we know this is not always the truth. Emotionally we feel committed to this belief because our society is purportedly founded upon the concept of justice and our popular culture continually reinforces it.

Blomkamp's films ignore this understanding. Max dies. Deon and Chappie are fugitives. Wikus must exist in an alien body apart from his wife. While each may have accomplished a level of justice for others in their social systems, it appears their personal fates are not necessarily what they deserved. Perhaps Blomkamp's disregard for the trope of a "happy ending"—or at least one with a sense of full satisfaction and reconciliation—accounts for some of the negative response to his films. Nevertheless, these films allow us to consider the ways in which relationships with the social system can be thwarted and relationships with the socially excluded can be strengthened.

These films identify the transformation of attitudes and beliefs about social change may require more than intellectual understanding. Leading social change may require tacit knowledge of exclusion through physical and emotional relationships offering new understandings of injustice and bringing about the self-awareness of empowerment to act. If we can dispense with our belief in a just world, we may be better able to face the realities of injustice in our society. We may be better able to understand that not everyone gets what they deserve and empower ourselves to take action for social change to remedy injustice.

REFERENCES

Appel, M. (2008), "Fictional narratives cultivate just-world beliefs," *Journal of Communication*, **58**, 62–83.

Caldwell, C., R.D. Dixon, R. Atkins and S.M. Dowdell (2011), "Repentance and continuous improvement: Ethical implications for the modern leader," *Journal of Business Ethics,* **102**, 473–87.

Chappie (2015), [Film] Neill Blomkamp, dir., United States: Media Rights Capital.

Clark, M.W. (2003), "Redemption: Becoming more human" *Expository Times*, **115** (76), 76–81.

District 9 (2009), [Film] Neill Blomkamp, dir., New Zealand: Wingnut Films.

Elysium (2013), [Film] Neill Blomkamp, dir., United States: Media Rights Capital.

Jost, J.T. and O. Hunyady (2005), "Antecedents and consequences of system-justifying ideologies," *Current Directions in Psychological Science*, **14** (5), 260 and 5.

Kearney, R. (2003), *Strangers, Gods, and Monsters.* New York, NY: Routledge.

Oord, T.J. (2010), *Defining Love: A Philosophical, Scientific, and Theological Engagement.* Grand Rapids, MI: Brazos Press.

Yost, K. (2012), *A search for home: Navigating change in* Battlestar Galactica, doctoral dissertation, Antioch University, accessed 23 September 2016 from Ohiolink ETD/ http://rave.ohiolink.edu/etdc/view?acc_num=antioch1347903521.

10. Ready, aim, feel: empathy, identification and leadership in video games

Kristin M.S. Bezio

INTRODUCTION

Since the 1980s, video games have widely been lambasted as a medium that is at best a waste of time and at worst a training ground for violence and aggression. Despite popularized media depictions of video games as corrupters of youth, to date, no study has definitively demonstrated any such link, at least to no greater degree than any other form of popular culture (Ferguson, 2013). As artifacts of popular culture, video games are just as capable of exerting influence—in fact, they may even be more capable of doing so by virtue of their immersive interactivity as a medium. It is important, however, to note that this notion of influence is distinct from the moral panic-induced accusations leveled at games by parental organizations, senators and disgraced lawyers, such as Jack Thompson. The participatory nature of games does demand more intensive interaction from its audience than novels or film, but such interaction does not translate to brainwashing or coercion. A video game player is no more likely than a book reader or film watcher to attempt to act out the violent fantasies that make up so much of Western popular culture. Rather, such media introduce narratives that either propagandize or problematize state-sanctioned violence, for instance, or place a hero in opposition to terrorists or oppressors, with specific ideological arguments at their centers.

In order to understand the distinction between game narrative and traditional, linear narrative, we must recognize that, in a video game, a player's actions form a part of a story made up of "both story events and gameplay events specific to one particular play-through of a game" (Bezio, 2014, p. 147). Every player's experience will be different—even if similar—from every other player's experience based on differences of reaction time, directional choices, skill or gameplay decisions. For example, one player may go left at an intersection while another may go right, and their experience of the game might change depending on which encounters each player has first, even though the specifics of the programming are identical for both.

In addition, in video games, players are able to do more than imaginatively identify vicariously with a hero in print or on a screen: they can control or occupy the positional body of that hero, making choices and taking actions on that hero's behalf. It is this imaginative identification that is vital to my argument. The key here is that imaginative identification all-but-requires the player to develop empathy for the hero, or player-character, who "is not simply a virtual 'skin,' but a specific persona associated with the game's narrative" (Bezio, 2014, p. 147; Voorhees et al., 2012, p. 17), although that persona may be either developer- or player-determined, depending on the game. This relationship of player to player-character permits video games to be used as a platform designed specifically to encourage and foster tolerance, self-reflection and empathy.

As Mary Flanagan argues, games "not only provide outlets for entertainment but also function as a means for creative expression, as instruments for conceptual thinking, or as tools to help examine or work through social issues" (2009, p. 1). The participatory nature of video games makes this working-through of "social issues" much more imaginatively immediate to players than if they are observing the events in film or reading them in print, as players are often asked to directly confront these "issues" by making a choice or engaging in gameplay that is directly impacted by them.

As is undoubtedly obvious, some games are designed to promote such positive social characteristics more than others, and there are certainly games that do not do so at all. However, I suggest that there are more games that engage in this practice on some level than are given credit for so doing and that there are some games whose primary intention is to direct their players' attention to concerns of social justice. In this essay, I will focus primarily on two game titles whose central intent is to use imaginative identification to produce and nurture empathy. I use these games as "case studies" in how digital games intentionally attempt to foster imaginative empathy through gameplay, thereby encouraging players to become active participants (and even leaders) in the process of social change.

The games in this study, produced in the decade between 2007 and 2017, intentionally craft narrative gameplay experiences that demand that players confront problems of intolerance, miscommunication, sexism and exploitation through both story and game mechanics. *Journey*, from 2012, combines simple gameplay, aesthetics and non-violent multiplayer interaction to teach players about cooperation and the universality of the human experience. Recent AAA games that incorporate combat and other "traditional" mechanics, such as exploration and loot collection, have also begun to include elements of empathy, ethics and moral choice into otherwise mainstream games. Titles such as *Mass Effect* (a series of third-person shooters set in a futuristic space setting, released 2007–17 by the game development company BioWare) mix elements of imaginative empathy—ethical decision-making, character-identification, issues of social justice—with more traditional mechanics, integrating critical and "serious" gameplay with popular gameplay in order to reach ever-wider audiences with messages of tolerance, diversity and the need for just leadership.

JOURNEY (2012)

Journey, created by thatgamecompany in 2012, was released on the Sony PlayStation 3 via the console's PlayStation Network and re-released on PlayStation 4 in 2015. At the 2013 DICE Summit, *Journey* won the Game of the Year Award, and its lead designer, Jenova Chen, gave a keynote on the importance of emotion in games, which included a story about a letter Chen received from a girl who had played *Journey* with her dying father, calling it "the game that changed my life, the game whose beauty brings tears to my eyes" (Takahashi, 2013). *Journey*, explained Chen in the talk, is "a metaphor for life and death" (Takahashi, 2013), the embodiment of the company's mission to "create timeless interactive entertainment that makes positive changes to the human psyche. If our games can help people, that's the best reward we can get" (Takahashi, 2013).

The premise of *Journey* is, quite literally, a journey undertaken through a desert to a mountain. The player-character is a robed figure, arguably human but of indeterminate gender or ethnicity. In *Journey*, players control movement and sound—they can walk, run, jump, fly or glide and chime at different volumes and for different durations. *Journey* can be played alone or with other players and was designed to be a cooperative experience. However, the game has no chat window or voice capabilities, unlike most multiplayer games. This means that players have to communicate using only the movements and chimes allowed to them by the game; Chen explains:

> I think words complicate things. Our vocabulary is limited. There are words that exist in one language and not in another language. It creates barriers that keep us from understanding each other. I'm often frustrated using words to talk to people. I guess that's why I have that craving for games like Journey, where it's not about language. (Takahashi, 2013)

In essence, the absence of language in *Journey* enables a primal, empathetic communication between players that is only hindered by the difficulty of language, particularly across cultural barriers. Chen joked in an interview that part of his struggle with language was that "I suck at writing English dialogue" (Takahashi, 2013), a practical (and personal) confession that nevertheless strikes at the core problem in cross-cultural communication.

Human beings communicate first and foremost in language. In our increasingly global society, we often find ourselves struggling to find the best way to communicate across barriers of culture, geography and semantic meaning, having to find the best translation for a word or phrase that ultimately fails to adequately communicate whatever it is we seek to transmit. Language, according to theorist Julia Kristeva, is a part of the hierarchical structure of social order, what she terms the "symbolic order," a system that "is determined by a set of signifying rules ... a general social law" of socioeconomic and political forces (1986b, p. 25). In simpler terms, Kristeva's symbolic order is autocratic and authoritarian, the often-unacknowledged power of our social institutions and paradigms to control our behavior, limiting us according to traditional (and often patriarchal) hierarchies that discourage creativity and innovation, the very things upon which we must draw to enact meaningful social and cultural change. This order uses language—and the social rules about who speaks it and in what contexts—to maintain a rigid institutional hierarchy of power and oppression.

Kristeva suggests that the means to escape the strictures of the symbolic order exist in the "semiotic chora," "a non-expressive totality formed by the drives and their stases in a motility that is as full of movement as it is regulated" (1986a, p. 93). In essence, the semiotic chora is a space of extra-linguistic communication that seeks to transgress the barriers constructed by social, economic, political and linguistic delineations, an imaginative space in which communication happens without the rigidity of words. The chora is thus a space that encourages the very kinds of innovation and creativity necessary for social change and transformational cultural leadership.

In gaming, the symbolic order exists, in part, in what Ian Bogost terms "procedural rhetoric," or "the art of persuasion through rule-based representations and interactions rather than the spoken word, writing, images, or moving pictures" (2010, p. ix). In gameplay, players relate to one another and to the objects in the game based on the mechanics offered by these procedural rhetorics. In most popular games, these mechanics—the game's verbs—consist of "shoot" or "stab" or "run" or "break," violent actions that situate players as hostile to other players and to their digital environment. In *Journey*, however, the players' set of rhetorical procedures are vastly different—they can "chime" or "glide" or "jump" or "walk," but there are no aggressive mechanics. The unconventional and non-linguistic mechanics of *Journey* align with Kristeva's chora, instead, encouraging players to use their creativity to solve problems and engage in cooperative, rather than competitive, play. Players are thus asked to relate to others in an empathetic rather than hostile fashion, asking how they can interact or help one another rather than how they can "beat" one another.

What this means is that players automatically become allies, companions in the game's goal of reaching the top of the mountain, a cooperative venture that requires imaginative empathy in order to succeed. Even in single-player, the player interacts with "cloth creatures," beings made of fabric that appear as dragons or serpents and that assist the player in solving the challenges presented along the way.

Narratively, *Journey* also subverts the conventional purpose of gameplay. Most conventional games are linear, progressing from the beginning to the end, which the player hopes will be a victory (in most single-player games, if the game is completed, the player wins; in multiplayer games, there can be winners and losers). *Journey* at first appears the same, with the "win-condition" being to reach the mountain in the distance.

Players begin in the desert, alone, on the edge of a vast field of stones that resemble tombstones. The player-character is a robed figure of nondeterminate gender or ethnicity. The abstraction of the figure enables players to more fully identify with it, in opposition to a set player-character with specific gender or ethnic characteristics that might contrast with those possessed by the player. Imaginatively, players can identify with what *might be* under the figure's robe, rather than having a potential disjuncture between their own identity and that of the player-character.

The figure, alone or joined by a companion, must navigate varied landscapes in the desert and underground by learning to glide, climb and "turn on" artifacts in the ruins by "chiming," eventually making his or her way to a snow-covered mountain, guided by pictographic glyphs and short "visions" presented by a large, white-robed figure (thatgamecompany, 2012). Chen explains that "The idea is that all these people are seeking enlightenment. They want to find the ultimate truth. But it's vague. It's a myth. No one knows what that ultimate truth is. Here, it happens to be on the top of the mountain. Everyone's trying to get there" (Takahashi, 2013). Through this common goal, *Journey* generates empathy through the universality of the experience, emphasizing the commonality of hope in spite of struggle and hardship.

Near the game's end, the player finds themselves staggering through the snow before falling, and the screen fades to black (thatgamecompany, 2012). But the game is not finished; the figure "resumes consciousness," and continues through the clouds into an oasis of waterfalls and blue sky, being supported by the "cloth creatures" who have been assisting along the way (thatgamecompany, 2012). The game ends as the player walks into the center of the mountain filled with a bright, white light; a shooting star emerges from the top, streaming across the desert to land in the dunes—in the precise place where the figure originally began (thatgamecompany, 2012).

The purpose of *Journey*, then, is to show players the universality of the human experience; we are born, we struggle through life's triumphs and challenges, we die. Chen explains that the figure does, in fact, die on the snowy mountain:

> The final level is not in the world. If you look closely at it, it has all this water. It has a blue sky. Everything there indicates that it isn't real. You've died. It's a flash. According to some people who've seen the moment of death, they see white, and then they see the past flashing by. That's why, in the summit level, you see all the things you've seen in the past—the strands of fish, the whale, all these wonderful things. You're fooled by it for a moment. We wanted to simulate that feeling of death. (Takahashi, 2013)

Journey thus presents a distilled simulation of life—and death—designed to foster imaginative empathy not only between players in the act of game-play, but also between people and across cultural, social, political, national, economic and ethnic boundaries, encouraging creativity and innovation in hopes of fostering social change. In demonstrating our common human journey, *Journey* asks us to recognize and celebrate our common humanity and to help one another along the way.

IMAGINATIVE EMPATHY IN AAA GAMES: *MASS EFFECT* (2007, 2010, 2012, 2017)

One might argue that an example like *Journey* is atypical, a game not designed to appeal to the mass market saturated by violent shooters. And that is true. However, there are many popular and successful games—AAA games, as they are called in the industry—that also incorporate elements of imaginative empathy in an attempt to teach toleration and foster diversity and inclusivity. Many newer games are beginning to focus on styles of gameplay which do not feature violence: *Mirror's Edge* is a game about parkour and city exploration; the *Portal* series features no weapons in its three-dimensional puzzle-solving physics games and *No Man's Sky* focuses on vast space-exploration and conservation.

All that being said, there are still many more games with violent central mechanics than without. Typical AAA titles include *Call of Duty*, *Battlefront* and *Halo*, all of which are first-person shooter games with a military setting (whether on earth, in an alternate universe or in space).

Even traditional role-playing games, like *World of Warcraft* or *Final Fantasy* (although very different in style), tend to be focused on combat skills and require combat to progress. But the inclusion of combat does not inherently preclude such games from including empathetic lessons or arguments for social change. BioWare's titles, including four each in the *Mass Effect* space opera series and *Dragon Age* fantasy series, are particularly strong examples of AAA games that openly advocate for diversity and inclusion in terms of gender, race and sexuality, including player-characters with customizable skin tones, genders and sexualities, as well as non-player characters (NPCs) with a wide variety of races, genders and sexual preferences.

In particular, the *Mass Effect* series focuses specifically on how these issues of diversity manifest in a leadership context, with the player-character of the first three games, Commander Shepard, attempting to negotiate both the internal politics of a diverse crew (both human and alien), the external politics of a vast galaxy and, when necessary, the logistics of combat (BioWare, 2007, 2010, 2012).[1] Players are able to choose whether they wish to play as a Paragon (largely altruistic), a Renegade (largely task-oriented) or as a combination of both (BioWare, 2007). Different gameplay choices build what amounts to idiosyncrasy credit as either Paragon or Renegade, meaning that if a player has not repeatedly made the same type of choice, they are not able to secure enough credit with various NPCs in order to convince them to take certain actions. As such, players have to decide what kind of leader they are—as well as what kind of leader they want to be.

Over the course of the first three games, players are repeatedly asked to make significant leadership decisions: which of their companions must go on a suicide mission (BioWare, 2007), who should lead an alternative strike team (BioWare, 2010), whether or not to end a genetic sterilization program (BioWare, 2012), whether to save human beings or an alien galactic council (BioWare, 2007) and whether to choose to control or destroy the most powerful force in the galaxy (BioWare, 2012). Each set of choices—some large, some small—has repercussions that play out both in each individual game and in subsequent games in the series, requiring players to seriously consider the consequences of their actions and the reasons behind them.

It is possible—although not ideal, in terms of in-game rewards—to play the game biased towards humanity and against aliens (the series' stand-in for racial conflict), but to do so forces repeated confrontations—both narrative and combat—with different alien species, who demand accountability or reparations for the deaths or losses inflicted on their peoples (BioWare, 2007, 2010, 2012). Players are thus forced to come to terms with the consequences of racial bias and are given the opportunity as the series advances to attempt to repair any damage done.

BioWare's *Mass Effect* series—whose first three games rest on the premise that Shepard must fight a race of sentient machines attempting galactic genocide—relies on the mechanics of conversational choices and combat. As a "shooter" game (most of the player's actions happen in combat), *Mass Effect* is unusual in that its ultimate goal is actually the end of violence; it acknowledges that escaping violence is not always possible and has created Shepard as a leader who engages in violence because it is necessary, not because it is desirable.[2] In so doing, the series acknowledges the disparity between the desire for peace and harmony and the reality of a global society in which diverse ideologies frequently come into conflict. The player's job is not to eliminate diversity—that is what the enemy is attempting to do—but to maintain a balance of diversity and harmony, even at the potential cost of his or her life (BioWare, 2012).

BioWare reinforces this macro-message with microcosmic encounters throughout its games as the player converses with each member of his or her crew—both alien and human—and chooses to fulfill or refuse their requests. Side missions throughout the games also offer opportunities for players to make leadership choices: to help a crew member gain revenge for betrayal or convince him to be merciful (BioWare, 2010); to release an imprisoned man or to exploit his genius (BioWare, 2010); to save an ally's son or save an entire city (BioWare, 2012). These choices often force players to decide between power or politics and empathy, and reward players for their choice with points in either the Paragon or Renegade scales (BioWare, 2007, 2010, 2012). Neither set of choices is "wrong," but each one does contribute to the creation of a leadership style for a player's Shepard; a Shepard with a high Paragon score can use persuasion and non-violence to greater effect than a Renegade Shepard, who must rely more on force and intimidation (BioWare, 2007, 2010, 2012). As such, it benefits players to choose a style and to be consistent—to gain idiosyncrasy credit with their followers as either Paragon or Renegade—in order to maximize their effectiveness, a leadership lesson with clear implications in the real world.

Either a Paragon or a Renegade Shepard can win the game, but, interestingly, it is possible to "lose" the series by making a selfish choice during the third game and shooting the Catalyst (an artificial intelligence that appears as a child), a character whose creation is the product of extreme imperialism (BioWare, 2012). By silencing the Catalyst (which is extremely tempting), the player refuses to hear its explanation of how genocidal colonial oppression is the ideal alternative to the chaos created by diversity; in creating this "loss-condition," BioWare emphasizes the importance of listening to the enemy, of understanding other perspectives and of negotiating with them, as the player cannot "win" the game until he or she has negotiated with the Catalyst, convincing it that genocide is not the best solution to cultural complexity (BioWare, 2012).

In the end, then, the *Mass Effect* series attempts to convince its players that the richness of the universe is found in diversity, rather than conformity. Irrespective of his or her leadership style, Shepard needs the skills and assistance of a variety of other characters (of different genders, races and sexualities), just as the galaxy needs the help of a variety of civilizations in order to defeat their enemy (BioWare, 2012). In short, players end the series with the notion that they can only succeed if they gain the support of as many different planets and organizations and species as possible; the greater the diversity, the better. In the process, the series attempts to instill a similar set of values—based on imaginative empathy—in its players, encouraging them to promote diversity and toleration in the real world as they do in the world of *Mass Effect*.[3]

CONCLUSION

These types of games—with choices that impact options later in the game—are becoming increasingly popular, with series such as *The Witcher*, *Red Dead Redemption*, *Dishonored* and *Fable* also including similar mechanics. What this means, from a leadership studies standpoint, is that more and more popular games—*The Witcher 3* and *Dragon Age: Inquisition* were both winners of Game of the Year for their respective years from different media outlets—are including leadership choices as part of their gameplay in an effort to force players to imaginatively empathize with the complex and difficult (sometimes impossible) choices leaders have to make. In *Mass Effect 2*, for example, Shepard has to choose between destroying or erasing the memories of an entire civilization of artificial intelligence, and neither choice feels "good" in the process of gameplay (BioWare, 2010).

In essence, video games, like every form of media that has come before them, are able to imaginatively engage their players in a variety of ways, using that engagement in order to foster not only empathy with the games' characters but also to implicitly encourage players to engage in socially affirming behaviors outside of the game. Playing games thus serves not only as a means of escape from everyday drudgery, but also as a way to temporarily inhabit another persona, to imagine living in that other person's proverbial shoes. The very process of play demands awareness of equity and inclusivity, a desire for a world that is better than the one in which we live, as Edward Castronova suggests:

when game players complain about why their games are enjoyable or not, they talk about justice, they talk about equity, they talk about growth, they talk about efficiency. And the underlying objective in the real world for our policies is the improvement of human well-being. Successful game designs improve well-being. (Castronova, 2007, p. 17)

When we think about the implications for leadership—and leadership studies—games thus offer us not only an avenue for study, but also a popular culture means for educating people for and about leadership, asking them not only to imagine empathizing with another, but also to imagine leading them into a better, more diverse global society.

NOTES

1. The fourth title, *Mass Effect Andromeda*, has a different player-character, although the themes and inclusivity of characters remain consistent. My analysis will focus primarily on the first three games in the series.
2. In *Mass Effect Andromeda*, the player-character, Ryder, is also required to choose between conquest and exploration, and is similarly encouraged by the game to choose the more peaceful options while balancing the safety of the ship's crew and colonists.
3. As a company, BioWare is openly vocal about advocating for diversity and inclusivity. There is a famous incident between David Gaider, a lead BioWare writer, and a fan complaining about the existence of non-heterosexual romances in BioWare's games. Gaider wrote:

    The romances in this game are not for 'the straight male gamer'. They're for everyone. We have a lot of fans, many of whom are neither straight nor male, and they deserve no less attention . . . [and] have just as much right to play the kind of game they wish as anyone else . . . The majority has no inherent "right" to get more options than anyone else. (Gaider, 2011)

REFERENCES

Bezio, K.M.S. (2014), "Friends and rivals: Loyalty, ethics, and leadership in BioWare's 'Dragon Age II'," in D.J. Hickey and J. Essid (eds), *Identity and Leadership in Virtual Communities: Establishing Credibility and Influence, Advances in Social Networking and Online Communities*. Hershey, PA: IGI Global, pp. 145–69.

BioWare (2007), *Mass Effect*, Edmonton, AB: Electronic Arts.

BioWare (2010), *Mass Effect 2*, Edmonton, AB: Electronic Arts.

BioWare (2012), *Mass Effect 3*, Edmonton, AB: Electronic Arts.

BioWare (2017), *Mass Effect Andromeda*, Edmonton, AB: Electronic Arts.

Bogost, I. (2010), *Persuasive Games: The Expressive Power of Videogames*, Cambridge, MA: MIT Press.

Castronova, E. (2007), *Exodus to the Virtual World: How Online Fun is Changing Reality*, New York, NY: Palgrave Macmillan.

Ferguson, C.J. (2013), "Violent video games and the Supreme Court: Lessons for the scientific community in the wake of Brown v. Entertainment Merchants Association," *American Psychologist* **68**, 57–74.

Flanagan, M. (2009), *Critical Play: Radical Game Design*. Cambridge, MA: MIT Press.

Gaider, D. (2011), "To the OP . . ." *Dragon Age II Official Campaign Quests and Story (SPOILERS)*, accessed 23 August 2013 at http://social.bioware.com/for um/1/topic/304/index/6661775&lf=8.

Kristeva, J. (1986a), "Revolution in poetic language," in T. Moi (ed.), M. Waller, (trans.), *The Kristeva Reader*, New York, NY: Columbia University Press, pp. 89–136.

Kristeva, J. (1986b), "The system and the speaking subject," in T. Moi (ed.), M. Waller, (trans.), *The Kristeva Reader*, New York, NY: Columbia University Press, pp. 24–33.

Takahashi, D. (2013), "An interview with Jenova Chen: How Journey's creator went bankrupt and won game of the year," *VentureBeat*, 8 February, accessed 21 July 2016 at http://venturebeat.com/2013/02/08/an-interview-with-jenova-chen-how-journeys-creator-went-bankrupt-and-won-game-of-the-year/.

Thatgamecompany (2012), *Journey*, San Mateo, CA: Sony Interactive Entertainment.

Voorhees, G.A., J. Call and K. Whitlock (eds) (2012), *Dungeons, Dragons, and Digital Denizens: The Digital Role-Playing Game, Approaches to Digital Game Studies*, New York, NY: The Continuum International Publishing Group.

11. "War. War never changes": using popular culture to teach traumatic events

Kimberly Klimek

Educators face the difficult task of creating secure scholastic spaces in which to discuss traumatic events. War. Rape. Slavery. Cultural Destruction. Genocide. Whether we teach ancient or modern history, history of the world or history of a specific place, hatred, anger, death and fear all find their ways into our lectures and our sources. We have a responsibility to show this ugly side of history along with the sublime beauty. We also have a responsibility to the students in our classrooms. The question then becomes, how do we teach the hard topics in a responsible and effective way? This chapter seeks to outline how educators can use video games, comics and cosplay alongside primary source materials to teach about the horrors, politics and economics of historical warfare and misogyny, while staying true to educational principles and acknowledging the very real cost these events may have had on our students.

Using popular culture in conjunction with historical primary sources provides opportunities for students to safely visualize themselves in dangerous situations, to distance themselves from trauma or to sympathetically experience it (Decker, 2012; Dong, 2012; Babic, 2014). Popular culture is an effective and affective way to both distance and contextualize traumas, while allowing diverse groups access to various historical ways of understanding war and misogyny.

In history courses, we assign primary source readings to our students. In reading these sources we are engaging with and analyzing the points of view of people from the past. The best sources humanize the past; they put names and feelings on those distant events. Using primary sources is one way for students to look at the past through its own lens, as opposed to the lens that we, as professors, set up. Doing so gives them a personal window into the past. This can, however, be a grimy window through which to see. Primary sources can be very difficult for students to access. As professors, we are used to the voices of the past sounding and looking differently than we do today. We are good at creating connections. We expect our students to be able to read, understand, evaluate and use the sources written by people during and around the period they are discussing. Yet students have a hard time with the translated sources, word usage, the allegories and metaphors used by peoples in the past. Our students can understand allegory and metaphor, however, for they abound in popular culture, in the literature and in the movies and the music to which they listen. The key is finding connections between primary source works, secondary source works and popular culture. Relating events of the past to popular culture, particularly through comics, video games and cosplay, allows our students to build more meaningful connections for themselves to the peoples of the past.

Comparing and using popular culture works alongside primary sources allows for both effective and affective understanding of the source materials. The sources are effective in that they can aid in understanding the historical reality and in evaluating the authenticity and validity of a source. They are affective in the experiencing of emotional responses and connections between characters, historical actors and the students themselves. What we want our students to understand is more than the listing of historical facts. In looking at primary sources of the past, I want them to see the past as individuals, often leaders, who had to make difficult decisions. Our goal is the analysis and synthesis of evidence to create an historical narrative about individuals and their actions. To do so, we must create a connection between the past and the present.

There are two major ways that I have seen the popular culture sources aid students in the understanding of a traumatic historical past. The first is an emotional understanding, particularly for traditional students who have not suffered trauma. This lens allows them to peer into the lives and feelings of those in historical traumatic situations. The second is a distancing mechanism for students who have experienced trauma. As one student put it, "Comics are less stressful than movies or monographs. I can shut the book if I need to and take a minute. And I can read the pictures first, to see how the text might affect me."[1]

Our classrooms are more diverse than at any time in history. A traditional student, fresh from high school, is most likely an 18-year-old female. About one-quarter of those female students will already have experienced a violent sexual trauma (RAINN, 2016). In the West, she has a high likelihood of speaking more than one language. She may be an immigrant or from an immigrant family, and in some places, she may be undocumented herself (Mulhere, 2015). Our non-traditional students often have experienced job insecurity or job loss. They may be single parents, working full-time jobs, military veterans, refugees or homeless. My signature classes on Medieval History often tempt, in particular, veterans with an interest in warfare. When I have asked why, my former students tell me that it is because of my acknowledgement of their veteran status. Not every veteran has a traumatic past and many decry the modern conception of a permanent and widespread PTSD amongst veterans. Nevertheless, their time in the military has given them different stories and different experiences that deserve acknowledgement.

My other popular class is Women in World History, where 98 percent of the students identify as female. Many of them have had traumatic experiences that can affect how and what they learn within a history class. Teaching about women's history is fraught with examples of mistreatment and subjugation of women by personal, governmental, religious and societal means. Acknowledging the facts of patriarchal and kyriarchal ("Kyriarchy," coined by Elisabeth Schüssler Fiorenza (1993), adds the intersectionality of race, class and religion to the idea of patriarchy, in that race/class/religion and so on can change the patriarchal dimensions under which people operate) damage done to women and women who have personal experiences with the structures currently in place is another important factor to consider when teaching.

This is not to insinuate that all college students have had traumatic experiences. Many have not. For these students, popular culture is a way to create an affective link to the past. Many students see history as a listing of names, dates and events to which they have very little connection. Popular culture is a way for us to create a compassionate connection to the pain and the joy of the past.

The beauty of using popular culture in teaching historical trauma is that it can aid both groups, by giving voice to those who have experienced trauma and giving emotional context to those who have not. We have a responsibility to teach Whole History—history that shows the joy and pain, the beauty and the ugly of the past. We cannot understand the twelfth century without the Crusades, and we cannot understand the Crusades without understanding how Europeans demonized their enemies and slaughtered in the name of God. We must not avoid difficult topics like war, racial disparities, cultural destruction, rape and slavery. In no way should we refrain from teaching any event that may be hurtful to students, but, nonetheless, we should be compassionate in how we teach those subjects.

Treating our students as adults with histories of their own can aid them when these unexpected events come up in the readings or the classroom. Knowing that they are seen, heard and acknowledged can allow students to feel comfortable enough to sit through a lesson on trauma, remove themselves from the situation, or speak to the professor after class. In a class about topics like American slavery or Nazi Germany, the entire semester may be difficult. And in those classes, it may be worthwhile having a discussion at the beginning that deals with the triggering and traumatic events that the semester will be discussing.

Setting up a respectful space helps once traumatic historical topics come to the fore. This is not about the creation of a benign and sterile space, but one where students feel empowered to learn and talk about problematic topics. We endeavor to create classrooms where consideration and respect are paramount—a good learning environment is one where students respect the professor and each other and where the professor respects her students. Using popular culture also aids in these difficult discussions as they can create both connecting and distancing sources for students in understanding the past.

I will now be discussing specific examples about how to use popular culture with primary sources within difficult classroom conversations. These are obviously just examples and each professor should use what works best for them and their own classroom topics. I have, however, found that this works fairly well within my own classes.

TEACHING WAR

Teaching about warfare can be quite complicated. Listings of dates and descriptions of battle tactics make few students excited and discussions of causes and effects leave little room for connections with the past. Teaching about the very real human costs of war and how those causes/effects and battles related to actual humans is much more inviting and important. For example, the Middle Ages are distant enough for most students not to feel the traumatic events of the past affecting them in any major way. Nonetheless, teaching the Crusades can be difficult when a classroom has several combat veterans within it—men and women who have seen the landscape on which the Crusades were fought, who have seen the people with whom the Crusades were fought, who have seen combat so similar and yet so dissimilar to that which the Crusaders fought—teaching these wars can be quite fraught. The veterans understand both the landscape and the people better than the traditional students do, often gravitating toward the Muslim immigrant students in class. Often, a traditional student will denigrate the Muslim religion during our discussion on the Crusades, referring to jihad and "cultures of death" they have heard about in the news. Before I can speak, a veteran will speak up to defend Islam and the Middle East—one spoke of his own conversion to Islam, another talked of her love for the Afghani people as a whole. The Muslim students, used to such micro-aggressions, stay quiet until the conversation gets moving, and they will often point back to our texts and try to show how modern movements like ISIS subvert their faith and cultures.

Understanding the ideology of warriors is one way to bring students into a discussion of warfare that uses compassion for current soldiers and immigrants while understanding the very real cost of war. In a class on Early World History, students read primary sources such as Sun Tzu's *The Art of War* (6th cent. BCE [2006]), Machiavelli's *The Art of War* (1521 [2005]), Musashi's *Book of Five Rings* (1643 [2010]) and a Crusade Chronicle, generally Jean de Joinville's *Chronicle of the Seventh Crusade* (13th–14th cent. [2009]). The students are asked to compare/contrast these sources. The readings exemplify how early societies viewed war as a legitimate career choice and how they wanted warriors to be more than killing machines, men who fought with honor and dignity, who cared for their families and who appreciated the arts. These men were rarely separated from their cultures and societies in the way we remove and house our soldiers on closed and locked bases. While there are some very distinct commonalities for which we were looking, such as the fact that soldiers needed to be trained in warfare and political machination, the reading itself was quite difficult. Because these sources rarely spoke about their ideologies in clear and concise language, at least to the modern reader, students struggled to see through the allegory and metaphor.

One way to create an emotional link between the past and the present, then, is to ask students to find popular culture references and connect them to the primary sources they are reading for the class. I asked students to find connections with modern examples that discussed the concepts of the Art of War with these older readings. The video game *Fallout* (1997–2015) became a major source for many of my students, as did other games like *Assassin's Creed* (2007–16) and *Call of Duty* (2003–16). Print sources also became important, as students brought in works by Neil Gaiman, such as *The Sandman Omnibus Vol. 1* (2013), and John Scalzi's *Old Man's War* (2007). Probably the most eloquent modern connection was between Sun Tzu's *The Art of War* and the modern-day U.S. Marine code. Linking these two ideologies of soldiers and their lives allowed students to see how connected the Art of War was across time and space.

Video games are an easy way for students to gain an affective understanding of warfare. *Fallout*, *Gears of War* (Microsoft Studios, 2006) and *Call of Duty Black Ops 3* (Activision, 2015) are three popular war games with easy access for students. Even if students do not play them, all three games have entered into the lexicon of popular culture. The first day discussing the Art of War, one student begins the discussion with "War." And another immediately chimes in, "War never changes"—the tagline for *Fallout*. It began a great talk on how war does and does not change over time and space, and what connections we can make between ancient warfare and modern warfare. *Fallout* gave my students an easy "in" to the readings. *Gears of War* and the incredibly popular *Call of Duty* also give affective understandings to warfare: the language and banter between soldiers, the group connections, the images and colors all represent facets of warfare students can use in understanding past conflicts. The "cutscenes" that interrupt game play to show conversations between players, introduce emotional connections or reward players are also especially helpful for this. One group of players spliced together all the *Call of Duty Black Ops 3* cutscenes to make a three-hour long movie about the game itself (*Call of Duty Black Ops 3 All Cutscenes Full Movie Gameplay*, 2015).

Comic books are another excellent avenue for both effective and affective understanding of warrior ideology and warfare. Although fewer comics discuss ancient battles, using modern wars can be just as useful. Comic books offer something that video games do not: the ability for the reader to close the book and leave the scene. This is very helpful to students who have experienced trauma, as it gives them ultimate control over the experience. As one student wrote, "The comics make everything feel very real. At the same time I can get at the material in a slower pace than a video, and that is helpful to me. I can take time to understand it." The series *War Stories* by Garth Ennis is both an effective and affective way of teaching the warrior ideology. This comic gives many readers a heavy emotional response to the characters within the stories. Students informed me that the characters seemed very real, very lifelike and they could understand what was happening to and through the characters.

The comic was especially useful to veterans. Veterans felt the banter between the characters was so real that many thought the author must have been a veteran himself (he is not a veteran, but a history buff). The visuals were also very realistic to veterans: "Either the artist had seen pictures of these events or had intimate knowledge of these events personally." A student also felt the command structure described within the book was very accurate. Additionally, they were able to use this to explain to their non-veteran peers how life in the military worked for them. At this point, the classroom became a full discussion about the ideology surrounding warriors and warcraft, and it included both veterans and non-veterans in the discussion. Everyone felt they had enough information to contribute to the conversation. Popular culture gave the students an entrance into a discussion of modern and ancient warcraft as they compared these modern sources to ancient Chinese and European ideals.

Using older comics, such as *Sgt. Fury and His Howling Commandos* (1963–81) and *G.I. Combat* (1957–87), engendered fewer emotional responses for students. They did, however, give students a good sense of twentieth-century warrior ideology and how it could relate to the earlier ideologies we were reading. These comics are distanced from bloody warfare and death as shown in modern renditions of warfare. Written during the 1940s and 1950s, these comics spoke to a different time, but they show how civilians wanted their soldiers to embody an American ideology of warriors. The soldiers were strong, educated, amusing and hyper-masculine. They had a bond with each other and a connection with the enemy, who is often seen as fumbling and ridiculous, but with enough strength and power that our heroes must work hard to win the day. The civilian ideals work well in contrast to the early ideologies of warfare that wrote of warriors as more than just fighters, but as integral parts of their society.

The two previous comics are completely fiction, but one can also use fictionalized accounts of "real" history within the classroom to great effect. One cannot ignore Art Spiegelman's *Maus* (1973) in any discussion of teaching historical trauma. His artwork and his words give a visceral emotional response to Jewish life under a Nazi regime. The horrors of warfare and genocide are contained neatly in simple sketches and simple words, creating both an effective and affective understanding of the past. There are many other impactful historical comics, such as *Sgt. Rock* (2009), *Tet* (2016) and *Dong Xoai* (2010). These modern historical comics show the drama of death, action and character within beautiful and poignant drawings and text. Fictionalized accounts of historical events, however, can be more difficult for students to extrapolate and generalize from, as they are concerned about the presented history over generalized ideals.

It was my students who first gave me the idea of using popular culture within the classroom. Their immediate link between *Fallout* and our readings connected them in a way I could not have produced through lecture. For other students, using these popular culture narratives allowed them a way to bond with the primary source material. Understanding how a twelfth-century knight felt while on Crusade can be very difficult for an 18-year-old fresh into college. However, using popular culture like *Fallout* and *War Stories* (2015) gives these students an important avenue into emotionally understanding the past. Students are given ways of emotionally connecting with people who are fundamentally unlike them, particularly with games that require cooperation and interaction between different players and that offer a long narrative arc. Additionally, students who struggle with the triggering aspects of traumatic events such as war have the ability to distance themselves from the difficult narratives, like the Crusade Chronicles, and connect to something that, while vivid, is also fiction. In essence, using the popular culture allows the students to have a break from the truth of the past, and understand this truth through narratives that were less dangerous because they were less real.

TEACHING MISOGYNY

This way of looking at reality through graphic narrative also aids students in understanding gender history and the nature of patriarchy. Popular culture offers a way to discuss the patriarchy that has existed within our past in ways that both give students an emotional connection to the past, as well as a way to distance themselves from difficult events. Considering that the majority of women, probably at least 75 percent, have experienced unwanted sexual contact, it is important for us to understand the triggering nature of events such as genocide, war, rape and cultural displacement. Again, it is not that we should not discuss difficult topics within the classroom; it is about how we do so with the sensitivity towards the people sitting within that room. Comics and cosplay provide a fertile ground for the discussions of modern misogyny.

Using the same techniques as those described earlier, the professor can assign various texts from the past and ask students to find modern equivalencies. For example, one could use St. Augustine's discussions on marriage and ask students to find modern counterparts that exhibit similar discussions. Looking in particular at medieval sources, there is a plethora of authors who discuss women as gateways to Hell. In one class, a student connected this to Neil Gaiman's *American Gods* (2001), where one of the goddesses swallows men through her vulva. This also has very close connections to ancient goddess worship and culture that we were then able to bring into the class discussion with the ideas and ideology of women's sexual nature and how it moved from fertility to fear throughout history.

Using more feminist works, students can find how the modern world has also subverted the misogynistic leanings of the past. Works like *Persepolis* (2004) and *Citizen 13660* (2014) are easy to use in the classroom as a way for students to connect to women's voices of the past. Both of these works are autobiographical graphic novels, written and illustrated by young women during the most difficult periods of their lives. Marjane Satrapi wrote of her experiences as a young woman during the Iranian Revolution. Her style mirrors Miné Okubo's memoir of life as a Japanese internee during World War II. Simple black and white graphics in both works portray the mundanity of horror during traumatic wartime events. Instead of large tomes of reading, students appreciate the graphic nature of the comics, where the drawings add to the text in subtle and stirring ways. For example, Okubo inserts herself into almost every picture, showing herself as an observer as well as participant in the world of the internment camps. One student wrote that the book was like "a hard jab in the nose" and made her see the emotional drama much more clearly.

There are many new comics available that teach the historical reality of women's lives in graphic form. *Abina and the Important Men* (2016) is another narrative that can be difficult for many students to access, about slavery and the modern world, but the graphic form of the novel allows students an entrance into this topic that gives them an emotional understanding while allowing them some distance from the topic itself. The beauty of *Abina* is that we are given access to the actual words of the young woman as she takes her slave master to court for enslaving her, giving us insight into African slavery in the late nineteenth century, as well as giving voice to the voiceless.

While few of our students have a direct understanding of slavery, many students of color have a cultural connection to slavery that runs deep. The destruction caused by slavery is inherent in the creation of the modern Western world—particularly relating to the culture, the institutions and the very bodies of peoples of color—and is an important and valuable part of our history. It is also a difficult one that has cultural resonance for many who sit in our classrooms. Giving these students voice, without making them "the voice" for their race or culture, is an important part of creating a classroom ready for deep learning, which can lead us toward cultural change. It is also an important step in dismantling the patriarchal notions of white supremacy inherent in our institutions and leaders.

While fictionalized accounts like *Abina*, *Persepolis* and *Citizen 13660* provide effective means of understanding past events at the same time as also giving us some affective understanding of women's lives, fictional characters offer students a way to understand patriarchy and kyriarchy in more visceral terms. The new additions of *Ms. Marvel* (2014) and *Bitch Planet* (2015) are two such sources.

Ms. Marvel (Marvel) of February 2014 features Kamala Khan, a Pakistani-American, as the lead character. She is the first Muslim character to lead a comic book line-up. She is an American teenager in Jersey City who has to deal with her protective immigrant parents and an older brother. Her religion plays a central role here, as does her age, as we watch Kamala become the superhero she is meant to be. Students are instantly attracted to Kamala and her familial and internal struggles. My Muslim students love discussing her family relations, especially with her religious and loving elder brother, and her own struggles to find a "cool, contemporary, and modest" superhero outfit. My non-Muslim students find entrance to a world they felt to be alien and unknown. Both groups easily find common ground—families and growing up are universal themes. The comic also allows us to discuss racism and religious discrimination. Paring *Ms. Marvel* with readings from India and China on women's roles and rights gives students an excellent emotional understanding of how young women in those countries sought, and continue to seek, more roles for themselves.

Bitch Planet (Image), by Kelly Sue DeConnick and artist Valentine De Landro, takes misogyny to a dystopian level, as The Fathers decide to remove non-compliant women to another planet, where they are imprisoned as examples to the people left on Earth. The comic, drawn in a style similar to 1970s blaxploitation films, is overtly feminist and can complement early feminist writings like Wollstonecraft's *Vindication of the Rights of Woman* (1792 [1995]). The main character is black and the comic is full of women of different races, sizes and temperaments. The Fathers are mostly white, wealthy older men. Conversations around race, class, gender and sexuality are so inherent in the comic that the collected volumes include Discussion Guides at the end.

Fictionalized accounts about the past, particularly surrounding the women's rights movement of the late nineteenth and early twentieth century, give a background for students in understanding the primary source material that they are reading. Almost every student has heard of Wollstonecraft's *Vindication of the Rights of Woman*, but few have read the original. Using comics and clothing allows students an affective understanding of this past—looking at how women dressed in society and how it affected their lived experiences, at how the industrialization of Europe changed those lives so quickly and drastically, at how abolition and American Independence affected the ideals of European societies can all be accomplished quickly and effectively through Steampunk cosplay.[2]

Cosplay can also be an important way for students to create for themselves an understanding of women in the past. The importance of Steampunk as a movement to the understanding of women's rights and women's history should not be understated. Even looking at images of cosplay outfits based on Steampunk and comparing these two actual patterns or visuals of Victorian women's costuming gives students an understanding of how connected we stay to the past. It also gives an opportunity to see a period where women were constrained by their clothing, by their society and by their government. Students need not participate in cosplay for them to understand and see the connection between modern cosplay and early modern renditions. Despite the growing trend of women participating in popular culture fan-world (often referred to as "fandom"), anyone attending a Comic Con or similar popular culture convention understands the pervasive misogyny female cosplay engenders. Denver Comic Con, among other conventions, has created a Rules and Consent banner that explains to attendees that costumes are not permission—look and appreciate, but don't touch: "Cosplay is not Consent!" (Denver Comic Con, 2017).

Every woman has experienced misogyny in one form or another. At least one-third of women have experienced it as violence and rape ("Unite to end violence against women fact sheet," 2008). Many other students have experienced oppression based on their race, culture, religion or class. Allowing these students the opportunities to discuss misogyny and oppression within areas like comics or cosplay gives them safe spaces to work on dismantling the traumatic experiences of our past, both personal and historical. More and more, women are expressing themselves through characters like Ms. Marvel or Zoë Washburne of *Firefly* (2002) to experience the newer versions of women in the popular culture world: strong and assertive female characters who take control and of whom others cannot take advantage. Research shows that seeing characters as strong and capable leaders encourages both women and men to accept women as societal leaders in "the real world." As Marian Wright Edelman famously said, "You can't be what you can't see" (*Miss Representation*, 2011). Seeing women in powerful leadership positions allows young people the opportunity to see themselves in those roles—perhaps not as a space pilot or superhero, but easily as a first officer and pilot or as a social justice warrior (Baxter, 2009; Klenke, 2011).

Using popular culture to find emotional connections between us and historical primary sources allows students the opportunity to delve into the sources with something more than an answer to a professor's question. Students take the opportunity to educate each other on popular culture icons and iconography, on comics they have read and on new versions of old tropes. Students who have broad knowledge of popular culture materials have an easier time deciphering, evaluating and interpreting the primary sources. These sources also aid students by giving them the space they need to respond to triggering events in their own lives.

The ability to use graphic novels, video games and cosplay gives us a way to discuss these difficult topics in a way that is true to the historical past while understanding the emotional needs of those people within our classroom walls. Popular culture offers a way to contextualize traumatizing events. We live during tumultuous and traumatic times, where great beauty exists alongside great tragedy. Showing how artists have conceptualized our own traumas, whether through *Call of Duty* or the *Saga* comics, allows students to see ways of understanding our present. Reading and evaluating primary sources, which often parallel our modern problems, allows students the ability to distance themselves from the modern, and using the popular culture artifacts allows them to emotionally connect to the past. In this way, students have a better chance of fully integrating their own knowledge with that of the past. Popular culture can be an effective vehicle for understanding the traumatic events in history—events that we must teach and our students must learn. Comics, video games, cosplay and others allow students a distancing mechanism as well as an emotional route to understanding the people of the past. They offer us a veil through which to see and teach the past in compassionate and pedagogically true ways.

NOTES

1. Quotations taken from student ratings of instructors are anonymous and will thus appear unattributed.
2. "Steampunk" as a culture can be understood as a fusion of Victorian aesthetics with a much more modern ethos of egalitarianism and scientific exploration. The movement's name comes from the frequent use of "steam-powered engines" (real or simulated) to drive modern machinery in the genre, such as steam-powered robots or aircraft.

REFERENCES

Allor, P. (author) and P. Tucker (illustrator) (2016), *Tet*, San Diego, CA: IDW Publishing.
Assassin's Creed (2007–16), Playstation and Xbox [Computer Program], Rennes, France: Ubisoft.
Babic, A.A. (2014), *Comics as History, Comics as Literature: The Roles of the Comic Book in Scholarship, Society, and Entertainment*, Lanham, MD: Fairleigh Dickinson University Press.
Baxter, J. (2009), *The Language of Female Leadership*, Basingstoke: Palgrave Macmillan.
Call of Duty Black Ops 3 (2015), Playstation and Xbox [Video Game], Santa Monica, CA: Activision.
Call of Duty Black Ops 3 All Cutscenes Full Movie Gameplay (2015), [Film] MKIceandFire, dir., 5 November, United States: YouTube, accessed 30 July 2016 at https://www.youtube.com/watch?v=qf4obtLgDDE.
de Joinville, J. and G. de Villehardouin (13th–14th cent.), *Chronicles of the Crusades*, trans. C. Smith (2009), New York, NY: Penguin Classics.
Decker, A.C. (2012), "Teaching history with comic books: A case study of violence, war, and the graphic novel," *The History Teacher*, **45** (2), 169–87.
DeConnick, K. (author) and V. De Landro and R. Wilson IV (illustrators) (2015), *Bitch Planet*, vol. 1, Portland, OR: Image Comics.
Denver Comic Con (2017). Cosplay, accessed on 11 July 2017 at http://popculture classroom.org/dcc/cosplay/.
Dong, L. (ed.) (2012), *Teaching Comics and Graphic Narratives: Essays on Theory, Strategy and Practice*, Jefferson, NC: McFarland & Company, Inc, accessed 5 February 2017 at http://0-site.ebrary.com.skyline.ucdenver.edu/lib/auraria/reader.action?docID=10582792&ppg=114.
Ennis, G. (author) and D. Gibbons, D. Lloyd, C. Weston and J. Higgins (illustrators) (2015), *War Stories*, vol. 1, Rantoul, IL: Avatar Press.
Fallout (1997–2015), Bethesda Game Studios [Computer Program], Bethesda, MD: Bethesda Softworks, LLC.
Firefly (2002), Fox [Television series], Los Angeles, CA: Mutant Enemy Productions.

G.I. Combat (1957–1987), Burbank, CA: DC Comics.

Gaiman, N. (2001), *American Gods*, New York, NY: HarperCollins

Gaiman, N. (author) and S. Keith and C. Doran (illustrators) (2013), *The Sandman Omnibus Vol. 1*, New York, NY: Vertigo.

Gears of War (2006), Xbox 360 [Video Game], Redmond, WA, Microsoft Studios.

Getz, T. (author) and L. Clark (illustrator) (2016), *Abina and the Important Men: A Graphic History*, New York, NY: Oxford University Press.

Klenke, K. (2011), *Women in Leadership: Contextual Dynamics and Boundaries*, Bingley: Emerald Group Publishing.

Kubert, J. (2010), *Dong Xoai, Vietnam 1965*, New York, NY: Vertigo.

Lee, S. (illustrator) (1963–81), *Sgt. Fury and His Howling Commandos*, New York, NY: Marvel Comics.

Machiavelli, N. (1521), *The Art of War*, trans. C. Lynch (2005), Chicago, IL: University of Chicago Press.

Miss Representation (2011), [Film] J. Siebel Newsom (director), Ross, CA: Girls' Club Entertainment.

Mulhere, K. (2015), "Undocumented and stressed," *Inside Higher Ed*, 26 January, accessed 30 July 2016 at https://www.insidehighered.com/news/2015/01/26/stu dy-finds-undocumented-colleges-students-face-unique-challenges.

Musashi, M. (1643), *The Complete Book of Five Rings*, trans. K. Tokitsu (2010), Boulder, CO: Shambhala Press.

Okubo, M. (2014), *Citizen 13660*, Seattle, WA: University of Washington Press.

RAINN (2016), "Campus sexual violence: Statistics," accessed 30 July 2016 at https://www.rainn.org/statistics/campus-sexual-violence.

Satrapi, M. (2004), *Persepolis*, New York, NY: Pantheon.

Scalzi, J. (2007), *Old Man's War*, New York, NY: Tor Books.

Schüssler Fiorenza, E. (1993), *But She Said: Feminist Practices of Biblical Interpretation*, Boston, MA: Beacon Press.

Spiegelman, A. (1973), *Maus: A Survivor's Tale*, New York, NY: Pantheon Books.

Sun Tzu (6th cent. BCE), *The Art of War*, trans. J. Minford (2006), New York, NY: Penguin Books.

Tucci, B. (author) (2009), *Sgt. Rock: The Lost Battalion HC*, Burbank, CA: DC Comics.

"Unite to end violence against women fact sheet" (2008), *United Nations Secretary-General's Campaign*, accessed February 2017 at http://www.un.org/en/women/endviolence/pdf/VAW.pdf.

Walsh, C. (2015), "Media capital or media deficit? Representations of women in leadership roles in old and new media," *Feminist Media Studies*, **15** (6), 1025–34, doi: 10.1080/14680777.2015.1087415.

Wilson, G. (author) and A. Alphona and S. Pichelli (illustrators) (2014), *Ms. Marvel*, vol. 1, New York, NY: Marvel Comics.

Wollstonecraft, M. (1792), *A Vindication of the Rights of Woman*, reprinted in S. Tomaselli (ed.) (1995), *A Vindication of the Rights of Men and a Vindication of the Rights of Woman*, New York, NY: Cambridge University Press.

PART IV

Digital leadership

12. Between artifice and emotion: the "sad girls" of Instagram

Eileen Mary Holowka

INTRODUCTION: SELFIE CULTURE

This chapter will examine the ways in which feminism manifests on social media platforms, such as Instagram, through both a resistance to and compliance with the protocols of the medium. For example, by playing with the expectations of social media for complacency and objectification through self-imaging, selfie-takers are able to subvert the medium's expectations of beauty and, in doing so, gain control over their own objectification—turn object to subject. In the words of Derek Conrad Murray (2015), "[t]he selfie does not simply comment upon a narcissistic need to see oneself in an idealized state, rather it makes one aware of the predatory nature of looking: the voyeurism in gazing at others and the implied pleasure in knowing that one is being gazed upon" (p. 512). Although Instagram is often still a problematic space for feminist self-representation, the women artists mentioned in this chapter have found ways of using it to their (and others') advantage. As media theorist and feminist Instagram user Magdalena Olszanowski (2014) writes, the images these (often white, female) users present "are fragmented narratives, fragmented bodies, in part fragmented by *sensorship* [the censoring of the senses]—institutional, societal, and internalized" (p. 23). While online harassment and censorship/*sensorship* are problems that can face anyone using Instagram, especially those who engage with it subversively, I argue that the community of voices collected and mediated by the platform stand as an undeniably powerful collection of feeling, experience, sadness and resistance. Although particular users (such as artist Audrey Wollen) are more resistant to the online communities, feminist social media theorists such as Olszanowski (2014), Jessalynn Keller (2014) and Johanna Hedva (2016) have shown that community is a critical part of online leadership and activism. This chapter looks at the way the sad girls of Instagram function as a community and counterpublic. For the purpose of this chapter, I define the "sad girls of Instagram" as a broad and immeasurable category of people who post selfies (or other images of themselves) representing their sadness to Instagram. Because of the vastness of social media spaces, where users both produce and consume content, the "sad girls of Instagram" are often in contact with one another and not necessarily aware of being a part of a "community" or collective. I do not wish to use this category to generalize all the differing intentions these users have, but to refer to a noticeable trend that involves posting self-image representations (selfies) of sadness on Instagram, particularly when it is done as a method of resistance. By paying attention to these self-representations and other manifestations of feminism on social media, we can begin to understand not only some of the importance of online feminism but also the ways in which we use presumed "artificial" platforms to express affect and have an effect on the "real" world.

SELFIE CULTURE AND AUTHENTICITY

Selfies, most commonly defined as smartphone images taken of oneself, are most often critiqued within pop culture with regard to their authenticity. They are often labeled "fake" for being filtered, constructed and performed, although they may be tagged and categorized using the hashtag "#authentic" if the picture is unfiltered or the subject is not wearing makeup. One of the most famous recent examples of this cultural desire for online authenticity occurred in late 2015, when social media celebrity Essena O'Neill quit Instagram in order to prove that "social media is not real life" (McCluskey, 2016). Before quitting, O'Neill edited all her photos so that they described the ways in which they were "fake." Her rejection of social media reinforced the idea that social media interactions are vapid, narcissistic and harmful (particularly for young girls). Although I do not want to invalidate O'Neill's claim that social media was a negative space for her, I argue that there are more productive ways to discuss social media than with regard to its artificiality, particularly when talking about women's and young girls' use of platforms such as Instagram. The representation of social media as either authentic or fake is not a useful way to quantify its potential impact, especially with regard to selfies, where it is all too easy to reinforce the misogynist assumption that women are inherently narcissistic (Senft and Baym, 2015; Dobson, 2015).

The notion of authenticity is complicated in part by the fact that social media interactions increasingly encourage the branding of the individual and the intimacy of corporations. As Leigh Alexander writes in her article, "Good morning, user! Welcome to the new intimacy economy," "organizations [are] pretend[ing], with increasing intensity, that they are individuals" (2015). Alexander admits that this makes her unable to feel close to the people who give her positive feedback online because she is unable to distinguish between people and corporations. However, her article goes beyond her own personal experience to dismiss all possibility of feeling an affective connection online, thereby denying the empowering experiences of many other social media users.

Instead of framing social media interactions in regards to authenticity, I choose to look at them in terms of affect; however, this is with the acknowledgment that affect theory is a complicated and not-always articulate lens. I cite here *The Affect Theory Reader* edited by Gregory J. Seigworth and Melissa Gregg, who write that "[t]here is no single, generalizable theory of affect: not yet, and (thankfully) there never will be" (2010, pp. 3–4). There are three main ideas to which I will refer throughout this chapter—affect, youth and imagination—all of which Lawrence Grossberg, in Seigworth and Gregg (2010), characterizes as "inarticulate." I want to suggest that it is not necessary for this chapter to exactly articulate affect theory or social media interactions in a single, definite way. Instead, it is important to look at what these instances *do*—"the effect of affect" (Seigworth and Gregg, 2010, p. 24). In other words, it is important to look at *how* these online social spaces (particularly Instagram) are used, as well as the lived experiences of the people using them; to look at the borders and parameters of these platforms and how branding can be subverted in order to understand how performance and "constructedness" can still make way for important and influential communities with the power to create social change.

SAD GIRL THEORY

The base inspiration for my claims regarding social media and affect begin with Instagram celebrity and artist Audrey Wollen's "Sad Girl Theory," which she began documenting on Instagram using the hashtag "#sadgirl." The #sadgirl is most commonly characterized as a young, white woman who documents her affect (most often sadness) through a selfie. Sometimes these selfies include crying or smudged makeup, as seen in Figure 12.1. In Wollen's own words, Sad Girl Theory is:

> the proposal that the sadness of girls should be witnessed and re-historicized as an act of resistance, of political protest. Basically, girls being sad has been categorized as this act of passivity, and therefore, discounted from the history of activism. I'm trying to open up the idea that protest doesn't have to be external to the body; it doesn't have to be a huge march in the streets, noise, violence, or rupture. There's a long history of girls who have used their own anguish, their own suffering, as tools for resistance and political agency. Girls' sadness isn't quiet, weak, shameful, or dumb: It is active, autonomous, and articulate. It's a way of fighting back. (Wollen in Tunnicliffe, 2015)

Figure 12.1   Audrey Wollen on leaving Instagram (@audreywollen)

Sad Girl Theory provides the promising possibility for young women to reclaim and become leaders of their own bodies. Although this ideal experience may not always be the reality for young Instagram users, there is a truth to Wollen's claim that political thought can occur online, whether to incite a protest (Gerbaudo, 2012) or begin to explore critical thinking (Keller, 2014).

Selfies and self-representation are integral to Sad Girl Theory, its main objective being to take the fetishization of female sadness and reframe it as subversive and potentially empowering. In Sad Girl Theory, women take leadership over their own images and bodies, with the added possibility of having their actions inspire other users to do the same. As Wollen is quoted as saying:

> I perpetuate my own objectification every day. But I'm interested in the idea that objectification itself has radical potential—we can use the products of oppression as the tools to dismantle it. I wish I could just be a person, and not a walking photograph of a naked girl. But I wasn't given a choice. I was being treated as if I was only a photograph of a naked girl long before I started taking photographs of myself naked. (Wollen in Barron, 2014)

Wollen is objecting to a long history of the over-sexualization of women's bodies across all media and the irony of how this contrasts with the fear of women's self-representation on social networking platforms, such as

Instagram (Dobson, 2015). Of course, Sad Girl Theory is often problem-atic in its celebration of sadness, which can be re-fetishized into the cele-bration of self-harm or used as a method to exclude disabled, non-white, non-idealized bodies. At its core, Sad Girl Theory is neither intersectional nor inclusive. Wollen herself has described the "sad girl [as] white," and she, in particular, has resisted the idea of a community forming around her words and theory (Wollen, 2016). The difficulties with the #sadgirl extend beyond Wollen's theory and become a trend. She becomes a poster girl and leader for the #sadgirl, despite not wanting to be, and her role as "leader" depends a lot on celebrity, as well as her position as having a body that is considered societally beautiful and sexually acceptable. In May 2016, she posted on Instagram to say she was going to take a hiatus from social media because she was uncomfortable with the way her theory was being cited by "[people] whose work [she doesn't] respect" in ways she found "reductive" (Wollen, 2016).

While I agree with many that Sad Girl Theory should be critiqued, espe-cially in regards to its lack of inclusivity, I disagree with the representation of the "Sad Girl" as solely vapid and narcissistic. Despite the exclusivity of Wollen's theory, the #sadgirl community stands as an important example of how young women—even if predominately middle-class and white—use social media as a space to subvert the expectations of their objectified bodies and experiment with their own representation. These social media interactions allow these users to explore leadership and activism in ways they may not be able to in their offline lives and become active critics of feminist thought, affect theory and self-representation before even knowing what these conversations might be.

BEYOND THE #SADGIRL

Other theorists and writers, such as Leslie Jamison (2014) and Johanna Hedva (2016), have written more articulate and inclusive theories similar to Wollen's Sad Girl Theory. In the "Grand Unified Theory of Female Pain," Jamison writes about the stereotype of the wounded and sick woman and how easy it is to fall into this representation. Although similar to Wollen's Sad Girl Theory, Sick Woman Theory is much more inclusive to marginalized, poor, non-white, non-binary bodies. Like Sad Girl Theory and Jamison's Theory of Female Pain, Sick Woman Theory addresses "[t]he *trauma of not being seen* [and questions] who is allowed to be visible" (Hedva, 2016). Jamison argues that this fetishizing or stereotyping of pain and sadness is no reason to stop representing it: "Sometimes [the wounded woman] is just true [. . .] Pain that gets performed is still pain. Pain turned trite is still pain" (Jamison, 2014). Jamison's idea is evocative and relatable. Although the ability to determine something or someone as "just true" is subjective and vague, her encouragement to treat these complicated states of being as articulate and authentic is appealing. Although not always directly related to social media, both Hedva's and Jamison's theories address the importance of self-representation and online collective spaces for those who are not necessarily able to march down the street in protest or those who are still too young to explore feminism and self-identification in an offline community. Like Wollen, Hedva and Jamison aim to make these people (particularly young girls) and their ideas more visible, through unapologetic self-representation and visualization. By including more voices, these theories open up the possibilities for social change, particularly in that they offer sad, sick, young or marginalized people a new way of thinking about themselves so that they can find ways to lead the way in shaping their own representations beyond societal constructions.

AUTHENTICITY AND AFFECT IN INSTAGRAM COMMUNITIES AND COUNTERPUBLICS

Instagram selfies have the power to share experiences and feelings on a large scale, thereby making potentially marginalized voices heard. Not all Instagram artists resist community the way Wollen has, and many young feminists have benefited from the influential counterpublics selfie-culture can foster. For example, Petra Collins and Madelyne Beckles curated the selfie exhibition *fuckboifuneral* (cited in Newell-Hanson, 2015), which reclaimed personal spaces and crafts that are often dismissed due to their presumed femininity. Collins and Beckles' *fuckboifuneral* resists assumptions of narcissism, reframing the selfie as a positive way to witness, perform and define the self. In order to claim the selfie as theirs, they created an archive of images that resist the dominant representations of women by including images of women not normally represented in popular media. Likewise, feminist Instagram artist Ashley Armitage also uses Instagram to create an archive of marginalized experiences. Her work also focuses on what is considered abject in female bodies, such as pubic hair, menstruation, body fat or wrinkles. Armitage's work takes a leadership role in representation and changes the way bodies are represented and celebrated in media.

The work of Collins, Beckles, Armitage and other Instagram artists who experiment with self-representation and subversive imaging are not that different from that of early feminist self-portraiture and performance artists such as Ana Mendieta, Hannah Wilke or Carolee Schneemann,

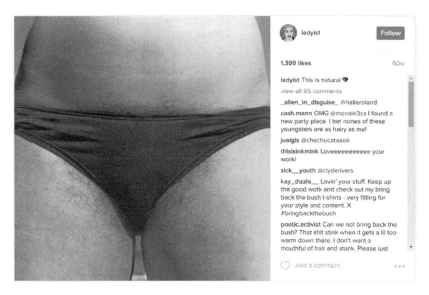

Figure 12.2   Image by Ashley Armitage (@ladyist)

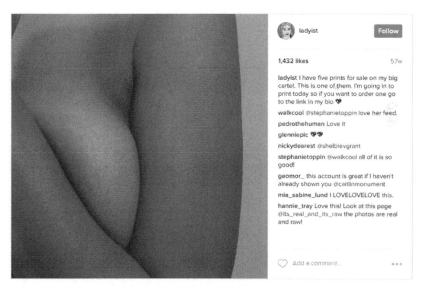

Figure 12.3   Image by Ashley Armitage (@ladyist)

whose works were often ignored, erased and rejected by arts communities. Many contemporary Instagram artists pay homage to these feminist icons by posting these earlier iconic photos amongst their own, drawing out important conversations between the generations. Work such as Mendieta's often reflected the all too real violence in her own life as a result of her experimental art practices, as well as, in her case, her Cuban-American identity and gender. Like many Instagram artists, Mendieta's art was popular and prevalent but has since been overshadowed by her partner and minimalist artist Carl Andre, and this experience is not unique to her (O'Hagan, 2013). Likewise, Wollen's selfies were appropriated by "artist" Richard Prince and hung in an art gallery without her permission (Barron, 2014). Just as self-imaging is not a new phenomenon, neither is the dismissal of these images for being vapid. Although, in both Mendieta and Wollen's cases, these erasures actually ended up making their work more visible later, that is not the case for many feminist artists (O'Hagan, 2013; Barron, 2014). The main difference between these eras of self-representation is that the Internet has provided not only a much larger and far more accessible audience but also the ability for the audience members to become quite easily producers and critics themselves. By taking a selfie and using a hashtag such as "#sadgirl," a young girl can visibly place herself into a feminist dialogue without ever having to leave the couch. In other words, a user does not need to have any higher education, ability to travel, access to a library or understanding of what feminist dialogue is to be able to begin exploring her own political, feminist, activist or artistic identity.

Online platforms, such as Instagram, provide new opportunities for young feminists to experiment with identity and representation. Although these spaces are by no means utopian, that does not mean their potential for experimentation and imagination should be ignored. In her article on contemporary feminist girl bloggers, Keller (2014) argues that although the conversations taking place in these online spaces may be conducted mostly by young girls, they still contain very serious and real discussions. Furthermore, the Internet is "often one of the only places in which they can engage in such practices" due, for example, to their not being able to take to the streets or not having access to feminist discourse within their own communities (Keller, 2014, p. 2). Young feminists can use the voice provided by this space to "perform various identities [and] develop [. . .] dissident feelings, intuitions, and desires"—in other words, creating the potential to develop feminist, political or activist identities (Keller, 2014, p. 11). Keller further points out that even *"being a feminist publicly* [is] in itself an activist strategy" in the ways that it makes feminism public and visible to people who might not be able to access feminism otherwise

(Keller, 2014, p. 15). Keller's theories of feminist girl bloggers tie into the visibility of female pain, sadness and suffering of which Wollen, Hedva and Jamison all speak. Like young girl bloggers, the representation of marginalized and abject bodies through selfies and Instagram photos creates a large and visible archive of images and feelings that are widely available in contrast to the usual representations seen in mainstream media. When alternatives to bodies most commonly depicted in ad culture are circulated and celebrated on Instagram, they begin to shift the conversation outside of the smaller circles in which they originated. The popularization of these images can create the possibility for alternative representations of female bodies and female sexuality in mass media.

In her article on Instagram's content censorship policies, Magdalena Olszanowski describes how, even though Instagram excludes a lot of content, these parameters actually provide room for even more subversion. For example, Instagram does not allow women's nipples to be shown; yet Olszanowski (2014) describes the way one user got around this policy by photographing herself naked, covered in smaller photos of her own naked body: "censoring [her]self with [her] own naked body" (p. 88). Similarly, users will cover the un-showable bits of their bodies with red or black bars, not just as a way to avoid being censored, but also as a commentary on and resistance to those censorship policies. Olszanoski's article shows how people can use potentially restrictive social media platforms subversively in order "to destabilize [a dominant mode of communication's] repressive power," to create new bodies, new spaces and new communities (2014, p. 93).

Instagram users are creating whole archives of experiences, feelings and existences that resist the popular assumption that online activism is purely superficial with no real-world impact. The lived experiences of social media activists and feminist Instagram artists also prove this assumption false. Collins herself would argue that the importance of online activism is that it is not that different from "real" life:

> If the internet mimics real life, then there is no doubt that real life can mimic it. That if we allow ourselves to be silenced or censored, it can happen in real life too. That if an online society of people can censor your body, what stops them from doing so in real life? (Collins, 2013)

Collins' quotation here questions the popular fear that the Internet is "unreal" by beginning to break down the distinction between the virtual and the actual. I argue that there is no way to distinguish a "real" self from an online avatar and that it is actually impossible to divide the digital self from our offline identities. Our offline identities are tied up with the images of ourselves that we share. The networks that users participate in online impact their offline networks and vice versa. This is a process of continuous overlapping, where multiple identities are performed and experimented with both on and offline, that have been characterized by Zizi Papacharissi (2011), Nick Yee (2015), Malcolm R. Parks (2011) and others. It is not a new phenomenon to say that constructedness and performance are parts of our identity (see Jacques Derrida, Judith Butler, Erving Goffman). Therefore, it seems clear that selfie-expression (self-expression through selfies) would also be a key part of many people's identities, particularly when that self-expression is so tied up with affect and potential political identification—the "ability to engage in collective action" and have "shared rituals [and] social regulations" (Parks, 2011).

INSTAGRAM AS AN "ARCHIVE OF FEELING"

As Mehreen Kasana (2014) argues in "Feminisms and the social media sphere," "social media is that one large digital archiving domain where women can give voice to their aspirations and make bonds with other women, materialize activism in favor of their goals and be heard" (p. 247). Although in many cases the Internet is used to silence women and minority activists, as seen with harassment campaigns or online bullying, online activism can at least function as a form of *"collected* memory"—as a space "for a worldwide audience to bear witness to events that would never go uncensored in mainstream (Western) media" (Arthur, 2009, p. 71; Gies, 2008, p. 312).[1] What I propose is that these online archives not only represent collected memories but also feelings and experiences. Although I characterized affect as inarticulate earlier, it is important to also understand affect as an important connecting force that bridges the inarticulate gaps of meaning created by the complexities of identifying on the Internet. As Sara Ahmed (2010) describes in her chapter "Happy objects," affect is "what sticks, or what sustains or preserves the connections between ideas, value, and objects." Likewise, I argue that it is affect that pulls together the unique—but related—forms of identification occurring under the hashtag #sadgirls and creates this powerful archive of images and emotions.

In *An Archive of Feelings: Trauma, Sexuality, and Lesbian Public Cultures*, Ann Cvetkovich (2003) argues that queer trauma narratives should be archived to preserve and recognize marginalized experiences in order to prevent the erasure of these bodies and their stories. Although, as discussed earlier, online movements such as Sad Girl Theory can be quite exclusive of many marginalized groups and therefore might not be the best queer archives in and of themselves, there is still validity in how the

#sadgirl records and makes visible the experiences and feelings of many young feminists who might not have any other outlet. Other theories, such as those in Jamison's (2014), the "Grand Unified Theory of Female Pain," and Hedva's (2016), "Sick Woman Theory," are reflected in the more inclusive work of artists like Armitage and Vivian Fu, whose images become a part of this ever-growing online selfie archive counterpublic of experience and feelings.

The faults of the #sadgirl allow room for other artists to take over and improve on the space. As Sidonie Smith and Julia Watson write, Internet users are "simultaneously self-presenters, self-curators, consumers of others' lives, and bricoleurs of individual and collective subjectivities" (2014, p.92). The visual, online archive made possible by Instagram is inarticulate and ever-shifting because it is always being redefined. Like Jamison's claim that a woman in pain can be "just true," these online archives—despite their faults, exclusivity and lack of order—can still have a "just true" or authentic offline impact—they can still be "real" (2014). Cvetkovich (with Carland, 2014) writes that:

> Words like "original" and "authentic" are so loaded for us because we were taught to be suspicious of them, but the archive of feelings gives us permission to turn down the volume on the voice of critique and pay attention to the strong feelings that get attached to things.

These online archives have inspired more users to document themselves and others, grow out their armpit hair, criticize their lack of space in the archive and then force themselves into the record. As Olszanowski (2014) points out, Instagram is an exceptional space for users to make "their own space where there isn't space for them." In other words, to become the leaders of their own space. As complex, problematic and inarticulate an archive like the #sadgirl can be, there is undeniable value in the communities and visibility it can foster—the personal made public, collective and visible.

NOTE

1. The Internet can be a very unsafe space for women and minority activists. Although I do not get into detail about online harassment in this chapter, I considered articles by Janet Morahan-Martin (2004), Katherine Cross (2014), Shira Chess and Adrienne Shaw (2015), as well as first-hand responses from Instagram artists during my research.

REFERENCES

Ahmed, S. (2010), "Happy objects," in M. Gregg and G.J. Seigworth (eds), *The Affect Theory Reader*, Durham, NC: Duke University Press, pp. 29–51.

Alexander, L. (2015), "Good morning, user! Welcome to the new intimacy economy," *NY Mag*, accessed on 10 March 2016 at http://nymag.com/select all/2015/11/welcome-to-the-new-intimacy-economy.html.

Armitage, A. (2016), *@ladyist*, Instagram, accessed 10 March 2016 at https://www.instagram.com/ladyist/?hl=en.

Arthur, P. (2009), "Trauma online: Public exposure of personal grief and suffering," *Traumatology*, **15** (4), 65–75.

Barron, B. (2014), "Richard Prince, Audrey Wollen, and the sad girl theory," accessed 10 March 2016 at https://i-d.vice.com/en_gb/article/richard-prince-audrey-wollen-and-the-sad-girl-theory.

Chess, S. and A. Shaw (2015), "A conspiracy of fishes, or how we learned to stop worrying about #GamerGate and embrace hegemonic masculinity," *Journal of Broadcasting & Electronic Media*, **59** (1), 208–20.

Collins, P. (2013), "Why Instagram censored my body," *Huffpost Women*, accessed 10 March 2016 at http://www.huffingtonpost.com/petra-collins/why-instagram-censored-my-body_b_4118416.html.

Collins, P. and M. Beckles (2015), "Petra Collins gives us the 411 on her Art Basel exhibit about girl stuff," *Oyster Magazine*, 2 December, accessed 10 March 2016 at http://www.oystermag.com/petra-collins-gives-us-the-411-on-her-art-basel-ex hibit-about-girl-stuff.

Cross, K. (2014), "Ethics for cyborgs: On real harassment in an 'unreal' place," *Loading . . . The Journal of the Canadian Games Studies Association*, **8** (13), 4–21.

Cvetkovich, A. (2003), *An Archive of Feelings: Trauma, Sexuality, and Lesbian Public Cultures*, Durham, NC: Duke University Press.

Cvetkovich, A. and T.R. Carland (2014), "Sharing an archive of feelings: A conversation," *Art Journal*, **72** (2), 70–77.

Dobson, A.S. (2015), *Postfeminist Digital Cultures: Femininity, Social Media, and Self-Representation*, New York, NY: Palgrave Macmillan.

Fu, V. (2016), *@vivianisvulgar*, Instagram, accessed 10 March 2016 at https://www.instagram.com/vivianisvulgar/?hl=en.

Fu, V. (2016), *vivanfu.com*, accessed 1 July 2016 at http://vivianfu.com/.

Gerbaudo, P. (2012), *Tweets and the Streets: Social Media and Contemporary Activism*, London, UK: Pluto Press.

Gies, L. (2008), "How material are cyberbodies? Broadband Internet and embodied subjectivity," *Crime Media Culture*, **4**, 311–30.

Hedva, J. (2016), "Sick Woman Theory," *Mask Magazine*, accessed 10 March 2016 at http://www.maskmagazine.com/not-again/struggle/sick-woman-theory.

Jamison, L. (2014), "Grand Unified Theory of Female Pain," *VQR Online*, accessed 10 March 2016 at http://www.vqronline.org/essays-articles/2014/04/grand-unified-theory-female-pain.

Kasana, M. (2014), "Feminisms and the social media sphere," *Feminist Women's Studies Quarterly*, **42** (3/4), 236–49.

Keller, J. (2014), "Making activism accessible: Exploring girls' blogs as sites of contemporary feminist activism," in C. Mitchell and C. Rentschler (eds), *The Politics of Place: Contemporary Paradigms for Research in Girlhood Studies*, New York, NY: Berghahn Books.

Maschger, M. (2016), "Vivian Fu: Identity, relationships, & the power of selfies," *Bust*, accessed 1 July 2016 at http://bust.com/arts/12838-photographer-vivian-fu-on-identity-relationships-the-power-of-selfies.html.

McCluskey, M. (2016), "Instagram star Essena O'Neill breaks her silence on quitting social media," *Time,* 5 January, accessed 10 March 2016 at http://time.com/4167856/essena-oneill-breaks-silence-on-quitting-social-media/.

Morahan-Martin, J. (2004), "Women and the Internet: Promise and perils," *CyberPsychology & Behavior*, **3** (5), 683–91.

Murray, D.C. (2015), "Notes to self: The visual culture of selfies in the age of social media," *Consumption Markets & Culture*, **18** (6), 490–516.

Newell-Hanson, A. (2015), "Petra Collins and Madelyne Beckles curate a 'fuck boi funeral'," *I-d Vice*, 2 December, accessed 10 March 2016 at https://i-d.vice.com/en_us/article/petra-collins-and-madelyne-beckles-curate-a-fuck-boi-funeral.

O'Hagan, S. (2013), "Ana Mendieta: Death of an artist foretold in blood," *The Guardian*, 21 September, accessed 10 October 2016 at https://www.theguardian.com/artanddesign/2013/sep/22/ana-mendieta-artist-work-foretold-death.

Olszanowski, M. (2014), "Feminist self-imaging and Instagram: Tactics of circumventing sensorship," *Visual Communication Quarterly*, **21**, 83–95.

O'Neill, E. (2016), *@essenaoneill*, Instagram, accessed 10 March 2016 at https://www.instagram.com/essenaoneill/?hl=en.

Papacharissi, Z. (2011), "Conclusion: A networked self," *A Networked Self: Identity, Community and Culture on Social Network Sites*, New York, NY: Routledge.

Parks, M.R. (2011), "Social network sites as virtual communities," *A Networked Self: Identity, Community and Culture on Social Network Sites*, New York, NY: Routledge.

Seigworth, G.J. and M. Gregg (2010), "An inventory of shimmers," *The Affect Theory Reader*, Durham, NC: Duke University Press.

Senft, T.M. and N.K. Baym (2015), "What does the selfie say? Investigating a global phenomenon," *International Journal of Communication*, **9**, 1588–606.

Smith, S. and J. Watson (2014), "Virtually me: A toolkit about online self-presentation," in A. Poletti and J. Rak (eds), *Identity Technologies: Constructing the Self Online*, Madison, WI: University of Wisconsin Press.

Tunnicliffe, A. (2015), "Artist Audrey Wollen on the power of sadness," *Nylon*, 20 July, accessed 2010 March 2016 at http://www.nylon.com/articles/audrey-wollen-sad-girl-theory.

Wollen, A. (2016), *@audreywollen*, Instagram, accessed 10 March 2016 at https://www.instagram.com/audreywollen/?hl=en.

Yee, N. (2015), *The Proteus Paradox: How Online Gaming and Virtual Worlds Change Us—and How They Don't*, New Haven, CT: Yale University Press.

13. How light painters lead change through popular culture

Laura DelPrato

Imagine someone standing in front of a tripod and camera, holding a flashlight aimed towards the camera's lens in the darkness of night. The individual opens the camera shutter with a wireless remote, draws a figure in the air with the flashlight still facing the camera lens and closes the shutter upon the figure's completion. Through this process, the individual has created a long exposure photograph that reveals an image painted in light that could not have otherwise been seen in its entirety by someone watching the process from the side. This process is the essence of light painting, a form of light art that involves choreographing and recording the movement of light through space-time with long exposure photography.[1] The resulting photograph is a light painting, and the person leading the composition is the light painter. Light painting is an emerging art form in popular culture whose works and community provide valuable examples of leadership in the digital age.

While light painting as a technique dates back to the 1930s (Page, 2017), many artists who practice it as a primary form of expression did not emerge until the early 2000s. The creation of social media platforms and digital technology catalyzed the large-scale emergence of light painters and set the stage for an active online community. Light painters leveraged these social media platforms to build relationships and promote their work as an independent art form. Ultimately, both the art and community of light painting incorporate elements of pop culture into narratives and practices that illuminate the desire and ability to transform place into space, using light and pixels to give purpose, unity and meaning to an increasingly fractured and digitized world. Light painters, in particular, cultivate spatial-temporal awareness to demonstrate ways people can engage in meaningful, holistic interactions both with each other and the world around them, with the ultimate goal of achieving global harmony and synergy. Furthermore, by looking at light painting and the development of the community around it as an example of leadership, we can learn how to productively collaborate across cultures to achieve positive social change.

LIGHT PAINTING THEORY—THE ART

Light painting as an art blends digital technology and interaction with the physical world to promote harmony and alignment in modern society. Responding to art theory from the early 1900s, light painting has advanced artistic expression by incorporating aspects of time and movement that are integral to the human condition. In particular, light painting suggests that one of the most unique aspects of humanity is imagination and the ability to choose to interpret the world in a positive light. Furthermore, light painting encourages people to not only interpret the world in a positive way, but also to see possibilities and actively transform them into positive social change.

To understand how light painting evolved artistic expression in the technological age, one must be familiar with earlier concepts of art theory responding to earlier advancements in technology. In the 1920s and 1930s, Hungarian artist László Moholy-Nagy promoted a theory of photography called "the new vision" that emphasized the need for photography to develop its own unique theory separate from that of painting. Moholy-Nagy argued that artists should integrate art, science and technology in artistic works (Kirkpatrick, 1988, pp. 63–76). In his book *Malerei, Photographie, Film* (*Painting, Photography, Film*), he emphasized that art needed to include an element of space-time, a dimension that painting alone lacked (Marien, 2011). In space-time, space and time are relative rather than fixed coordinates. As art historian Jeannine Fiedler explains, "the champions of the New Vision demanded that the [modern man] actively seize the speeding space-time continuum, bursting with energy, by making machines productive according to his needs" (Moholy-Nagy et al., 2006). In the mid-1930s, Moholy-Nagy intentionally created artistic long exposure photographs of metallic sculptures that emphasized light and movement. As Churkin (n.d.) notes, such works became known as representations of "lumino-kinetic art." According to Rycroft (2012), kinetic art refers to "visual art that represents or reproduces real or illusory movement," and the added prefix "lumino" makes the phrase refer to the movement of light specifically. Although the kinetic art movement occurred on a small scale, its emphasis on the representation of movement through time aligns with Moholy-Nagy's new vision and makes his theory relevant to the work of contemporary light painters.

Light painting has evolved Moholy-Nagy's vision and lumino-kinetic art in a way that responds to popular culture and the modern technologically advanced world. This emphasis on integrating art and technology also reflects the way that contemporary light painters leverage social media to share their art, as well as how they use long exposure photography to emphasize the need to increase human interaction with the physical world. The light painting process itself blends technology with art as light painters use the camera as a tool to capture choreographed light performances that combine physical and photographic arts into a single composite image. Based on Moholy-Nagy's integration of art, science, technology and space-time, "Fourth Space" will be used as an overarching theory to analyze light painting artwork. Fourth Space is a concept that helps explain the significance of the unique space that light painters create during the artistic process. The creation of this space distinguishes light painting from photography and offers a unique way to reflect upon the advancement of technology and globalization in the twenty-first century.

To expand the concept of Fourth Space further, the term "Fourth" relates Fourth Space to scientific conceptions of physical dimensions. In general, the number in front of a physical dimension indicates the number of coordinates necessary to define the location of an object within that dimension. For example, objects in the first dimension can have a position along a single axis, while objects defined by the second dimension can have a position along two orthogonal axes. Three-dimensional objects have a position along three orthogonal axes (length, width and depth), while four-dimensional objects have a fourth coordinate, space-time. Although we live in a four-dimensional world, we can only perceive three dimensions at any given moment; consequently, four-dimensional objects are very difficult to conceptualize. Nonetheless, Fourth Space allows light painters to interact with the fourth dimension and create works of art that reflect such activity. Specifically, light painting's Fourth Space is a two-dimensional representation of three-dimensional objects moving through the fourth dimension, a photographic documentation of the artistic process over time.

To conceptualize this movement of three-dimensional objects moving through the fourth dimension, consider a three-dimensional car. In a light painting, the viewer can perceive the movement of a three-dimensional object through the fourth dimension as a single "stretch instant" in time. Think of the "stretch instant" as a car stretched out through time. The "stretch" car exists at all instants within the slice of time captured during the long exposure photograph. Accordingly, the stretch instant allows us to see all of the locations through which the car traveled, and we can return to different points in time by looking at the image. The "stretch" car as subject exists in several moments of time and yet in no single moment of time. Consequently, the viewer can "see" the evidence of how three-dimensional objects move through space-time by observing light painting images. One might say that the viewer of a light painting can "see" spatial travel through time.

To enter and create Fourth Space, the light painter must possess a strong spatial-temporal awareness that allows her to conceptualize and interact with the fourth dimension. One of the easiest ways to relate this awareness to the physical act of light painting is to think of the flashlight as a paintbrush and darkness as a three-dimensional canvas. As in sculpture, the light painter must be aware of depth when she paints with light. Similar to painting, the light painter must be aware of the color of light or "paint" she chooses and the size of the brush or light. However, what is unique to the act of painting with light, instead of with pigment, is the change in intensity of light with the change in time of exposure. If a painter holds her paintbrush on a page, a certain amount of paint adheres to the paper and then ceases to change. When a light painter holds a flashlight towards a camera during a long exposure, the intensity of her light increases as the time of the exposure increases. Essentially, the light painter is still painting even when she stands still during the long exposure. Thus, light painters must connect with the physical world to develop the spatial temporal-awareness necessary to create Fourth Space.

The second part of Fourth Space involves the concept of space. The term "space" relates to the way light painters conceptualize their interactions with the world. More specifically, "space" is the environment that results from actions that occur within a particular geographic location. As Daphne Spain (1992) suggests, "'space' distinct from place only exists because social processes exist" (p. 5). It is "the actions that people take in a space that give it a special rather than geographical valence" (Spain, 1992, p. 5). This is also true in digital space. For instance, when people talk about what happens in a Facebook group online, they do not mean the physical location of the servers that store digital data. Instead, they mean what happens in "cyberspace," or a digital representation of space defined by a particular online community. Similarly, light painters create space out of place through the act of light painting by creating meaning through the artistic process. It is in Fourth Space that this transformation occurs.

In dimensional terms, place is location in the four-dimensional world defined by three coordinates—longitude, latitude and altitude. Inadvertently, Spain invokes the fourth dimension in her concept of space by tying space to social interaction. In order for events or interactions to occur, they must take up time, which means that space must also possess a space-time dimension. In Spain's conception, space is sacred because it contains particular social interactions that define it. From a light painter's perspective, place is three dimensional, lacking human interaction, while space is four dimensional, since it has gained meaning through interaction over time. Therefore, Fourth Space gains its sacredness from the physical act of light painting.

Finally, the theoretical and cultural impact of Fourth Space also relates to Homi Bhabha's theory of Third Space. Bhabha presents Third Space as an environment where individuals can resolve the conflicting identities that result from globalization. He explains, "My purpose here is to define the space of the inscription or writing of identity" (Bhabha, 1994, p. 49). As in Spain's definition of space, Bhabha emphasizes that particular actions that occur in a location define the essence of the environment. He further describes the challenge that Third Space strives to resolve as "we are faced with a dimension of doubling; a spatialization of the subject" (Bhabha, 1994, p. 49). Thinking in terms of dimensions, the doubling to which Bhabha refers can be thought of as dual cultural identities. According to his theory, one cannot simply find identity in a two-dimensional place where the two identities exist side by side in contrast to each other. Instead, one needs to link the two identities as a whole with a third dimension, thus "spatializing" the subject by adding a third dimension where the two identities harmonize to become one entity, one identity. This process also takes time, and, as a result, Third Space is not a physical setting on Earth, but instead a four-dimensional locus in space-time that depends upon action to obtain its sacredness. While the process of resolving identity creates Third Space, the act of light painting extends that articulation of global identity into Fourth Space.

In Fourth Space, the goal of light painting is not to choose an individual identity in a particular moment, but to understand humanity as a whole throughout time. Instead of "resolving" identity, light painters create and maintain multiple identities in Fourth Space. For instance, they are light painter, artist, technician, director, subject and photographer all at the same time. Fourth Space allows light painters to explore a universal human identity that unites us in a world that is constantly undergoing globalizing change. By focusing on unique human qualities such as imagination, light painting transcends cultural, language and temporal barriers that segregate individuals in order to achieve global harmony. This universal identity of humanity not only emphasizes common characteristics, but also highlights them in a positive way. In particular, light painting illuminates the possible realities we can achieve if we choose to interpret our environment in a particular way. Consequently, Fourth Space goes deeper into the fourth dimension than Third Space and explores what it means to be human and constantly changing through space-time rather than resolving individual identity at one point in time.

The creation of Fourth Space demonstrates how light painting has evolved art theory in the twenty-first century. Reflective of Moholy-Nagy's new vision and the kinetic art movement, light painters integrate science, technology and the fourth dimension through artistic works to tell stories that can more easily reflect human interaction with space-time. The emphasis of the fourth dimension and a universal human identity empowers light painting art to respond to modern society in a form that more closely mirrors its content. The birth of the light painting community itself occurred in a digital space, reflective of the place to space transformation its artwork creates. Ultimately, Fourth Space offers an opportunity for both light painters and viewers to more intentionally engage in the evolution of society through space-time. Specifically, light painters use international communication and collaboration to engage people in timeless tales represented in a modern, global context that reflects the universality of the human condition.

Overall, light painting as an art aims to achieve global harmony by illuminating humanity's ability to create positive change in an increasingly global and digital environment. The art strives to unite humanity through four main functions: transforming object into subject, transforming place into space, illuminating the intangible and infusing magic into the mundane. The art itself has led change in artistic expression and serves as an example through which society can learn to better visualize the positive changes that may be possible with proper collaboration, communication and motivation.

FOURTH SPACE NARRATIVES IN POPULAR CULTURE

Light painting expands its leadership beyond the art community by incorporating popular culture subjects into Fourth Space narratives, which include fantastic elements and infuse magic into the mundane, emphasizing the power of creativity and the human imagination to transform the world. Combined with the spatial-temporal awareness that light painters cultivate, such images promote a philosophy similar to happiness engineering through which all humans can engage in meaningful, holistic interactions with each other and the world around them (Baucells and Sarin, 2012). While light painters do not suggest that everyone should physically engage in the act of light painting, their artwork illuminates the positive change people can create by transforming place into space, whether through art, cultural practice or another form of social interaction. Ultimately, light painting incorporates elements of pop culture into narratives that illustrate the ability to cultivate proactive and creative mindsets with the potential to create positive social change.

Light painters incorporate numerous popular culture subjects from movies, television series and video games into Fourth Space narratives in order to infuse the magic of these fantasy media into the mundane, everyday world. In typical light painting images, dinosaurs roam freely, trash cans transform into monsters, aliens invade Earth and Pacman meets the Human Torch. Light painters have even illuminated specific characters and objects from media such as the Mach 5 from the television series *Speed Racer* (1967–68), Mario from the *Super Mario* video game (1985), Pikmin from the *Pikmin* video game (2001), aliens from the *Space Invaders* video game (1978), Ghostbusters from the television and film series (1984, 2016) and many others. Though many of the subjects are specific to popular culture in the twenty-first century, themes emerge that link such modern stories to more timeless tales, reflective of how light painting seeks to investigate a universal human identity throughout time. The most prevalent themes include "death," "time travel," "aliens and UFOs," "myths and legends," "gods and religion," "magic powers" and what will be called "creature creations," a trend in which light painters invent or reinvent creatures out of their own imaginations and the environment around them.

Illuminating universal themes, Fourth Space narratives tend to depict the human condition from a positive perspective. For instance, death becomes a reason to celebrate life rather than a reason to be cautious or afraid to the point of failing to live life to the fullest. Aliens and other creatures of the unknown come in peace to expand our understanding of the universe. Creature creations explore the ability to change perspective and create someone or something out of an otherwise inanimate object or even out of proverbial "thin air." Overall, such Fourth Space narratives seek to give life and soul to timeless tales and to unite the global community of human beings through the human imagination. While different cultures may have unique folklore that was once specific to a particular geographical location, such as the kraken, light painters illuminate these archetypes in a modern context, sharing the digital interpretation with a more global community. Instead of being limited to a particular culture, light painters illuminate these stories to transcend physical boundaries and enhance global communication. By focusing on timeless tales of the human imagination and our capacity to view the world in a positive light, we can reify positive visions of both the present and potential future.

Such an approach to storytelling supports the idea that humans can control the way they choose to perceive the world. This idea of being mindful about the way we interpret the world around us reflects recent research in positive psychology and happiness engineering, as well as the spatial-temporal awareness light painters cultivate through the practice of light painting. Manel Baucells and Rakesh Sarin (2012) explain that happiness is "the state of mind that comes from feeling that you are no longer yearning for some unmet need" and suggest that readers "reframe at least one experience from negative to positive" every day to increase their level of happiness (p. 79). This emphasis on transforming internal perceptions instead of striving to change external factors over which we often have little control is similar to the place to space transformations of light painting. Light paintings offer transformed perspectives of the real world that allow us to marvel at things we might otherwise miss due to the focus on everyday tasks. By focusing on the possible realities that light paintings illuminate, we can visualize and act upon our ability to create positive change. As a result, light painting encourages individuals to cultivate an internal locus of control and collaborate with others to achieve our potential as both individuals and as the human race at large.

Additionally, light paintings illuminate figments of the human imagination that allow us to reconnect with the childlike creativity that we may have lost in the process of maturing into adulthood. Such images encourage us to not only explore imagination but also to play. Fourth Space narratives assert that adults can play and still fulfill their adult responsibilities. In fact, positive psychology and happiness engineering also encourage people to play in order to achieve a more meaningful, fulfilling and holistic lifestyle. As psychologist Mihaly Csíkszentmihályi suggests, we can "create more happiness by structuring real work like game work" and solve our most pressing problems like "depression, helplessness, social alienation, and the sense that nothing we do truly matters" (McGonigal, 2011, p. 36). Accordingly, light paintings invite us to play with our childhood dreams, participate in ancient myths and develop our own super powers to unite humanity in a globalizing digital world. By uniting humans through universal experiences, light painting helps society harmonize and synergize across cultures to develop innovative solutions to challenges, instead of becoming the challenge.

While light painters are not suggesting that everyone should physically engage in the act of light painting, their artwork illuminates the magic that humans can infuse into the mundane by transforming place into space and the social change that can result. For example, consider the Fourth Space narrative in Stephen Humpleby's *Hide and Seek* light painting (2014), which explores the way humans relate to and interact with nature. His image illustrates the way people play with nature that simultaneously evokes awe and gives significance to the presence of humanity in the universe. While the Milky Way's large size overpowers the Earth, the rock, the light orb and human beings on a physical scale, the intensity of the light orb gives humans a vibrant significance.

Hide and Seek reifies the awe that we feel in the presence of nature by highlighting its large physical size and tangible permanence. The universe is more durable than humanity both in terms of the length of its physical existence and its physical state. The boulder and stars in the images will

Figure 13.1   Hide and Seek by Stephen Humpleby

have a physical form much longer than a single human life and even longer than the lifetime of the human species. The light orb serves as the primary trace of human existence and is covered by the boulder, as nature has great power to dictate the agency of the human species and protect it from the life-threatening conditions outside of the Earth's atmosphere. The overall composition invokes a respect for the power of nature and reifies the awe that we often feel in connection to it.

While evoking an awe of nature, *Hide and Seek* assigns important significance to humans in relation to the universe. Although the universe is physically vast and impressive, the intangible significance of humans is impressive, as well. The light orb hiding behind the large boulder may be small in size relative to the universe, but its vibrancy asserts a bright voice for humanity. Our lives take on intangible forms that become as timeless as nature itself. The presence of humanity inspires awe in another sense;

even though we are small and fragile in comparison to materials of nature like boulders and stars, we are powerfully present. In leadership terms, the image shows the power and influence we have on the environment and suggests that we should integrate and harmonize with nature, rather than try to assert a false sense of control over it. Such imagery also encourages viewers to cultivate an inner locus of control, so that more people will strive to create positive change, rather than stagnate due to the belief that one person is too small to make a significant impact. Humpleby himself made an impact by choosing to use light painting for this artistic expression, a form of art that does not negatively impact the environment, rather than draw graffiti on the rock or damage the natural environment. By simply "leaving no trace," Humpleby chose to support the environment, a choice that others can easily make, too, by simply be aware and intentional about our actions.

The title and composition of *Hide and Seek* emphasize our human ability to change perspective of the world around us. Humpleby chooses to compose the image from an angle that makes the image resemble a solar eclipse as the large boulder blocks the light orb. An eclipse itself is a symbol of the power of perception. Due to the specific angle of this photo, the boulder appears to be bigger than the light orb as it covers it. From a different perspective, the light orb could be bigger than the boulder as the sun is much bigger than the moon in reality. Similarly, the boulder could be read as a barrier to humans' agency, yet the playful imagery and title turn the relationship between humans and nature into a playful game when we change our perspective. It is in this intentional choice of perspective that the images allow us to view humans as small in physical size, yet significant with respect to the universe. Similarly, leaders can have a seismic impact on a project based on the way both they and their followers interpret a situation. By choosing to look at nature as a gift and form of protection, rather than an obstacle to human agency, humanity can develop an appreciation for nature and incite change to create environmentally friendly solutions to challenges.

Jediimind's *Look out Mario! You've got company!!* (2012) is a light painting that uses a Fourth Space narrative to demonstrate that humans can play and engage in meaningful interactions with each other and the world around them in order to increase well-being and collaborate with others. In the Fourth Space narrative, Jediimind transforms the physical setting of a metal bridge into an intangible journey through pop culture. While many viewers will immediately notice the title's reference to Nintendo's video game character Mario, Jediimind's choice of a bridge for the light painting's physical location adds symbolic depth. Bridges serve as transportation networks that link people from different locations together. Similarly, video games and elements of popular culture, such as Mario, a globally popular video game figure created in Japan and modeled after an Italian immigrant to the United States, serve as digital immaterial networks that unite people from different places and cultures together. Both physical bridges and intangible networks of pop culture provide links that connect people to one another. Rather than passively watch the *Mario* television series or play the *Super Mario* video game alone, Jediimind's narrative shows how humans can bond over popular culture stories and blend technology with the physical world to infuse magic into the mundane.

By infusing magic into the mundane, Jediimind's Fourth Space narrative allows humans to more holistically engage in the universal human activity of play. Like Mario, we all will face obstacles, such as Koopa Troopas and Piranha Plants, which may interfere with the pursuit of our goals. Additionally, we may encounter bridges or transitions in life where we are not sure what lies on the other side. Yet following Mario's lead, we can choose to persevere and overcome those challenges. Instead of giving up and letting Bowser hold Princess Peach prisoner, we can choose to accept the hero's journey and take responsibility for our actions. In life, we may not be able to see what lies on the other side of the bridge, but we can choose to view our surroundings in a positive perspective and adapt to change. Similarly, like the two women interacting with the illuminated Mario world in Jediimind's light painting, we can choose to play and see possibilities rather than focus on what appears to be reality. By thinking of life as a fun game with different challenges to overcome at every level, we can better enjoy our journey through it. Furthermore, we can interact with others in a positive way by partnering with them along our journeys. *Look out Mario! You've got company!!* challenges viewers to learn to see possibilities in unconventional places, play in the mundane world and embrace life in a positive way.

By creating Fourth Space and exploring a universal human identity, light painters invite people to reflect upon the way society responds to the advancement of technology and globalization. Rather than fight technological progress and globalization, light painters' art suggests that human beings can harmonize with technology, as Jediimind shows in his image. In particular, the spatial-temporal awareness that light painters cultivate demonstrates ways people can engage in meaningful, holistic interactions with each other, with technology and with the world around them to transform place into space and encourage people to take a positive outlook on their ability to impact society.

Furthermore, and most importantly, light painters create Fourth Space narratives that invite us to find beauty in urban decay, connect with nature and reconnect with our childlike creativity through play and the deliberate

Figure 13.2   Lookout Mario! You've got company!! by Jediimind

choice to view life from a positive perspective. They challenge us to embrace life holistically and take responsibility for our happiness by actively pursuing our passions and being mindful of the way we interpret the external world. The "bigger mission" that light painting strives to introduce is the ability to appreciate the interconnectedness and universality of the human condition even in the twenty-first century (McGonigal, 2011, p. 36). In leadership terms, light painting encourages leaders and followers to focus on shared experiences that transcend cultural and physical boundaries in order to collaborate to achieve positive social change and global harmony. Leaders, in particular, can cultivate strong, positive visions of the future to engage followers in a shared mission.

LIGHT PAINTING COMMUNITY AS A MODEL OF LEADERSHIP

With the invention of the World Wide Web, the rise of Web 2.0 and the advent of the affordable digital camera, the social media age helped light painting emerge as an independent art form and simultaneously created a connected environment appropriate for the birth of several online communities. We can learn real-world leadership lessons by examining these online communities to determine examples of what does and does not work. The light painting community has excellent examples of effective leadership and positive impact of community engagement. Before the launch of Flickr in 2004, most light painters were isolated from each other unless they lived in close geographical proximity.[2] While they were often able to post their images to websites if they were practicing artists, such outlets did not allow light painters to interact with each other on a personal level so easily. Social media platforms, such as Flickr and Facebook, helped bridge this physical gap by creating an online space where light painters could share their work. For example, Flickr created an online community where photographers could upload their still photographs and gain feedback from other members. It provided various capabilities that allowed for interaction on multiple levels, such as the ability to create online groups with other users where members could post photos of a similar characteristic in the same place. The groups also provided forums where members could discuss techniques, tools and resources, which enabled members to learn from one another and develop common techniques.

While Flickr and the Internet in general fostered connections between artists, light painters specifically leveraged social media platforms to bridge physical gaps and create a supportive community focused on their chosen form of art. In April 2008, photographer Trevor Williams took advantage of Flickr's social capabilities by creating the Flickr light painting group called Light Junkies (2008).[3] The creation of Light Junkies led to a thriving online community where light painters shared their works, ideas and resources with each other to promote their collective creative potential. Williams, known as TDUB303 on Flickr, used the Light Junkies group to lead the community in a way that cultivated artistic creativity and member engagement. In the description of the group, he emphasized that its purpose was to be an inspirational environment where light painters could share ideas and learn from each other: "The more people we have the more inspiration and knowledge we will gain so try to invite new people so we can grow this group into a great resource for techniques and inspiration" (Light Junkies, 2008). Such a description paved the way for the creation of a supportive and collaborative community. This intentional choice to foster collaboration and support, rather than safeguard individual discoveries, allowed light painters to exponentially increase the speed with which they collectively gained knowledge. Had Williams not intentionally created this culture, artists might have used the group as simply a forum to showcase their masterpieces and not share their artistic discoveries, slowing the collective progress of the group.

Williams also created multiple tutorials and led several discussions aimed at increasing member engagement. The group currently has over 600 discussion threads and an up-to-date discussion directory that helps members navigate through the group's forum. Following Williams' collaborative leadership example, other avid light painters started to lead their own discussions, and Light Junkies evolved to become one of the main communication and collaboration outlets for the light painting community. In one interview, light painter Jeremy Jackson, known as Tackyshack, reflected, "It wasn't until I discovered the light junkies Flickr group back in 2008 that I figured out what light painting was, and even more blown away by what others had already done with the art form. From that point on I was hooked" (Light Junkies, 2008). Since 2008, numerous other online light painting groups have emerged on both Flickr and Facebook, as well as lightpaintingphotography.com, a website founded by light painter Jason D. Page dedicated to sharing the most current light painting news.

In addition to using social media to share a wealth of knowledge and resources, light painters use it to create opportunities for artistic collaboration. For instance, light painters in the Light Junkies group created the LJ Drinks Menu thread, where members contributed light paintings of their favorite types of drinks, including the recipes. Today, the LJ Drinks Menu includes over 70 illuminated beverages (Petersen, 2014). Additionally, five prominent light painters, Jeremy Jackson, Aaron Bauer, Dennis Calvert, Mike Ross and Johnny Dickerson, united to host a light painting booth at FloydFest in Virginia in 2010 (Light Junkies, 2009). Such in-person collaborations strengthened the online light painting community and demonstrate the potential impact of online community-building in "real world" spaces. One notable collaboration involved a group of 12 artists, East Coast Light Painters, who collaborated to light paint 200 light orbs in a single image, which became a Guinness World Record on 19 July 2014 (Bauer, n.d.). East Coast Light Painters' large-scale collaboration demonstrates both how social media facilitated light painter interaction and how light painters leveraged it to collaborate. Learning from the light painting community, others can use social media as a tool to communicate and catalyze real-world interaction. Furthermore, this example of leadership encourages others to not only meet in person, but also plan more meaningful and purposeful "real-world" interactions to accomplish specific goals. If light painters can achieve a world record through online collaboration and dedication to transforming that interaction to real world change, imagine what other groups might be able to accomplish.

Around 2010, light painters came together and used social media to create an international light painting community known as the Light Painting World Alliance. To lead this initiative, Sergey Churkin sent out Flickr mail messages to several light painters active in the online Flickr community. He hoped to receive feedback about the possibility of forming an official light painting alliance that would promote the art form on a global scale. After receiving encouragement from several members, Churkin launched the official Light Painting World Alliance (LPWA) website in 2012. Since then, the LPWA has created annual action plans available in 13 different languages. In addition to providing direction and guidance, LPWA has made several notable achievements. One of the most prominent achievements is the light painting world exhibition, five of which have occurred as of May 2016 (Page, 2017). Such activity in the light painting community demonstrates how the Internet and social media facilitated international collaboration among artists of an emerging art form. Using the light painting community as an example of leadership, leaders can learn to specifically target followers who have expressed interest in a particular mission to gain buy-in to accomplish common goals. Rather than impose a particular strategy or vision over others, leaders can intentionally collaborate and include participants of diverse backgrounds and perspectives to create a common vision and alliance. Furthermore, we can choose to harmonize with others through common interests and value diversity as a way to increase knowledge, rather than clash due to differences.

Additionally, the light painting community also leverages social media to share art with the public and engage followers. Anyone with access to the Internet can see the images posted in Light Junkies on Flickr because it is a public group and, depending on specific users' privacy settings, the public can usually see images uploaded to individual users' photo streams. Online and social media platforms, such as Flickr, Facebook and Instagram, have empowered light painters to gain recognition for their artwork at an accelerated rate—for instance, light painter Darius Twin has over 70,000 followers on Instagram—that would not have previously been possible. Darius Twin's following is significant because it illustrates how leaders can effectively engage with others to gain a following. Darius Twin has built his following over several years, posting images consistently and responding to viewer feedback. By collaborating with audience responses and establishing a strong personal brand, Darius Twin has been able to gain significant support and has even attracted companies such as Honda, Reebok and Apple to request commissioned light painting work. By consistently delivering high quality work, engaging with followers and successfully collaborating with commission partners, Darius Twin has significantly contributed to the advancement of light painting. Completing projects commissioned by major brands, Darius Twin has both set a precedent for valuing light painting monetarily and gaining exposure so that other companies see the value of light painting and want to commission additional artists. Following Darius Twin's lead, non-light painting leaders can engage with followers, build a consistent brand over time and use that brand to create positive social change.

Overall, social media created the opportunity for large-scale growth of the light painting community, and light painters take advantage of this opportunity by using collaborative leadership to help establish light painting as an independent art. Light painting leaders establish creative cultures of experimentation, collaboration and open sharing of ideas. Valuing knowledge as power, light painters openly share information about the tools and techniques they use and increase the rate at which their art advances. This supportive community not only evolves light painting works, but also encourages new members to join the growing light painting community. Such methods also attract non-light painter followings of light painting art, thus establishing light painting as an emerging and growing independent form of light art. By following the light painting community's example, others too can engage followers, increase community growth and achieve social change.

NOTES

1. See https://www.flickr.com/groups/lightjunkies/pool/ for some examples of light painting.
2. Flickr is an online community where photographers can share and comment on photographs. Light Junkies: https://www.flickr.com/groups/lightjunkies/pool/.

REFERENCES

Baucells, M. and R. Sarin (2012), *Engineering Happiness: A New Approach for Building a Joyful Life*, Berkeley, CA: University of California Press.
Bauer, A. (n.d.), "FloydFest 9 2010," [Digital Image Album] Flickr, accessed 30 July 30 2016 at https://www.flickr.com/photos/drtongs/sets/72157624471936701.
Bhabha, H.K. (1994), *The Location of Culture*, New York, NY: Routledge, accessed 11 September 2012 at http://www9.georgetown.edu/faculty/irvinem/theory/Bhabha-LocationofCulture-chaps.pdf.
Churkin, S. (n.d.), "Painting with light – How it all began (part one)," Light Painting World Alliance, accessed 31 July 2016 at http://www.lpwalliance.com/index2.php?type=publicationview&id=15.
Ghostbusters (1984), [Film] Ivan Reiman (director), USA: Columbia Pictures.
Ghostbusters (2016), [Film] Paul Feig (director), USA: Sony Pictures.
Humpleby, S. (2014), "Hide and Seek," [Digital Image], Flickr, 21 May, accessed 30 April 2014 at https://www.flickr.com/photos/picturesbysteve/12878860044/.
Jediimind (2012), "Look out Mario! You've got company!!," [Digital Image], Flickr, 21 May, accessed 30 April 2014 at https://www.flickr.com/photos/jediimind/7241386152/.
Kirkpatrick, D. (1988), "Time and space in the work of László Moholy-Nagy," *Hungarian Studies Review*, Spring 1988, **XV** (1), 63–76.
Light Junkies (2008), "Overview," Flickr, accessed 31 July 2016 at https://www.flickr.com/groups/lightjunkies/.
Light Junkies (2009), "The LJ Drinks Menu," Flickr, accessed 28 July 2016 at https://www.flickr.com/groups/694160@N25/discuss/72157617920883557/.
Light Painting World Alliance (2016), "23.05.2016 5th LPWA exhibition total list of participants," Light Painting World Alliance Events, 23 May, accessed 30 July 2016 at http://www.lpwalliance.com/event/87.
Marien, M.W. (2011), *Photography: A Cultural History*, 3rd ed., Upper Saddle River, NJ: Pearson Prentice Hall.
McGonigal, J. (2011), *Reality Is Broken: Why Games Make Us Better and How They Can Change the World*, New York, NY: Penguin Books.
Moholy-Nagy, L., J. Fiedler and H. Moholy-Nagy (2006), *László Moholy-Nagy: Color in Transparency: Photographic Experiments in Color 1934-1946 = Fotografische Experimente in Farbe 1934–1946*, 1st ed., Göttingen: Steidl; Berlin: Bauhaus-Archiv.
Page, J.D. (2015), "Light painting Guinness World Record, 200 Orbs," *Light Painting Photography*, accessed 27 February 2015 at http://lightpaintingphotography.com/light-painting-photography/light-painting-guinness-world-record-200-orbs/.
Page, J.D. (2017), "Light painting history," *Light Painting Photography*, accessed 30 July 2016 at http://lightpaintingphotography.com/light-painting-history/.

Petersen, C. (2014), "Tackyshack's epic light masterpieces are a feat of DIY ingenuity," *The Creators Project*, accessed 20 January 2014 at http://thecreatorspro ject.vice.com/en_uk/blog/tackyshacks-epic-light-masterpieces-are-a-feat-of-diy-in genuity.

Pikmin (2001), Nintendo [Video Game], Japan: Nintendo.

Rycroft, S. (2012), "Art and micro-cosmos: Kinetic art and mid-20th-century cosmology," *Cultural Geographies* **19** (4), 447–67. doi:10.1177/1474474012447538.

Space Invaders (1978), Video Computer System [Video Game], Japan: Taito.

Spain, D. (1992), *Gendered Spaces*, Chapel Hill, NC: University of North Carolina Press.

Speed Racer (1967–68), Fuji TV [Television Series], Japan: Tatsunoko Production.

Super Mario (1985), Nintendo [Video Game], Japan: Nintendo.

14. Beyond bans and beyond the classroom: Wikipedia, leadership and social change in higher education

Holly Connell Schaaf

INTRODUCTION TO WIKIPEDIA

A prominent declaration on the main page of Wikipedia's English-language version beckons users: "Welcome to Wikipedia, the free encyclopedia that anyone can edit" (Wikipedia, 2017b). Visitors wishing to heed this call gain further information through various pages on the website, including "Contributing to Wikipedia," which enticingly affirms:

> You do not even have to log in to edit articles on Wikipedia. Just about anyone can edit almost any article at any given time, even without logging in. However, creating an account is free and has several benefits (for example, the ability to create pages, upload media and edit without one's IP address being visible to the public). (Wikipedia, 2017a)

Those who do not create a Wikipedia account can make edits that are attributed to their IP addresses, numbers that identify particular computers or other devices within networks. Once registered, edits that users make are publicly attributed to usernames they choose rather than IP addresses. This system means that while editors can choose not to create an account, the website can still monitor sources of change to articles, an approach that enables broader participation while avoiding risks of absolute anonymity.

Wikipedia promotes itself as a collaborative collective always eager for new members. "Contributing to Wikipedia" explains that the site was created by:

> thousands of editors' contributions, each one bringing something different to the table, whether it be researching skills, technical expertise, writing prowess or tidbits of information, but most importantly a willingness to help. Nobody owns articles, so if you see a problem that you can fix, do so. (Wikipedia, 2017a)

This invitation affirms that diverse skills are prized as part of the collective effort and asserts the rights of new users to revise articles because no one person or group controls them. In addition to directly revising articles, Wikipedia's editors can also click on "Talk" tabs at the top of articles, which allow them to converse with collaborators about revising parts of that article or to cooperatively plan more comprehensive strategies for adding content.

Users have freedom to edit and many decisions about pages are reached through egalitarian consensus building, but Wikipedia does have a complex structure of administrators who deal with vandalism and resolve disputes that the users involved cannot. Dariusz Jemielniak in *Common Knowledge?: An Ethnography of Wikipedia* concedes that there is "[s]tatus, power, and hierarchy enactment in a community so officially antihierarchical" (Jemielniak, 2014, p. 6), but ultimately reveals the power of consensus to resolve most disagreements. In addition to Wikipedia's human editors, he acknowledges that "some Wikipedias employ bots (software scripts)" to revert vandalism, to perform other basic edits, and, even, "to automatically create articles . . . This expansion strategy has been used by most Wikipedias since October 2002, when a bot added thirty thousand stubs on American cities and towns to the English Wikipedia in little over a week" (Jemielniak, 2014, pp. 12–13). Although the nature of Wikipedia means that articles in their early phases may have errors and bias, Jemielniak (2014) affirms the power of the collective to achieve revisions so that "[i]n general, any purposeful, long-term universal bias on Wikipedia, detouring from the dominant beliefs of the general academic and para-academic community, does not prevail" (p. 5).

Despite the work of editors, administrators and bots to correct errors and resolve most bias, Wikipedia's creation by volunteers rather than paid experts who must follow mandates of one central authority means that it "routinely reflects the interests of its contributors and not necessarily that of the general audience of English speaking readers" (Rand, 2010, p. 926). For example, "there is dense coverage of literature topics but this is artificially emphasized by the presence of long articles on the Harry Potter series" (Rand, 2010, p. 926). This freedom to write about popular culture topics without scholarly oversight has caused some academics to ban use of Wikipedia in their classes but has also contributed to the website's astounding growth since its 2001 inception. Beyond its own success, Wikipedia's model has also inspired other wikis focused on diverse popular culture phenomena. Numerous forms of popular culture from film to fan fiction have also recently found expanded roles in university classrooms, becoming acceptable topics not only for traditional thesis-driven papers, but also making their presence felt as genres in which to work directly. Wikipedia has taken on new roles of this kind, as well.

In order to explore how the nature of leadership in college classrooms shapes the decisions university faculty make about Wikipedia's inclusion in their courses and the choices available to students, I discuss the presence of Wikipedia in assignments that analyze it as the focus of traditional papers and that use it as a direct platform. My analysis stems from a definition of popular culture akin to what Stacy Takacs (2014) describes in *Interrogating Popular Culture: Key Questions*:

> "popular" reminds us of our focus – people and their practices of creation, interpretation, and agency. The term embodies a distinct orientation to cultural study, one which emphasizes people's power to create and discriminate, to make choices about whether and how to use the expressive resources available in their societies. (p. 8)

Although I address the effects of using Wikipedia in assignments of different genres, I argue that the genre has less effect on potential student experience than the degree to which faculty embody qualities associated with integrative and collaborative leadership. These models involve connections across organizational boundaries that owe much to the networking processes of Wikipedia and other open-source software that enable pubic collaboration.

TWENTY-FIRST CENTURY TECHNOLOGY AND MODELS OF LEADERSHIP

Twenty-first century technology that allows for collaboration, like Wikipedia, is profoundly shaping contemporary leadership by transforming our relationships with information and each other. As Janis Bragan Balda and Fernando Mora (2011) observe, technology like Wikipedia promotes "collaborative knowledge building," and "tools developed within this methodology quickly find adoption in non–software environments" (pp. 16, 18). In many academic and professional contexts, as well as across a variety of technological platforms, collaborative approaches to processing and representing knowledge that recent technology encourages create the need for continued collaboration, even beyond these technological platforms.

Leaders should not ignore these shifts in the proliferation of information, though facing them as a university instructor does not mean suggesting that our students accept them in unqualified ways. Brian Davenport (2014) argues that:

> [b]ecause of the radical changes in technology, information is now available from a variety of sources. As a result, the wise leader will not limit the sources

they consult for information. Additionally, the wise leader will also be acutely aware that it is no longer possible to control the spread of information. (p. 43)

Although Davenport's focus is not the college classroom, if applied to the role of technology in higher education courses, his observations suggest that extreme attempts to control knowledge that students access, such as banning Wikipedia, are unlikely to be successful. He concludes that leaders should "seek to embrace the possibilities created by the massive amount and rapid proliferation of information while at the same time being cognizant and cautious of the negative possibilities this new reality holds" (Davenport, 2014, p. 44). Although college instructors should not behave as if these new modes of spreading knowledge do not exist, acknowledging them does not mean encouraging or allowing our students to be uncritical consumers of knowledge.

The observations about emerging relational twenty-first century leadership from Davenport, as well as Balda and Mora, resonate with facets of integrative and collaborative leadership. These models provide helpful theoretical frameworks for exploring the use of Wikipedia in the classroom in relation to faculty leadership. Both integrative and collaborative leadership emphasize building relationships, often across previous boundaries, to face collective challenges.

Collaborative leadership focuses on creating connections across organizational boundaries to harness the power of collective abilities rather than relying on the directives of a central authority to make decisions. Chris Ansell and Allison Gash (2012) demonstrate how "[c]ollaborative leaders typically play a facilitative role, encouraging and enabling stakeholders to work together effectively" (p. 2). Montgomery Van Wart (2013) explains that collaborative leadership "deemphasizes the roles of both leaders and followers in order to emphasize the needs of the network, system, environment, or community, resulting in a collaborative style" (p. 559). To suggest that leadership emphasizing needs of a collective did not exist before twenty-first century technology would be unconvincing, yet a collaborative enterprise of Wikipedia's scope and global reach would not have been possible without the contemporary technology that also aids in making positive results of this collaboration more widely known.

In addition to transforming knowledge creation through collaboration, integrative leadership strengthens relationships through an approach called informed mindfulness. In "The pebble in the pond: How integrative leadership can bring about transformation," Adam Perlman et al. (2014) describe how, "[i]nformed mindfulness naturally includes the qualities of curiosity and inquisitiveness . . . it requires having an attitude of openness and the release of preconceptions and prejudices as one studies a subject in order to educate oneself in the most accurate and honest way" (p. S3). This approach is useful for college instructors grappling with new technology. Being inquisitive will enable us to explore and assess the merits and drawbacks of particular technologies instead of ignoring these platforms due to preconceived notions about them. In addition to building more open relationships with the technology itself, strategies from integrative leadership can help us connect more fruitfully with our students. It is "[t]hrough relationship building [that] the Integrative Leader cultivates and unifies mindful teams. In turn, these teams develop their own relationships with others" (Perlman et al., 2014, p. S1). In higher education, cultivating relationships with classes and individual students creates open environments in which students help each other and even spread useful strategies we have taught them beyond our classrooms.

These approaches are intertwined with collaborative technologies like Wikipedia, yet many aspects of their integrative qualities do not depend on gluing students to screens; instead, they emphasize building relationships and forging connections through experiential learning outside the classroom. As Julie E. Owen (2015) discusses, "[i]ntegrative approaches to leadership explicitly connect academic study with the rest of one's life. Integrative leadership development does not distinguish between curricular, cocurricular, and extracurricular" (p. 52). She further argues that, "if leadership is going to address systemic social issues such as global poverty or environmental challenges, leaders must be capable of multimodal thinking and be educated in interdisciplinary, integrative, and intentional ways" (Owen, 2015, p. 49). The effects of these real-world problems threaten to force destructive, uncontrollable social change, but can potentially be resolved through collaborative approaches that are shaped by or use twenty-first century technology, but are capable of creating change beyond flat screens.

Although I believe in the existence of social change due to this evolving relationship with Wikipedia, I also warn against overly dramatic views about the degree of this change. As Joseph Michael Reagle (2010) cautions: "[a] hazard in thinking about new phenomena—such as the Web, wiki, or Wikipedia—is to aggrandize novelty at the expense of the past" (p. 13). Looking for social change can lead to seeing more change than actually exists. In *Social Movements and Global Social Change: The Rising Tide*, Robert K. Schaeffer (2014) argues that when we analyze social change, "it is important to keep in mind *both* developments – growing liberty and persistent inequality" (p. 8). Wikipedia has transformed knowledge production, but the degree of social change it creates in and through university classrooms depends on how fully instructors are willing to embrace models such as integrative and collaborative leadership, to surrender exclusive authority over student work by allowing their participation in open-collaborative composition and to lead by helping students discover possibilities they may not otherwise have considered. I explore in my conclusion some ways in which platforms like Wikipedia and leadership theories that move away from authoritarian models create opportunities not just for student use of technology, but also for engagement beyond the classroom.

WRITING ABOUT WIKIPEDIA

Using Wikipedia itself as an object of analysis appears to offer opportunities to understand the possibilities of wikis, yet many challenges arise. In a 2012 article, Paula Patch describes how she uses Wikipedia in her composition course. Her detailed analysis reveals how these types of assignments can explore the site yet fail to fully grasp the potential of Wikipedia, but her collaborative leadership style does enable some successful pedagogical outcomes.

Many aspects of Patch's class demonstrate changes from the strategy of fully banning Wikipedia and reveal what a collaborative leadership style in the classroom makes possible. Ansell and Gash make clear that "the distinctive quality of collaborative leadership is that it is facilitative rather than directive: it must create the conditions that support the contributions of stakeholders to the collaborative process and effective transactions among them" (Ansell and Gash, 2012, p. 18). Discussions about Wikipedia in Patch's course are productive not because she delivers authoritative knowledge, but because she creates an environment that facilitates honest student contributions that foster collaborative understanding. Patch's students confess their preconceptions about Wikipedia, including their belief that "use should be avoided or, at least, undisclosed, based on some of their professors' warnings that Wikipedia use is always unacceptable" (Patch, 2010, p. 279). Her students do not fear admitting to a professor that former teachers' attitudes have caused them to use the site furtively and not deepen their understanding of how it works, a fact that reveals benefits to Patch's collaborative leadership and perils of more authoritarian classroom management. Creating open environments enables us to lead, not by dictating what knowledge should be useful to our students, but by showing we can help them develop the understanding to find and evaluate the information they need.

In addition to classroom discussions, strengths also exist in Patch's approach to having students analyze Wikipedia. She suggests that Wikipedia entries are good for analysis because "[a] wiki's layers are transparent in a way that print and most other online texts are not; every

Wikipedia article includes a History page showing who has edited the article and when, as well as a Discussion page on which editors and other interested users can discuss changes" (Patch, 2010, p.279). Making these pages aspects of analyzing an entry is a crucial step toward students appreciating how knowledge is constructed through a wiki with collaborative leadership.

However, limits of students' exploration of Wikipedia are shown in Patch's description of her assignments. Students write "a critical, rhetorical analysis of a Wikipedia article" (Patch, 2010, p.280) and adapt it to a longer essay "in which they make the case for or against the reliability . . . of their selected article. Their assessment of the reliability of the article should lead to a more general argument about Wikipedia, online media, collaborative media, encyclopedias, or something else related to the Wikipedia phenomenon" (Patch, 2010, p.280). Analyzing multiple versions of the entry and debates that helped shape them enables students to discover distinctive qualities of the wiki, yet the assumption behind the assignment—that they can generalize about the whole website from one entry—risks creating misunderstandings of the system. Individual entries can be extraordinarily unrepresentative. As Jemielniak (2014) concedes, although biases do not ultimately tend to prevail, "the chances that an article on a sensitive or controversial topic will be unbalanced at some point in time are very high" (p. 5). Interpretations in individual student papers about reliability will be skewed by the entry they pick and the specific time during which they analyze that entry. Although the longer essay's argument appears to open up possibilities, the initial directive to evaluate reliability restricts the areas students could persuasively address.

The assignment ultimately seems to focus solely on testing reliability, and Patch's reflections show this was the primary purpose. She notes that "most students deemed their articles unreliable according to the criteria, and I thought this signaled the effectiveness of the activity: students emerged with an understanding of the problems associated with Wikipedia and other online sources" (Patch, 2010, p.281). Though the opportunity to explore Wikipedia directly grants students some agency, there remains a danger that we as instructors will (perhaps unconsciously) stack the deck. Although it is important to have goals and clear purposes for assignments, planning tasks to yield an overly narrow result or viewing work as successful only if it makes our students think precisely what we wanted them to believe does not move as far beyond giving direct orders as we might wish.

However, Patch's further reflections suggest her willingness to facilitate her students' discoveries and not be primarily directive. She realizes "most students find that Wikipedia can be a good starting point for personal and even academic research, and I have come to agree" (Patch, 2010, p.281).

Rather than basing an assignment's success on her students reproducing her own unshakable opinion, Patch suggests that her assignment design enabled students to assess Wikipedia in ways she did not anticipate. This description reveals a class environment that facilitates student inquiry and an instructor open to changes in her own perspective.

WRITING AS WIKIPEDIANS

The more radical type of Wikipedia assignment—students contributing to Wikipedia entries—opens up new possibilities that using Wikipedia as a subject for a traditional thesis-driven paper does not. And yet, it is not immune to the negative effects of authoritarian leadership styles. Aspects of integrative leadership have bearing on these choices, particularly the fact that "[f]or the Integrative Leader, understanding when and how the dynamics at work push for conformity to an old norm and when one should encourage acceptance of a new norm can mean the difference between success and failure" (Perlman et al., 2014, p.S8). The ways in which instructors frame opportunities and choose to lead students affect assignments profoundly. Although individual feedback from instructors remains crucial to student success, continuing to make private directives from professors the exclusive force through which students revise their work misses opportunities that collaborative platforms offer for enhancing student ability to work collaboratively and write for diverse audiences. In this part of my argument, I will examine assignments described by Cullen J. Chandler and Alison S. Gregory, Megan Sweeney and finally, Michael Kuhne and Gill Creel.

Chandler and Gregory

The humorous title of Chandler and Gregory's 2010 article "Sleeping with the enemy: Wikipedia in the college classroom," suggests a playful atti- tude, which Thomas Leitch emphasizes as important when engaging with Wikipedia (Leitch, 2014, p.101). The article describes how Chandler was "[a] purist" who thought "traditional publications like books and journals are still the gold standard" and, "[t]ired of seeing Wikipedia in his students' bibliographies," created a policy for all his classes: "[u]se Wikipedia and the paper would receive a grade of zero, no questions asked" (Chandler and Gregory, 2010, p.249). On the surface, the article chronicles a change in Chandler's classroom procedures. In 2007, he learned of a project in which students deliberately entered false information on Wikipedia (Chandler and Gregory, 2010, pp.249–50), but instead of replicating this practice, he decided to have his students write the articles (Chandler and Gregory, 2010, p. 250). Despite the shift in approach to Wikipedia, a close analysis of the article suggests that the assignment is profoundly informed by Chandler's initial attitude and by his classroom leadership style, an influence that limits his students' exploration of Wikipedia's collective compositional environment.

Transforming his students into Wikipedians might appear to be a dramatic reversal of Chandler's original convictions, but his structuring of the assignment suggests continued aspirations to more traditional classroom authority. The article makes clear that "all content had to receive approval from Chandler before the students were allowed to add their work to Wikipedia. These hard-copy papers, rather than the Wikipedia entries, were the basis for the students' grades on the project" (Chandler and Gregory, 2010, p. 252). We are accustomed to grading unchanging texts, yet by requiring that writing gain his approval before being added to Wikipedia, Chandler denies his students the opportunity to experience the community's feedback on their initial work. Grading these papers is argued to be justified because "given the ever-changing nature of Wikipedia, we anticipated that some of the students' work would be almost immediately changed and we wanted to be sure that the unadulterated work was what was graded" (Chandler and Gregory, 2010, p. 252). This policy willfully or unwittingly misses the fact that the students' versions of their entries would be available on Wikipedia, even if current entries were revised. The negative connotations of "adulterate" imply that each composition as the work of one author was pure and its emergence on Wikipedia creates an inferior text.

Claims about why the assignment was successful also suggest little change in Chandler's attitude about Wikipedia and missed opportunities to more deeply engage with Wikipedia's collective knowledge production through collaborative leadership in the classroom. The article describes how "students started off as avid Wikipedia fans," conceding that, "[o]ne of the many hidden benefits of this project (from the professors' viewpoint, anyway) was that the students could not use Wikipedia – there was no information on their topics because they were to create it!" (Chandler and Gregory, 2010, p. 255). Although this vision of creation can be seen as encouraging students to use other sources and take an active role in Wikipedia, Chandler's continued excitement about students not using Wikipedia contrasts starkly with actual engagement in the site's collaborative compositional environment. Rather than encouraging students to join the conversation, Chandler's purpose appears to be blocking their use of the site as a one-stop shop for information without giving them any transferable new relationship to Wikipedia. The outcome is similar to Patch's conclusions from her students' more traditional essay: "By the end of the project, the majority of students in the class (roughly 80%) said that they now thought Wikipedia was less useful than they originally thought, but that it is still a good place to find citations directing readers to usable sources" (Chandler and Gregory, 2010, p. 255). Reaching a similar place to Patch's assignment seems counterintuitive since students writing for Wikipedia would experience direct interaction with Wikipedians that Patch's students as outside observers would not, but given Chandler's control over student texts, it should not be surprising.

Chandler's students' responses to the limited interaction they have with Wikipedia's compositional environment vividly reveal that the students do not see collaboration as an opportunity and are restricted by narrow conceptions of authority. At the end of the course, some students' entries on Wikipedia had been revised while others' had not yet been edited. The responses of both groups as presented by Chandler replicate his initial atti- tudes toward academic authority. The actions also suggest that students did not develop awareness of the potential advantages of writing in a col- laborative compositional environment and thus missed the opportunity to find features transferable to later contexts.

The article celebrates the students' perspectives at the end of the course, noting excitedly, "The students' ownership of the articles was overwhelm- ing!" (Chandler and Gregory, 2010, p. 252) and describing this as "[a]n unintended – but most welcome – project outcome" (Chandler and Gregory, 2010, p. 254). A passion for their own writing is a feeling most of us try to instill in students—it is a force that can propel them to marvelous places. Yet Chandler does not even seem to disapprove of students who felt "indignation" when their entries were revised and referred to "the article's other editors as 'Wikijerks'" (Chandler and Gregory, 2010, p. 254). This is not a constructive attitude to have when writing in other genres or media, but student anger toward those who revised their articles is especially misplaced given that they are writing on Wikipedia where participants are encouraged to edit through the declaration that, "Nobody owns articles." Positive ownership of writing in genres that remain less collaborative has the potential to improve student composition, but rage toward other writers in an environment intended to be collaborative shows little to no development in understandings of genre.

The reactions of students whose work was not revised during the course also show little understanding of the collective commitment of non-experts that drove Wikipedia's success, suggesting that students will be unlikely to transfer potential strategies from Wikipedia's model to future contexts. The article states that, "those students now consider themselves to be the world's foremost experts (at least through Wikipedia) on the topic" (Chandler and Gregory, 2010, p. 254). Although the article indicates that students' pretensions were challenged, those challenges were based on reinforcing traditional academic authority and the students' lack of it (Chandler and Gregory, 2010, p. 253). Leitch asserts that these professors "never encouraged their students to reconsider their assumptions about authority in light of experiences that had highlighted the often playful negotiations behind authority, presumably because they shared these assumptions themselves" (Leitch, 2014, p. 102). Students whose entries were not edited view lack of revision as a victory, likely due to their association of edits with the corrections of an authority like their professor. They do not see the potential of revision to be an ongoing conversation through which collaborative leadership can lead to stronger writing.

Chandler's leadership isolates his students in ways that the relational elements of integrative and collaborative leadership aim to discourage. As Perlman et al. (2014) explain:

> [s]ilo-ing can occur for a number of reasons but at its core, it is a group's inward focus on its particular goals and objectives and a lack of recognition and perhaps even commitment to a truly shared sense of purpose. It is a 'my tribe versus yours' mentality in a world seen as having limited resources. (p. S10)

Chandler's approach encourages his students to believe that everything they write must be guided by an authority and then defended against the intrusions of others. Although students will still likely have their writing revised by other authorities in the workplace, they will experience collaborative work as well. Debra Humphreys discusses the results of several surveys of employers by the Association of American Colleges & Universities (AAC&U) from the past decade: "employers say that 'teamwork skills,' especially deployed effectively in diverse settings, are essential for success in today's world. More than 70 percent of those surveyed in 2010 said they thought higher education institutions should place more emphasis on developing this skill in all college graduates" (Humphreys, 2013, p. 4). Owen argues that if we want students who can lead by making "connections across silos, structures, and disparate activities, [we] need to be practicing integrative leadership development" (Owen, 2015, p. 54). Although more traditional writing assignments address abilities students should develop and so still have an important place in classrooms, Chandler's Wikipedia assignment is a missed opportunity for instilling collaborative skills in leadership and writing that could be transferred to multiple domains.

Sweeney

In "The Wikipedia project: Changing students from consumers to producers," Meghan Sweeney demonstrates qualities of integrative and collaborative leadership through her classroom management and evolving relationship with Wikipedia, and her students reap the benefits. Sweeney's approach to Wikipedia stems from a realization of how the presumed authority her students vested in her blocked them from engaging in critical thinking. Her observation enables her to be a catalyst, a collaborative leader who "[i]dentifies value-creating opportunities and mobilizes stakeholders to pursue them . . . [and] frames or reframes problems" (Ansell and Gash, 2012, p. 8). Sweeney was bothered by a perennial question she received from students: "whether or not I 'allow' Wikipedia" (Sweeney, 2012, p. 256). She explains that "[t]he question and answer end inquiry, problem solving, and critical thinking. So I stopped answering it. Instead, I redesigned my course to leverage Wikipedia as a source of inquiry" (Sweeney, 2012, p. 256). In contrast to each student writing an individual piece and receiving instructor approval before submitting to Wikipedia, Sweeney's approach focuses on students figuring out together how to join Wikipedia's ongoing conversation.

Sweeney develops her use of Wikipedia through strategies at the core of informed mindfulness. This concept "connects mindful self-awareness and self-regulation with educated decision-making [and] as situations arise and decision points are faced, [leaders are] able to place what is happening in its larger context and, having clear values and being sufficiently educated, make an informed choice" (Perlman et al., 2014, p. S1). Before her thinking evolved, Sweeney describes how "for several semesters, I 'allowed' students to use Wikipedia as a gateway to additional sources. But that rule did not prove successful, since several students kept using Wikipedia as a predominant source" (Sweeney, 2012, p. 257). Rather than merely penalizing individual students for not using Wikipedia as instructed, Sweeney was able to place the usage in a larger context and make curricular revisions based on the trend.

Sweeney's informed mindfulness moved into even more direct self-awareness that enabled her to create new classroom approaches to Wikipedia. Informed mindfulness involves "asking such questions as, do my actions reflect the values I say I have, or do I say one thing and do another?" (Perlman et al., 2014, p. S4). Sweeney confesses that limiting her students' access to the site "felt hypocritical because I have, on occasion, in the privacy of my own office, accessed Wikipedia for a quick reference" (Sweeney, 2012, p. 257). Integrative leaders focus on "understanding their greater purpose and prioritizing that purpose over their own fears or the difficulties that a particular situation may create" (Perlman et al., 2014, p. S4). Sweeney moved past anxiety about her students' use of the site in order to see greater pedagogical purposes beyond simply stopping students from using the site in unhelpful ways. Her integrative leadership makes it possible for her to create an assignment to transform student usage of Wikipedia and help her students acquire skills that can transfer to other collaborative contexts.

Sweeney optimistically embraces the potential of Wikipedia and its diverse universe of active contributors. She argues that "[b]y contributing to Wikipedia, students switch from consumers to producers and subsequently change their relationship with Wikipedia" (Sweeney, 2012, p. 256), and "[e]ven though class wikis are valuable in many ways, they do not teach students how to negotiate a wiki that is open to a global and diverse group of contributors, like Wikipedia" (Sweeney, 2012, p. 257). In the 2013 survey of employers by the Association of American Colleges & Universities, "more than a 90 percent agree that 'all students should have educational experiences that teach them how to solve problems with people whose views are different from their own'" (Humphreys, 2013, p. 4). Experience with the collaborative composition of Wikipedia can offer undergraduates opportunities to develop these collective problem-solving skills.

Sweeney's desire to change students' relationships to Wikipedia is intertwined with her teaching of popular culture topics and emphasis on outside-the-classroom learning. Like Chandler, Sweeney does precede contributing to Wikipedia with more traditional writing, but does not unite the two in a single assignment that puts primary focus on her approval. Sweeney's students craft a research proposal about a chosen youth subculture, written to engage with the current "conversations that experts are having (or not having) about their chosen subject and to convince their audience that an ethnographic study will further add to the conversation" (Sweeney, 2012, p. 259). Even this more traditional proposal places emphasis on intellectual conversation, a focus that helps prepare students for Wikipedia's collaborative nature. The emphasis on conversation also brings students outside the classroom by requiring that they observe and interview members of their chosen subculture. The multiple conversations in which Sweeney's students participate prepare them to think, write and lead in a variety of contexts in ways that a focus on a single directive conversation between professor and student cannot.

In addition to developing experience through interactions with Wikipedians on the site, Sweeney's students work in groups to figure out how they can enter Wikipedia's ongoing conversation. She notes that "[a]fter seeing the fairly ruthless discussion pages on the backend of

Wikipedia, they realize their contribution must add to the conversation in a meaningful and appropriate way" (Sweeney, 2012, p. 261). Providing students with genuine opportunities to engage with Wikipedia's collaborative design does not imply that all conversations will be pleasant interactions in which they easily triumph over interlocutors or communications in which more experienced Wikipedians become authorities students must follow. The work instead offers students meaningful practice in conversing with collaborators who may be half a world away or sitting directly beside them. By interrupting the hierarchical conversation in which students ask her to tell them whether they may use Wikipedia or not and ceding some of her direct authority, Sweeney's collaborative and integrative leadership enables her students to become involved in more constructive conversations with Wikipedians and each other.

Kuhne and Creel

In "Wikipedia, 'the people formerly known as the audience,' and first-year writing," Michael Kuhne and Gill Creel embrace integrative and collaborative leadership and the compositional environment of Wikipedia even more profoundly, describing how their students intensely engage with bots, human Wikipedians and the world. Although Kuhne and Creel acknowledge that imagined audiences can be useful in composition courses, they enthuse, "now when writers want to share their work, the imagining can stop because in less than a minute the Wikipedians may be here" (Kuhne and Creel, 2012, p. 187). They highlight how "[u]sing the highly collaborative and contested environment of Wikipedia as a writing platform allows a more concrete understanding of the new digitally embodied audience than traditional classroom writing" (Kuhne and Creel, 2012, p. 177). Embracing aspects of integrative leadership makes it possible for Kuhne and Creel to allow these vast, uncontrollable audiences into their courses. As Lori Knutson (2015) explains: "[t]he Integrative Leader trusts, lets go, and allows what wants to emerge . . . Integrative leadership is the capacity to awaken collective wisdom to attain the full potential of individuals and systems" (p. 408). Kuhne and Creel (2012) declare, "[w]hat we have here are robots and people, cranky and helpful, doing our jobs for us" (p. 186). Their use of the phrase "doing our jobs for us" highlights the constructively playful attitude they take toward their students' engagement with Wikipedia. They do not idealize the interactions their students have, understanding that these conversations will vary. Although their suggestion that net bots and larger human audiences are doing their jobs is somewhat tongue-in-cheek, they clearly take fuller engagement with Wikipedia seriously as a new opportunity they can give their students, and as a chance to engage with students more as facilitators and co-creators of knowledge than as authorities who decide what information is worthy.

Instead of being the sole authorities that evaluate student work or even the first authorities that give students' thoughts a seal of approval before allowing them to venture outside the classroom, they enable students to engage with Wikipedia more fully as Wikipedians. They argue that teaching writing is "impossible to do alone anyway, especially when it comes to questions of audience" (Kuhne and Creel, 2012, p. 186) and that "[w]riting in and about Wikipedia encourages students to think about the outcomes of their writing and, by extension, changes the student/teacher relationship in pedagogically useful ways" (Kuhne and Creel, 2012, p. 177). Kuhne and Creel embrace collaborative leadership by being catalysts and forging a "mutually reinforcing link between collaboration and innovation" (Ansell and Gash, 2012, p. 8). This experience does not simply prepare students to use the site, but also to write for diverse, real audiences and to work in the ever-expanding set of professional environments shaped by the view that "[f]ormal leadership tends to restrict and tightly control information flows ... [and] such restrictions cause dysfunction because good ideas and much enthusiasm come through informal networking, lateral communication, and nonhierarchical forms of innovation diffusion" (Van Wart, 2013, p. 559). Ultimately, working with Wikipedia does not have to mean idealizing it. A central purpose of giving students the chance to write as Wikipedians is to expose them to forms of collaboration akin to what they will likely encounter in a variety of other situations.

CONCLUSION

New possibilities for social change exist in aspects of Wikipedia's collaborative design and public platform. In his 2016 study, Piotr Konieczny (2016) praises recent positive developments of work with Wikipedia, arguing that:

> [c]ontributing to Wikipedia, seeing their work used, commented upon, and improved by others, can show students that they have the power to make a positive impact on the wider world. An incredible amount of creativity and labor is wasted around the world when students' papers are discarded after being graded. (p. 1528)

Unlocking student creativity does not demand using Wikipedia as a platform—a variety of new public contexts are emerging that enable students and their work to transcend the traditional university classroom.

In "Teaching students to be public intellectuals" an article in *The Chronicle of Higher Education* (2016), Sarah Madsen Hardy and Marisa Milanese describe the approach in their writing courses and the larger movement toward public writing. They emphasize "how much our students learn when they confront the challenge of translating their academic arguments for audiences who are intellectually ambitious but expect accessible prose and an immediate sense of the argument's relevance to their lives" (Madsen Hardy and Milanese, 2016). Students choose a single focus for the semester, research extensively, write a research paper and then "translate what they've learned into a form that will appeal to a public audience — say, readers of the [sic] *The Atlantic* or Slate" (Madsen Hardy and Milanese, 2016). This translation involves asking crucial questions such as "How do I reframe my argument for this new audience? How do I establish authority in this kind of public venue? What word choices and sentence shapes create the conversational style demanded by, say, the Opinion Pages of *The New York Times*? Which details should I drop?" (Madsen Hardy and Milanese, 2016). As fully engaging with Wikipedia can do, revising papers for specific reading publics heightens students' capacities to think critically about audience and authority. Madsen Hardy and Milanese (2016) describe how "[m]oving through that sequence, students recognize that scholarly and public practices and attitudes are, at their best, deeply intertwined" and affirm the importance of students entering public life in a variety of ways to facilitate social change.

Technology that facilitates collaboration and outside the classroom learning have parallel benefits and are now coming together in exciting projects in universities across the country. Owen (2015) brings together these elements, declaring that "[e]xperimental, technology-infused, and experiential approaches can invite intellectual curiosity and leadership" (p. 55). Technology can make organizing face-to-face outside-the-classroom collaboration possible, shape fundamental features of those interactions and also act as a tool for reflecting on and sharing further those collective endeavors through wikis and e-portfolios. Similar to collaborative technology like Wikipedia, experiential learning beyond the classroom nurtures central aspects of integrative and collaborative leadership. Tracy R. Rone (2008) argues that outside the classroom activities "foster collegial relationships between students . . . [and] diminish the status hierarchy between students and college faculty . . . and [that she] gained greater insights into [students'] strengths, skills, and creativity not revealed in the contexts of class meetings and office hours" (p. 243). Through informed mindfulness, Rone not only discovered more effective ways to help individual students harness their talents, but also modified future student trips based on her observations of how much an initial group of students gained from a series of less-structured interactions with members of the community they were visiting (Rone, 2008, p. 241). Learning outside the classroom can enable students to collaborate and innovate if we give them the opportunity to develop relationships and make crucial choices that shape their own experiences.

Experiential learning has been around long before technology like Wikipedia, but it is increasingly becoming a cornerstone of institutional policy in higher education. Humphreys (2013) stresses the need for increased faculty collaboration and describes how "select leaders in student and academic affairs have exercised collaborative leadership to advance more experiential learning opportunities for students. Such efforts have resulted in community-based research and service-learning opportunities" (p. 5). In "Collaborative leadership on a liberal arts campus: Supporting student engagement" Elsa M. Núñez, president of Eastern Connecticut State University, stresses the key roles that collaborative leadership and experiential, outside-the-classroom learning played in the new strategic plan for her university. She argues that in higher education "leadership is not vested in one person or housed in a suite of offices" (Núñez, 2013, p. 17) and "[s]enior management's task is to facilitate and support the leadership potential of everyone on campus" (Núñez, 2013, p. 17). Núñez links the need for collaborative leadership on every level of campuses to experiential learning made possible by relationships her university has built "with employers in Connecticut and beyond" (Núñez, 2013, p. 18) as well as their Center for Community Engagement which facilitates service-learning initiatives, each of which "has proven to be an effective way to apply student learning in real-life situations while meeting critical community needs" (Núñez, 2013, p. 19). Humphreys (2013) maintains that, "private and public institutions must collaborate with one another, create tighter connections to their own local communities, and use information technology to connect their students to broader learning communities around the world" (p. 6). These webs of experiences and interactions can help drive social change in higher education and in the communities that colleges and universities serve.

Rather than being a force that divides us from students who are left to their own devices, technology paired with new models of leadership and new adventures outside the classroom can enable us to engage more deeply and successfully with our students. Wikipedia can be a force for social change not just through direct student engagement with the platform itself, but also as proof that collective enterprises once thought impossible can be realized and as evidence that innumerable people will become involved in communal projects they find inspiring, even without monetary incentive. Whether or not we choose to work extensively with Wikipedia itself in college classrooms, drawing back from micromanagement and overdetermined final outcomes, offering choices rather than just commands to undergraduates and enabling them to work with each other and broader communities can help our students transform academia and the many worlds outside it.

REFERENCES

Ansell, C. and A. Gash (2012), "Stewards, mediators, and catalysts: Toward a model of collaborative leadership," *The Innovation Journal: The Public Sector Innovation Journal*, **17** (1), 3–21.

Balda, J.B. and F. Mora (2011), "Adapting leadership theory and practice for the networked, millennial generation," *Journal of Leadership Studies*, **5** (3), 13–24, accessed 5 August 2016 at Wiley Online Library.

Brox, H. (2012), "The elephant in the room: A place for Wikipedia in higher education?" *Nordlit*, **30**, 143–55.

Chandler, C.J. and A.S. Gregory (2010), "Sleeping with the enemy: Wikipedia in the college classroom," *The History Teacher*, **43** (2), 247–57, accessed 4 August 2016 at JSTOR.

Davenport, B. (2014), "From A to Google: How technology is impacting information and leadership," *Journal of Leadership Studies*, **8** (2), 4–5, accessed 4 August 2016 at Wiley Online Library.

Horrigan, B. (2016), "Integrative leadership means partnering," *EXPLORE*, **12** (2), 139–40, accessed 10 October 2016 at Elsevier ScienceDirect Journals.

Humphreys, D. (2013), "Deploying collaborative leadership to reinvent higher education," *Peer Review*, **15** (1), 4–6.

Jemielniak, D. (2014), *Common Knowledge? An Ethnography of Wikipedia*, Redwood City, CA: Stanford University Press.

Knutson, L. (2015), "Integrative leadership: An embodied practice," *EXPLORE*, **11** (5), 407–9.

Konieczny, P. (2016), "Teaching with Wikipedia in a 21st-century classroom: Perceptions of Wikipedia and its educational benefits," *Journal of the Association for Information Science and Technology*, **67** (7), 1523–34.

Kramer, M. and D. Crespy (2011), "Communicating collaborative leadership," *The Leadership Quarterly*, **22**, 1024–37.

Kuhne, M. and G. Creel (2012), "Wikipedia, 'the people formerly known as the audience,' and first-year writing," *Teaching English in the Two-Year College*, **40** (2), 177–89.

Leitch, T. (2014), *Wikipedia U: Knowledge, Authority, and Liberal Education in the Digital Age*, Baltimore, MD: Johns Hopkins University Press.

Madsen Hardy, S. and M. Milanese (2016), "Teaching students to be public intellectuals," *The Chronicle of Higher Education.* 29 June, accessed on 6 August 2016 at http://chronicle.com/article/Teaching-Students-to-Be-Public/236944.

Núñez, E.M. (2013), "Collaborative leadership on a liberal arts campus: Supporting student engagement," *Peer Review*, **15** (1), 17–20.

Owen, J. (2015), "Integrative and interdisciplinary approaches to leadership development," *New Directions for Student Leadership*, **145**, 49–58.

Patch, P. (2010), "Meeting student writers where they are: Using Wikipedia to teach responsible scholarship," *Teaching English in the Two-Year College*, **37** (3), 278–85.

Perlman, A., B. Horrigan, E. Goldblatt, V. Maizes and B. Kliger (2014), "The pebble in the pond: How integrative leadership can bring about transformation," *EXPLORE*, **10** (5), S1–S14.

Rand, A.D. (2010), "Mediating at the student-Wikipedia intersection," *Journal of Library Administration*, **50**, 923–32.

Reagle, J.M. (2010), *Good Faith Collaboration: The Culture of Wikipedia*, Cambridge, MA: MIT Press.

Rone, T.R. (2008), "Culture from the outside in and the inside out: Experiential education and the continuum of theory, practice, and policy," *College Teaching*, **56** (4), 237–46.

Schaeffer, R.K. (2014), *Social Movements and Global Social Change: The Rising Tide*, Lanham, MD: Rowman & Littlefield.

Soules, A. (2015), "Faculty perception of Wikipedia in the California State University system," *New Library World*, **116** (3/4), 213–26.

Sweeney, M. (2012), "The Wikipedia project: Changing students from consumers to producers," *Teaching English in the Two-Year College*, **39** (3), 256–67.

Takacs, S. (2014), *Interrogating Popular Culture: Key Questions*, New York, NY: Routledge.

Turnbull James, K., J. Mann and J. Creasy (2007), "Leaders as lead learners: A case example of facilitating," *Management Learning*, **38** (1), 79–94.

Van Wart, M. (2013), "Lessons from leadership theory and the contemporary challenges of leaders," *Public Administration Review*, **73** (4), 553–65.

Walker, M.A. and Y. Li (2016), "Improving information literacy skills through learning to use and edit Wikipedia: A chemistry perspective," *Journal of Chemical Education*, **93**, 509–15.

Wikipedia (2017a), "Contributing to Wikipedia," accessed 4 August 2016 at https://en.wikipedia.org/wiki/Wikipedia:Contributing_to_Wikipedia.

Wikipedia (2017b), "Main page," accessed 4 August 2016 at https://en.wikipedia.org/wiki/Main_Page.

Epilogue

Kimberly Yost

Those of us who are artists, educators, leaders or a combination of the three may be intimately familiar with how plans and expectations can be thwarted by the nonconformity of human beings. And so it is with this volume. I had planned and expected this epilogue to be a summation of popular culture's effect on the ideological formation of leaders in the quest for social change and how this conceptual understanding can be pedagogically leveraged. I could have implemented this plan, and it would have been relatively successful for those who have stuck with us by reading all the way to the end. Critical analysis of the artists, creations, socio-political contexts and implications for future leaders and society is the foundation of academic endeavors. And yet, relegating the insights and efforts of the scholars who have contributed to this volume to a precariously tilting pile of dusty texts that should be considered for the classroom seems not only a disservice, but also too simplistic.

Popular culture is a ubiquitous force within our lives—whether we consider the mediums of the written word, film images, music or social media—that influences who we are and how we perceive ourselves and others. Capitalizing on newly available production modes of popular culture by artists, academics and leaders has led to a grassroots effort of social change initiatives on a global scale with the potential to succeed more quickly than other non-violent change efforts we have seen in history. The behavioral norms of our dominant cultures are being challenged by the ability of popular culture fields to create group identities quickly, reflexively and porously. In addition, the resolution of contemporary issues within imaginative works may ultimately lead to the creation of such worlds. Role models of leadership and social change in popular culture provides a safe space for exploration and experimentation. As consumers of popular culture, our emotional needs can be assuaged or inflamed and we can be motivated to challenge the status quo and become agents of change. At the time of this writing, activism for social change in American politics is burgeoning through social media, particularly Twitter and Facebook. Virtual communities are challenging the status quo through spreading information with the express understanding of moving the conversations to the "real" world with actions to elicit social change. Leaders have emerged from outside the traditional venues to provide visions of a more just and morally sound approach to our social contract. Future generations may study these events as part of an historical body of knowledge, but we must not consign these social change events to the classroom and history books just yet. We must continue living and contributing to their formation.

We are living in a transitional period of cultural production that is becoming more egalitarian, cheaper, faster and, thus, more pervasive. Writers can publish their fiction or non-fiction works electronically at nearly no cost. Scholars can publish weekly blogs to further their academic and research agendas. Filmmakers can upload their works to YouTube and create their own channels for distribution and viewing. Musicians have similar avenues for their works. In the digital age, artists working within this medium have multiple and varied opportunities for their work. These options bypass the traditional modes of cultural production—even the traditional modes of popular cultural production. Indeed, older works of popular culture, whether books, films or music, have been redesigned for dissemination through contemporary means.

In conjunction with the evolution of cultural production is the evolution of our understanding of what constitutes a leader. Leaders influence others towards common goals, which can be abstruse in the age of social media where movie stars, journalists, politicians, pastors and cats can all have tens of thousands of followers. As witnessed through many of the chapters in this volume, we may be at a tipping point in our understanding. Leaders are no longer only those who have legitimate authority and power, but can be pushed forward by followers or circumstances to serve others by providing a contextual shape—to make sense—of contemporary issues, principally the needs and desires of those who are marginalized. As evidenced, historical or fictional figures can be used in this way and may provide a clearer interpretative vision for social change than living leaders.

Social change often works at a glacial pace. When it does occur, we often dwell upon the spark that provided the impetus for the change. We look to see who was standing near the eruption. Who was there to point us in the direction of safety or to clean up the mess. We rarely look to see the length of the fuse or how many different hands created the path. The scholars in this volume help us to understand and perceive the intersection of popular culture, leadership and social change in an historical framework, as well as an emotional one. The arts play with and upon our emotions in a synergistic relationship with dialectical outcomes. It is the tension of emotional conflicts which leaders, broadly defined, can harness to influence follower actions toward social change in ways that may be hidden or slow to actualization.

For those who seek social justice in all its diverse meanings and embodiments, the journey continues. Utilizing popular culture artifacts as a means by which to witness, encourage and lead social change is another step upon the path; one more fuse to provide a spark.

Index